DESERT S...
JUNGLE LANDS

Also by Steve Eather

6 Squadron (RAAF) 50th Anniversary History
'Target Charlie': Australian Air Operations in Vietnam
'Magpie Strike': 2 Squadron (RAAF) in Vietnam
Flying Squadrons of the Australian Defence Force
Odd Jobs: RAAF operations in Japan, Korea, Malaya, the Berlin Airlift and at Malta 1946–1960
Get the Bloody Job Done: The Royal Australian Navy Helicopter Flight in Vietnam

Cover photo: Brigadier Ken Eather discusses the tactical situation with Major General Allen from his headquarters (a rock partially covered with a sheet of canvas) at Ioribaiwa Ridge, mid September 1942. It is possible that this very telephone conversation, photographed by one of his troops, is the one in which Eather asked for and received permission to withdraw to Imita Ridge, thus precipitating the Australian Army's most significant command crises of the war.

Photo courtesy of the Army History Unit via Captain Owen Eather

DESERT SANDS
JUNGLE LANDS

A biography of
Major General Ken Eather,
CB, CBE, DSO, DSC

BY

STEVE EATHER

First published by Allen & Unwin in 2003

Copyright © Steve Eather 2003

All rights reserved. No part of this book may be reproduced or transmitted in any form or by any means, electronic or mechanical, including photocopying, recording or by any information storage and retrieval system, without prior permission in writing from the pubisher. *The Australian Copyright Act* 1968 (the Act) allows a maximum of one chapter or 10% of this book, whichever is the greater, to be photocopied by any educational institution for its educational purposes provided that the educational institution (or body that administers it) has given a remuneration notice to Copyright Agency Limited (CAL) under the Act.

Allen & Unwin
83 Alexander Street
Crows Nest NSW 2065
Australia
Phone: (61 2) 8425 0100
Fax: (61 2) 9906 2218
Email: info@allenandunwin.com
Web: www.allenandunwin.com

National Library of Australia
Cataloguing-in-Publication entry:

Eather, Steve.
    Desert sands, jungle lands: a biography of Major General
    Ken Eather.

    Includes index.
    ISBN 1 74114 182 6.

    1. Eather, Ken, 1901–1993. 2. Generals – Australia –
    Biography. 3. Soldiers – Australia – Biography. I. Title.

355.331092

Set in 12 pt Granjon by Midland Typesetters, Maryborough, Vic.
Printed by Ligare Book Printer, Sydney

10 9 8 7 6 5 4 3 2 1

About the author

Steve Eather was born at Newcastle in 1961, the son of an RAAF armament fitter. He moved around Australia with his family as a child, also spending three years in Malaysia. As he grew older he developed a strong interest in Australian history.

In 1979 Steve joined the Royal Australian Air Force and served in military logistics including seven years with an F111 bomber squadron. While still serving he became a curator at the RAAF Museum, Point Cook and, with Phillip Collins of Index Communications, played a pivotal role in developing that institution's highly successful Heritage Gallery. Since transferring to the RAAF Reserve and leaving full-time military service in 1995, Steve has made a successful career in the museum industry and has been employed at Werribee Park Historic Mansion, Scienceworks Museum and Museum Victoria in a variety of capacities. He has a Graduate Certificate in Environment and Heritage Interpretation from Deakin University and is currently the Assistant Manager of Museum Victoria's Moreland Annex artifact storage facility.

Dedication

This book is dedicated to the soldiers of the 7th Division—the unfortunately named 'Silent Seventh', so-called because of the lack of publicity they received in World War II. These gallant troops served in many bitter campaigns and played a pivotal role in protecting Australia from the Japanese threat.

Contents

Acknowledgments		ix
Abbreviations and terms		xiii
Foreword		xvii
Preface		xix
1	Early days	1
2	A call to arms	10
3	The North African Campaign	24
4	Syria: A promotion and a homecoming	44
5	Imita Ridge and the last line of defence	59
6	Taking the offensive on the Kokoda Track	81
7	Gona: A fight to the last man	105
8	The capture of Lae and the Markham and Ramu Valleys Campaign	129
9	Balikpapan: A final fight	155
10	Overlord of a Japanese bastion	165
11	A celebration of victory	179
12	Farewell to all that	189
Postscript		206
Appendix I	Command assessments	207
Appendix II	Promotions and command appointments	213
Appendix III	Honours and awards	215
Notes		219
Bibliography		227
Index		234

Acknowledgments

It goes almost without saying that preparing a book such as this required the support and assistance of many organisations and individuals. I gratefully acknowledge the contribution of:

Mr John Allen (the son of Major General A.S. Allen); Corporal 'Hook' Anderson (editor of *Forever Forward*, the newsletter of the 2/31st Battalion Association, NSW); The Army Museum; Mr Ron Austin of Slouch Hat Publications (for permission to reproduce material from 'From Kokoda to the Sea'); the staff of the Australian War Memorial—Ms Akemi Inoune, Major General Steve Gower, the director, for kindly giving permission to quote from the official history of the Australian Army in World War II and the Research Centre staff); Dr Jack Beale (former chairman of the Board of Trustees, Water Research Foundation of Australia); Mr Col Begg (Agriculture New South Wales); the editor of *Black & Blue* (the newsletter of the 2/25th Battalion Association); Lieutenant Colonel John Burrell (2/1st Battalion); Ms Lyndal Maree Caffrey; Mr George Carlia and Mrs Jen Carlia (my brother and sister-in-law for looking after me on my unexpected research trips to Sydney); Mr Neville Carlyle (secretary of the 2/31st Battalion Association, NSW); Central Army Records Office, Ms Averil Condren (former Abbotsleigh school archivist); Private Gerald Connelly (2/25th Battalion); Wing Commander R.C. Cresswell, DFC; Mr David Crotty (Australian War Memorial); Major General Paul Cullen, AC, CBE, DSO, ED, FCA (2/2nd Battalion); Mr Phillip Dandy; Colonel Wally Delves (2/1st Battalion); Mr Bill Eather (my father, for pushing me along when I needed it and providing support and useful suggestions); Lieutenant Terry Fairbairn (2/1st Battalion); Ms Julie Gleaves (Abbotsleigh school archivist); Corporal Barry Hennessy (2/1st Battalion); Mrs Kathy Hicks (Water Research Foundation of Australia); Professor David Horner (Australian National University, for his support and permission to quote from 'Crisis of Command'); Private John Hurwey (11th Australian Division); Wing Commander Rollo Kingsford-Smith, DSO, DFC (Australian Victory March Contingent for access to and permission to quote from his memoirs); Mr Konishi Hirofumi (Japanese war veteran); Mr Frank McCosker (2/35th Battalion Association); Sergeant Patrick Lowry (2/1st Battalion); Professor Tim McCormack (University of Melbourne); the late Sergeant Moriki Masaru (144th Japanese Regiment, for access to and permission to quote from his memoirs); Museum Victoria Library and especially Ms Sandra Winchester and Ms Val Hogan; National Archives of Australia Melbourne Office and in particular Mr Mark Brennan; the National Library of Australia and especially Ms Anna Skurowski; the staff of the Library Of New South Wales; Mr Paulo De Nicolo (Embassy of Italy, Canberra); Mr Nev Quick (Museum Victoria); Mrs Mildred Reynolds (my aunt and a noted genealogist, author, family historian and editor of the *Eather Family Newsletter*); the Returned Services League of Australia (Queensland, New South Wales and Victoria Divisions); Captain M.L. Roberts (2/31st Battalion); the editor of *Queensland RSL News*; Private Lou Smith (11th Australian Division); the staff of the State Library of Victoria; Associate Professor Yone Sugita; Ms Midori Treeve (for facilitating access to Sergeant Moriki's memoirs); Captain N.H. Travers (2/1st Battalion); Ms Elizabeth Triarico; Ms Kellie Ward (Australian National University Legal Office); Private Julian 'Doc' Waters (2/25th Battalion, for access to and permission to quote from his memoirs); and the staff of the Wyndham City Library.

My special thanks go to Mr Lex MacAulay, noted author on military topics. Lex's deep-seated knowledge of the allied military intelligence gathering service, the Papuan Campaign and the Australian War Memorial's collection has been of great assistance.

Dr Chris Coulthard-Clark, a senior researcher at the Australian War Memorial, read the manuscript, offered advice and provided support and encouragement throughout. The Army History Unit also provided substantial support for my project. I was very fortunate to receive a research grant from this body, which enabled me to make a lengthy research trip to the Australian War Memorial.

Others who have greatly assisted me by proofreading the manuscript include Kristen Thornton (Defence Science and Technology

ACKNOWLEDGMENTS

Organisation, who repeatedly read drafts and provided tremendous support); Mrs Norma Thornton; Ms Rebecca Marsh; Flight Lieutenant Dave Muscat; and Mr Rod Gray (Museum Victoria). Brigadier Phil Carey (historian of the Royal New South Wales Regiment) also proofed the manuscript and provided an interesting command assessment on Ken's career. Mr Rob McWilliams (Museum Victoria) undertook the extraordinary task of translating part of the official history of Italy in World War II, thereby providing a fascinating insight on the Italian perspective of the battles of Bardia and Tobruk.

I am especially indebted to members of General Eather's family. Mrs Isobel Elliott, the General's daughter, provided important information. Mrs Kathleen Eather, General Eather's wife, made herself available to talk about her husband's life at a time when she was recovering from a serious illness. Mr Chris Brookes, one of the General's nephews, and his wife Faye generously gave access to private papers, photographs and letters in their possession. These letters, none of which have been censored (although they were carefully written to not divulge classified information), offer an extraordinary insight into General Eather's Army service. Captain Owen Eather and his wife Julian offered hospitality and unstinting support of my project. They answered my incessant questions and provided many documents, including the historically significant and previously unaccessed Kododa Track private diary. Owen has also proofread the manuscript several times. Owen's son, Eamon, also assisted.

Due to its importance as a primary source document in a crucial period of Australia's history, I have often quoted from General Eather's 1942 diary. Because of lack of space and the pressures of the times, he often used abbreviations. AIF battalions are recorded simply as 25bn, 31bn and 33bn rather than their correct titles of 2/25th Battalion, 2/31st Battalion etc. The battalions were also referred to by using the battalion commanders' family names. This is at times confusing. For the record, the battalion commanders and their units are:

2/25th Battalion	Lieutenant Colonel Withy (later Lieutenant Colonel Marson)
2/31st Battalion	Lieutenant Colonel Dunbar (later Lieutenant Colonel Miller)

2/33rd Battalion	Lieutenant Colonel Buttrose
3rd Battalion	Lieutenant Colonel Cameron
2/1st Battalion	Lieutenant Colonel Cullen

At the start of each diary quotation I have inserted the battalion name where General Eather refers to his units by the commander's name to assist with unit identification. I have also taken the liberty of writing most of the abbreviated words in full for ease of reading.

General Eather kept diaries for the entire war and for a period thereafter, but with the exception of his most important 1942 diary, these no longer survive. Owen, fully aware of the importance of the documents in his possession, has gone to considerable lengths to ensure their survival so that they could help tell a remarkable story. I am very grateful to him for unfettered access to this significant document.

In conclusion, I must especially thank General Peter Cosgrove, Chief of the Australian Defence Force, for kindly writing the foreword for this book. I am also particularly grateful for the Allen & Unwin team for taking this book on and especially Ian Bowing, Alexandra Nahlous and Emma Singer. Their assistance and support have been greatly appreciated.

Notwithstanding the information supplied and support received from many people and groups, the opinions and conclusions expressed in this book are the author's alone.

Abbreviations and terms

ADC	Aide-de-camp
AIF	Australian Imperial Force: the all-volunteer army formed to serve outside Australia as the Militia could not, by legislation, be compelled to fight on other than Australian soil
AMF	Australian Military Forces: the small pre-war permanent forces. The Militia and the AIF were all part of this larger army organisation
ANGAU	Australian New Guinea Administrative Unit: an Australian Army unit formed especially to administer the indigenous populations of Papua and New Guinea while civil administration was in abeyance
ANZAC	Australian and New Zealand Army Corps
Anzac Day	Australia's national day of commemoration for its war dead
Bangalore torpedo	Tube-like explosive device often used to destroy barbed wire entanglements
BBC	British Broadcasting Commission
Bde	Brigade
Bn	Battalion
BP	British Petroleum
Bren	British-designed light machine-gun
Bren carrier	Light tracked armoured vehicle often fitted with a Bren light machine-gun or other weapon; designed to move weapons and troops across bullet-swept ground with some degree of protection
C47	American twin-engined transport aircraft
C in C	Commander-in-chief

Cmdr	Commander
CMF	Citizen Military Forces: the Army Reserve; also known at various times as the Militia
CO	Commanding Officer
Coy	Company
Creeping barrage	Artillery fire used to support advancing troops; the barrage is timed to move forward in front of the troops, subduing enemy opposition as they continue to attack
CSIRO	Commonwealth Scientific and Industrial Research Organisation: Australia's pre-eminent scientific research body
Dago	Disparaging term for an Italian soldier
DSC	Distinguished Service Cross
DSO	Distinguished Service Order
GOC	General Officer Commanding
HQ	Headquarters
HMAS	His Majesty's Australian Ship
HMS	His Majesty's Ship
HRH	His Royal Highness
Inf	Infantry
I Tank	Infantry Tank designation; refers to the British-built Matilda tank in North Africa
LO	Liaison Officer
LtCol	Lieutenant Colonel
MC	Military Cross
MDS	Medical dressing station
MID	Mentioned in despatches
Militia	Australia's pre-World War II Army Reserve which, at times, was composed of either conscripts or volunteers or both; during World War II the Militia was a largely conscript home defence force limited to fighting only in Australian territory (which included the territories of Papua and New Guinea, and later other areas near Australia)
MO	Medical Officer (doctor)
NCO	Non-commissioned officer

ABBREVIATIONS AND TERMS

NG	New Guinea
No-man's-land	Disputed territory between two opposing forces
OP	Observation platform
Pioneers	Troops trained with limited engineering skills who could also be used as infantry
POW	Prisoner of war
Provos	Regimental police
Qantas	Australia's national airline
RAAF	Royal Australian Air Force
RAF	Royal Air Force
RAP	Regimental air post: the forward medical treatment location for a battalion's casualties
RSM	Regimental Sergeant Major
Staff Corps	The pre-war regular army officer corps
U/C	Under command
USS	United States Ship
VD	Venereal disease
Vichy	French collaborative government set up under Marshal Petain after France signed an armistice with Germany in 1940
Wadi	Dried-up watercourse in the desert
WRANS	Women's Royal Australian Naval Service
WRFA	Water Research Foundation of Australia

Foreword

In its relatively short one-hundred-year history, the Australian Army has been extremely fortunate in the very high quality of its leaders at all levels. Names such as General Sir John Monash and Field Marshal Sir Thomas Blamey are well known to generations of serving soldiers. There are many others whose names are not so well-known but who, through brilliant leadership, personal bravery and superb battlefield skills, have written their place into our military history. Major General Ken Eather is one such leader. His biographer, Steve Eather—distant relative and ex-serviceman himself—has captured and recounted General Eather's story in a lucid, readable work that reflects credit not only on Major General Eather but on that fine fighting force, the Second AIF.

As the foundation Commanding Officer of the 2/1st Battalion, 2nd AIF, Ken Eather's leadership skills were first clearly demonstrated in the early battles in the Western Desert in 1941. His Battalion led the attack on Bardia and was prominent at Tobruk, performing well beyond expectations. Throughout the actions, he was in the front line, leading his men and making local tactical decisions that influenced the whole battle. His men greatly respected his judgment, personal bravery and willingness to share the same risks.

It was, however, in the command of the 25th Infantry Brigade of the 7th Division that the (then) Brigadier established himself as one of the finest Australian fighting commanders of the war.

Ken Eather's promotion to Brigadier coincided with the Japanese attacks and it was against this new enemy that he was to spend the rest of his fighting career. His introduction to jungle fighting was in the battle for the Kokoda Track. His Brigade was thrown into the battle at the lowest ebb of Australia's fortunes. He was under enormous pressure not only to stop the Japanese advance but to turn it back and drive them from the mountains. His leadership skills were again tested and he performed magnificently.

On 26 July 1945 Ken Eather was promoted to Major General and given command of the 11th Australian Division. The Division was given the role of occupying Rabaul and taking responsibility for the large Japanese garrison. General Eather ensured they were properly treated and prevented revenge attacks on them by the local populace. His biggest challenge, however, was keeping up the morale of his Division during the drawn out process of repatriating the Japanese and Australian troops. He did this with skill and aplomb.

This book is a gripping overview of one person's experience of war. It also is a valuable insight into what constitutes a great leader. By highlighting Ken Eather's own methods and experiences, the work is almost a student's primer on command leadership. I congratulate Steve Eather on an excellent study of a great Australian.

Peter Cosgrove, AC, MC
General
Chief of the Defence Force
Canberra, May 2003

Preface

Growing up in the late 1960s and early 1970s, I occasionally heard mention of Ken Eather, an elderly man, a distant relative who had been a soldier—an important one in fact.

Although I saw him from a distance during Sydney Anzac Day marches, I had not thought about him very much until one day in 1973. In sixth grade at Maitland Primary School, I slipped away from school at lunchtime with a group of friends and ran down to the local corner shop to spend our lunch money on lollies. We rushed into the shop in a rowdy group and one of my friends yelled out, 'What are you getting, Eather?' On hearing this the shopkeeper whirled around and stared at me. I thought I was in dreadful trouble for making too much noise. To my surprise, he asked if I was related to General Eather. I nodded timidly. To my further surprise, his face broke into a huge smile and he gave me a large bag of lollies—for free! The shopkeeper had been a soldier in World War II and had served under General Eather's command. I was over the moon at receiving such a windfall, but in the years to come often wondered why a shopkeeper would give a rowdy child he didn't know free lollies 30 years after a war on the basis of being a relative of someone I had never met. Who was General Eather and why would the shopkeeper feel such loyalty to his former commander?

This book owes everything to that shopkeeper and that bag of lollies. I later discovered that Major General Eather was one of Australia's foremost soldiers. After long and dedicated service in the pre-war Militia he was one of the first officers appointed to the AIF. Having formed the 2/1st Australian Infantry Battalion (City of Sydney Regiment), he led his unit in the key initial assault role at Bardia, the Australian Army's first major battle of World War II. After further service in North Africa and Syria, he returned to Australia as a brigadier. He then went to New Guinea where his troops, with others, finally stopped the Japanese advance on Port Moresby—Australia's darkest hour—before pursuing them back over the Kokoda Track and capturing Kokoda village. Further bloody campaigns followed. Near the end of the war he was promoted to major general and given command of the 11th Division.

After a period as military governor of New Britain and New Ireland, General Eather led the Australian Contingent at the 1946 Victory Parade in London. Upon completing this final task he retired from the Army, but soon made his mark as the president of the Primary Producers' Association of New South Wales and later still as the executive director of the Water Research Foundation of Australia, a nationally significant organisation. These were all substantial achievements for someone who had left school at the age of fourteen and at the outbreak of war in 1939 was a dental mechanic and an obscure part-time soldier.

The purpose of this book is not to glorify war—that most base of human activities and the ultimate failure of diplomacy; rather, I have tried to record the life and achievements of a truly notable Australian.

In the chapters relating to the war in the Pacific there are a number of references to the barbarous treatment of Australian soldiers and indigenous people by the Japanese Army. I do not apologise for this, and make the point that I am referring to the activities of *some* Japanese 60 years ago, and certainly not referring to the Japanese people today or, indeed, to all Japanese in the past. The Japanese Army of World War II was a ruthless and brutal organisation which felt itself in no way governed by the accepted rules of war. Their treatment of those who fell into their hands at that time reflected this thinking.

While Japanese war crimes are widely acknowledged, except in Japan itself, Australian breaches of the rules of war are not. In this book Australian breaches are also described. When the Japanese atrocities became known, the Australian soldiers became so enraged that for the rest of the war the Japanese were given little quarter, even if they asked for it—which they rarely did. Japanese soldiers were sometimes shot if they attempted to surrender. Occasionally they were killed after capture. The hatred and savagery felt by the Australians and Japanese towards each other in those days is perhaps hard for the young people of both nations to understand today, but 60 years ago both countries thought they were fighting for what was right and gave each other no quarter.

Steve Eather
July 2003

1
Early days

... the parsimonious treatment of the Australian Army in the years between the wars, with its night parades, its eight or ten days of annual training, its uncertain future and its constantly changing organisation, left gaps that were hard to remedy in the experience of the officers of the middle ranks. They came to the command of battalions and companies without full apprenticeship... However, this group included young leaders of great capacity who were destined to rank among the outstanding commanders of the Second A.I.F.—men such as Eather, Dougherty, Chilton, Walker and Porter...

Gavin Long, General Editor of the Official History of Australia in World War II

Although the Eathers are one of the oldest European families in Australia, their early connections would hardly have given rise to the expectation that the family would generate a truly great Australian. In fact, it has produced several such people and this story is concerned with arguably the most notable of these.

Thomas Eather (the original family name was Heather, but through the poor level of literacy marking early colonial times, it evolved into Eather) was born on 15 July 1764 at Bexley in Kent, England.[1] In October 1787, the illiterate 23-year-old was apprehended and charged with highway robbery. The theft was no small one—some 40 shillings and a silver watch valued at an additional 50 shillings were stolen from one George Cotton, Esq. Thomas was found guilty and sentenced to hang. This sentence was later commuted to fourteen years' transportation to New South Wales. Thomas had the misfortune of being assigned to the transport *Neptune*, one of the vessels making up the Second Fleet. As a result of its captain (an experienced slave-trader from the African run) withholding rations to sell for personal profit, the *Neptune* had the highest death rate of any convict ship ever to make the voyage to Australia. One hundred and fifty eight of the vessel's 427 convicts died; those who survived were desperately ill and suffering the effects of starvation, scurvy and neglect when they reached their destination. On 28 June 1790 the *Neptune* anchored in Botany Bay and the Eather family's association with Australia began, in chains.[2] Several years after Thomas was transported to the antipodes his nephew Samual was convicted of grand larceny and joined his uncle in Australia (the author is a descendant of Samual).

Thomas eventually won his freedom and married Elizabeth Lee, another convict. The couple were to have eight children and become the founders of one of Australia's largest families. Thomas began farming at what is now the town of Windsor; he also became a publican, established a freight carting service across the Blue Mountains and took up property on the Namoi River in the New England region.

Thomas's fifth child, also named Thomas, was born in October 1800 at Richmond. Thomas Junior, after operating a butchery and bakery, turned to farming and married Sarah McAlpin, later taking over Thomas Senior's cattle and sheep station Henriendi, on the Namoi River, and raising a family.[3] William, one of young Thomas's children, later worked Henriendi with a brother for some years. In 1853 William married Ann Senior and the couple had at least ten children, the last of whom was also named William.

In 1896 William Eather—great-grandson of the Second Fleet Eather—married Isabella Theresa Lees at Paddington, a suburb of Sydney.[4] Their son Kenneth William Eather was born in Sydney on 6 June 1901. Two sisters, Dulcie and Nancy, were later additions to the family.

William and Isabella had met while the young man was working as a property manager, probably at Henriendi. Isabella was a governess at another property in the area. William was remembered as a 'kindly, gentle man, whose heart was in the country'.[5] Relatives doubted that he ever really made the transition to city life. Isabella, however, had come close to having a very different life. According to the same relatives, she had:

an excellent soprano singing voice and played the piano. She was selected from 500 voices in Sydney Town Hall for further studies but, as her family did not believe in women working on the stage, she did not accept the offer. Isabella was a woman of very powerful personality and was the driving force of their home.

William was at one time a plantation manager in New Guinea so that, interestingly as later events would prove, as a young boy Ken lived for some years in Port Moresby. In Australia Ken went to school at Abbotsholme College, a boarding school in Wahroonga, Sydney. This school was founded in 1909 by John FitzMaurice but closed following the death of its founder in January 1924. The school buildings were subsequently destroyed by fire.[6] Abbotsholme was one of the best boarding schools in the Sydney area and also had a reputation for very strict discipline. Nonetheless, young Ken enjoyed school. He was good at mathematics and his love of reading was something that would become a lifelong pleasure. He enjoyed playing cricket, especially as batsman.[7]

It is interesting to reflect on the ways Abbotsholme made an impact on Ken's life. In the Army Ken himself would later have a reputation as a strict disciplinarian. It is also possible that he may have met two other students there—the future Liberal prime ministers Harold Holt and William McMahon—and that his time there could have contributed to his relatively conservative political views.

Growing up in the Eather household was enjoyable. The sisters and their brother played well together, even though the girls often became Ken's victims when playing Cowboys and Indians, at times ending up staked to the ground while their brother did war dances around them. The three siblings would remain close all their lives.[8]

Although Isabella was a very strong-willed woman, she doted on her children, especially her son. She was an excellent cook and cakes were a speciality. More than once Ken and his cousin Ike were caught having just eaten a whole freshly baked sponge cake between them—but the wayward pair usually escaped retribution.

Even at a young age, William's son seems to have had a focus on organisation and detail that was unusual. One of his sisters recalled how, on one family camping trip, Ken had drawn up a list of duties for Nancy and Dulcie to complete so that 'all would go smoothly'.[9]

Chris Brookes (Nancy's son) recalls his mother telling him that as Christmas approached, Ken was 'sometimes visited by Father Christmas' as he lay in bed. After a brief exchange of pleasantries, Ken would give a detailed report to Father Christmas about his sisters' behaviour. The girls would live in suspense for weeks before the big event, hoping that Father Christmas would still visit them.

In January 1911 Australia introduced universal compulsory military training (conscription) for the first time. From the age of twelve, boys had to join the junior school-based cadet units. When they turned fourteen they transferred to the senior cadets for four years. From the age of eighteen to 26 they became members of the Militia. Accordingly, young Ken Eather had his first taste of soldiering as a twelve-year-old. Junior cadets were not issued with uniforms but were obliged to complete 90 hours of training per year. Activities included drill, physical training, rifle shooting, swimming and first aid.[10]

One person who made a very definite impression on the young army cadet was Colonel James Lees, an uncle who had had a distinguished career in the British Army. Colonel Lees was a cavalry officer, one of the 'brave six hundred' immortalised in Tennyson's poem on the charge of the Light Cavalry Brigade at Balaclava during the Crimean War. Colonel Lees later came out to Australia and subsequently lived in New Zealand where he became a prize fighter.[11] Even in later life, family members noted that Ken often talked fondly of Colonel Lees, who must have died at least 50 years earlier. Colonel Lees's fame as one of the survivors of Lord Cardigan's epic cavalry charge had a powerful effect on Ken's decision to pursue a military career of some sort, despite his parents' discouragement.

When Ken transferred to the senior cadets at the age of fourteen he was issued with his first army uniform. Along with the other senior cadets, he completed weekend and night training and camps. Rifle shooting was conducted using modified Martini-Henry carbines. While the cadets had to complete a mandatory minimum of 64 hours' training per year, additional activities existed for those who were keen to do more.

As a result of his family's unfortunate financial situation during the early days of World War I, Ken was forced to leave school at the age of about fourteen.[12] He had not completed his education, although this was hardly an uncommon event at that time. He became an apprentice dental mechanic, a trade for which he showed considerable aptitude and flair. The prevailing patriotism of the times and Ken's interest in military matters and enthusiasm for cadets makes it likely that he was keen to enlist in the Australian Imperial Force when he was old enough, but the war ended before he could do so.

There is some suggestion that Ken wanted to join the small permanent army and attend Duntroon after the war. His parents, and in particular his determined mother, reputedly saw little future for their son in such a poorly regarded and remunerated profession and vetoed the idea, their attitude undoubtedly influenced by the recent hostilities in which so many Australians had been killed and maimed.

At the age of eighteen Ken was transferred into the Militia and shortly afterwards, on 31 June 1919, was commissioned as a second lieutenant. At this time, Militia training was of a low standard and trainees for the most part were uninterested. Being made an officer in a conscript force at such a young age demonstrates Ken's keen sense of responsibility and aptitude. Displaying unusual dedication and a flair for soldiering, Ken remained in the Militia after his mandatory training obligation was completed, where many others resigned. He was made a provisional lieutenant in March 1922 and served with the 53rd Infantry Battalion before transferring to the 56th Battalion in July 1925. In February of the following year he was promoted to captain and just two years later to major.[13]

Ken's rapid advancement was ample testimony to his developing skill, leadership abilities and knowledge of military matters. It was all the more remarkable for his lack of combat experience, for promotion in the Militia usually went to officers with war service, and there were plenty of veterans from whom to choose.

In 1923 Ken, by now a brown-eyed, fair-haired young man standing 180 cm tall, married Adeline Mabel Lewis at Canterbury.[14] From his mother, in particular, Ken had developed a quiet but forceful personality. He did not often lose his temper but he was determined. Not religious in any outward form, he was nonetheless a kind person, and had a rather dry sense of humour. On 25 June 1924 the couple's first child, Elsie Isobel, was born. A son, also named Ken, was a later addition to the family.

Parallel to Ken's outstanding success in the Militia, his career as a dental mechanic also flourished. Indeed, his work was of such a high standard that he was much in demand. So successful and well known did he become that he later went into practice with a partner in Sydney's elite Macquarie Street. Some of his customers—reputedly including a number of Indian rajahs—came from overseas to receive the benefit of his high quality work. He worked long hours building up his practice and his days were made longer by train travel between his home at Bankstown and the city. During the Depression years, Ken's practice did not fail like so many other businesses, although undoubtedly demand slowed down. However, his parents suffered substantially, losing inherited real estate in the Waverly area.[15]

What of the Army in which Major Eather was making a part-time career? Aside from a small permanent nucleus, the Australian Army of the 1920s and 1930s was modelled on the Australian Imperial Force

Happy times. The Eather family in the 1930s. Already known as an efficient Militia officer and a highly successful dental mechanic, the future major general sits with (from left to right) Adeline, Nance, his parents and daughter Isobel.

Photo courtesy of the Brookes family

of World War I and was equipped primarily with weapons from that conflict. Following the signing of the Washington disarmament agreements in the early 1920s, Australian defence spending was savagely reduced. Militia soldiers were now required to attend only six days annually in camp, with a further four training nights at local drill halls. Clearly, this level of training would not result in an effective force that could be mobilised at short notice in defence of Australia. In total the Militia consisted of just 31 000 partly trained troops.

When Australia along with the rest of the world was hit by the Great Depression, defence spending was further cut and any hopes that the Milita would become an efficient fighting force were dashed for those officers charged with training the troops. By 1935, the now voluntary Militia contained less than 30 000 'soldiers'.

Despite these disappointments, the Militia's core of highly motivated part-time officers continued to work hard and to the best of their abilities. On 1 July 1933, at the age of 32, Eather was promoted to lieutenant colonel and appointed Commanding Officer of the 56th Battalion, Riverina Regiment, which had its headquarters at Belmore in Sydney. This was his first unit command. It was said that this appointment made him the youngest battalion commander in the Militia. It also made him one of the first officers not a veteran of the 1914–1918 war to be given a battalion command. Certainly he was seen as a highly efficient and capable infantry officer by his peers and by the higher echelons of the Army. Nonetheless it appears that Army Headquarters harboured some reservations about appointing a non-veteran to a battalion command, for the initial recommendation was unsuccessful. It was only after Brigadier Allen and General Moreshead made strong representations to Headquarters that a second recommendation succeeded. After four years leading the 56th Battalion, in 1937 Eather transferred to the command of the 3rd Battalion—a Militia unit that would later play a distinguished part in the Kokoda Track fighting, again under his command.

In common with other dedicated Militia officers, Eather spent a great deal of his own time studying military and related subjects. In his case there was particular emphasis on administration, military law and logistics. He continued in the command of the 3rd Battalion until August 1938, when he transferred to the unattached list of

On behalf of his battalion, Lieutenant Colonel Eather accepts a trophy for having the best all-round infantry battalion in the Militia, circa 1936. Members of the battalion look on during the presentation.

Photo via the Brookes family. Reproduced with permission of the Army History Unit

officers—a reserve category with no active training obligations. The reason he took this step is unclear. Possibly he believed that there was little chance of further advancement in this career, although in view of his outstanding record of achievement and rapid promotion this seems improbable. It is more likely that family commitments were an issue, or that his dental mechanic's practice had developed to such an extent that it was no longer possible to devote sufficient time to soldiering. Transfer to inactive duty should have meant the end of his part-time military career but for the growing threat of war in Europe and Asia.

In 1931 Japan had invaded Manchuria, while in 1933 Hitler and the National Socialist (Nazi) Party came to power in Germany, that country subsequently resigning from the League of Nations. By 1937 Italy had annexed Abyssinia and the Spanish Civil War was being fought.

EARLY DAYS

As these alarming events unfolded, the democratic countries came to the reluctant realisation that they must re-arm. There could have been no country more reluctant to re-arm than Australia. By 1935 the defence budget had increased so microscopically that it *almost* equalled the 1928 allocation. While clearly disturbed by the unfolding situation in Europe and Asia, the government was desperate not to commit scarce funds for defence while even the slightest possibility remained that Australia would *not* become involved in a war.

Of the Australian Army in the mid-1930s, the following disturbing observation was made by Gavin Long, the official historian:

> The army whose rebuilding he [General Lavarack, the then Chief of the General Staff] had to control consisted of 1,800 'permanent' officers and other ranks, compared with 3,000 in 1914, and 27,000 militiamen compared with 42,000 in 1914. Its equipment had been supplemented hardly at all since the A.I.F. had brought it home from France and Palestine.[16]

In the late 1930s defence spending increased very substantially indeed. Sadly, it was by then too late to obtain military equipment from British factories, which were fully occupied filling orders for their own forces. The Militia was greatly expanded and by Christmas 1938 numbered 70 000; nonetheless, it was still a very poorly trained force.

2
A call
to arms

> *Fellow Australians. It is my melancholy duty to inform you officially that, in consequence of a persistence by Germany in her invasion of Poland, Great Britain has declared war upon her and that, as a result, Australia is also at war.*
>
> Australian Prime Minister R.G. Menzies in a national radio broadcast, 3 September 1939

Prime Minister Menzies's sombre announcement to the Australian people that they were at war with Germany was followed by a confusing period of many months in which the nation was not fully preparing itself for conflict. While the Navy and Air Force were mobilised for active service, for the Army the situation was different. The fighting elements of the Army almost wholly comprised the Militia which, by government legislation, could not be compelled to serve outside Australian territory. Nor could the Militia be mobilised without causing immense disruption to Australian industry and the economy. A new volunteer force would have to be specially enlisted if Australian troops were to proceed overseas on active service.

G.A. Street, the Minister for Defence, announced in parliament on 19 September that:

> the Government has decided to form a special force, consisting of an infantry division, for service either at home or overseas, according to circumstances. This force is to be enlisted for the duration of the war and twelve months thereafter, or until lawfully discharged. Arrangements have been made for troops to be enrolled and medically examined immediately at any training centre in Australia . . .

Somewhat surprisingly, it was announced that virtually all the command appointments within this new division, to be called the 6th Australian Division, would go to Militia officers rather than to available Staff Corps regular officers. This decision would lead to intensified acrimony between regular and Militia officers—worsening a problem that had existed for years—but it allowed a number of relatively junior Militia officers to rapidly make names for themselves. One of them was Ken Eather.

Lieutenant Colonel Eather was asked to accept an appointment in the AIF. He readily agreed and formally enlisted in the new force on 16 October. He was given command of the 2/1st Infantry Battalion, a unit to be formed from recruits enlisted in the Sydney area and known as the 'City of Sydney Regiment'. Apart from attaining this distinction, he was just the third soldier recruited into the 2nd AIF from New South Wales, as revealed by his low service number of NX3. Eather's decision to accept this appointment, which apparently he never regretted, would have a continuing financial impact for much of his life—his highly successful dental mechanic's practice being hastily sold for substantially less than it was worth.

On 25 October 1939, Warrant Officer Wally Delves, a permanent army infantry and light horse instructor, knocked on Eather's office door at Victoria Barracks. After saluting he said, 'Sir, I hear that you are forming an infantry battalion.' On receiving an affirmative reply, Wally said, 'I want to be your RSM.' This was the type of initiative which appealed to Eather. After some brief checks which revealed that Delves would be an outstanding asset, he was transferred the following day to the AIF and appointed Regimental Sergeant Major of the 2/1st, even before he received permission to leave the permanent forces.[1] At this early stage the unit comprised just its colonel and a few administrative staff. The new RSM would be of great assistance to his commanding officer, not just as the battalion was forming, but over succeeding years.

Other key personnel were selected for the 2/1st in various ways. Noting his own unusual selection, Captain Bill Travers, one of the unit's initial officers, recorded:

> Shortly after the war began Eather came to interview officers of the 1st/19th Battalion, CMF, for selection in the 2/1st Battalion, AIF,

which he had just been appointed to command. He carried out these interviews in the anteroom of 1st/19th Battalion's Officers' Mess at Victoria Barracks, each interview taking a half to three-quarters of an hour.

When it came to my turn to be interviewed I went into the anteroom in a considerable state of anxiety. The first question shot at me was 'Why do you want to join the AIF?' Such a question was designed to test my sincerity. The possible answers were legion and all could be misinterpreted. I think mine was unexpected.

Pointing to the various photographs hanging on the anteroom wall, I replied, 'Well that is a picture of my father, and that is a picture of my grandfather, and that is a picture of my great grandfather. They all served in Victoria Barracks [author's note: with the implication that they had seen no active service and done nothing of military value]. That was the end of the interview. It was over in ten minutes and I was a member of the 2/1st Battalion!'[2]

The 2/1st Battalion comprised one of the twelve (later reduced to nine) infantry battalions of the 6th Australian Division. The battalions were grouped into three brigades which, along with artillery, engineers and other support troops, made up the division. Of the twelve battalion commanders, eight had served in World War I; the other four—including Eather—had been too young to serve in that conflict. All, however, had extensive Militia service.

The 2/1st, 2/2nd and 2/3rd Battalions which formed the 16th Brigade, and some supporting troops also enlisted in New South Wales, were all located at Ingleburn. The 16th Brigade was commanded by Brigadier A.S. 'Tubby' Allen. Battalions enlisted from the other states formed the 17th and 18th Brigades. The whole force was commanded by Major General Sir Thomas Blamey, one of Australia's most distinguished military officers. (Coincidentally Allen, Blamey and Eather would later be involved in events of extraordinary military and political significance. All of their careers would be placed in jeopardy, and in some cases either damaged to some degree or destroyed, by the decisions they would make in New Guinea.)

Recruits allocated to the 2/1st Battalion were transported by bus to the newly constructed and spartan Ingleburn camp outside of Sydney. The first draft arrived in early November and, while Eather oversaw the training syllabus and devoted his time to the many other matters associated with the formation of a new Army unit, proceeded to prepare the camp site for the drafts soon to follow. Within four weeks, nearly 600 recruits had arrived.³ Militia recruits were selected from a number of local units including the 1st/19th, 17th, 18th, 30th and 36th Battalions. Eather gave considerable thought when appointing officers and NCOs, paying particular attention to their age. While some AIF battalion commanders quite deliberately selected a significant number of World War I veterans as leaders, in the 2/1st just one officer had seen service in that conflict. Eather took the view that many veterans would simply be too old to withstand the rigours of the coming conflict. He may also have questioned the relevance of their experience in what would be a mechanised and highly mobile war. The newly appointed non-commissioned officers were given only acting rank initially, which meant that they could be easily demoted and replaced if they did not meet their colonel's expectations.

Facilities at Ingleburn were very basic and there were complaints over the quality of food, camp hygiene and lack of facilities. Tensions exploded one evening in mid-November, when the troops rioted over the exorbitant prices and lack of variety of goods available at the contractor-operated canteens. Complaints to the contractor had been met by abuse and ignored. The troops set fire to one canteen and it would seem that no attempt was made to put the fire out. Troops of the 2/1st Battalion along with others were involved in this incident, which unfolded literally before their colonel's eyes. The historian of the 2/1st Battalion noted that Eather was having a meal with some of his officers when the fire started and that the orderly officer, appalled by the sight visible from the window, made to organise firefighting operations. However, he was told by his apparently unconcerned commanding officer, 'You have had a long day, finish your meal.' A few minutes later, the orderly officer again suggested that he should organise a fire-fighting party but Eather, looking outside again, told him, 'Have your coffee first. It's still not thoroughly alight!'

On becoming aware that the troops intended burning down a second canteen, Eather finally acted. He formed his officers in a line between the canteen and the soldiers before telling his men to stop being foolish and to go back to their quarters.⁴ His orders were obeyed and the angry troops dispersed. Although many of those involved in the riot could be identified, no one was charged. Clearly, Eather was in sympathy with his men's actions. His failure to act immediately to control the troops is in contrast to his reputation as a strict disciplinarian, however. It would appear that he felt drastic action against the contractor was warranted. The ultimate result supports this supposition, for the contractor was replaced by a more efficiently run Army-managed canteen.

Eather's rigorous training was starting to weld the 2/1st into a highly disciplined and effective battalion. Initially he had centred his efforts on drill, weapons training, field craft and section manoeuvres before developing more complex and larger troop manoeuvres. Training proceeded apace for some weeks until the 16th Brigade received orders to prepare for embarkation overseas.

Prior to embarkation, a farewell march for the 16th Brigade through Sydney was held. This event was well reported in the media. According to the *Sydney Morning Herald* on 5 January 1940:

> Six thousand young soldiers of the Second A.I.F., proud bearers of the standard bequeathed to them by the original Anzacs, marched through the streets of the city yesterday.
>
> A tumultuous reception was given them by dense crowds, estimated to number nearly 500,000 . . .
>
> The superb bearing of the men, their smart appearance, and the precision of their marching excited universal admiration and the unqualified praise of their leader, Lieutenant General Sir Thomas Blamey, who will take them overseas.

While Adeline Eather may have been a proud spectator at the parade and all that had gone on in the lead-up to it, she must have been desperately sad now that the moment had come for her soldier husband to leave. Having lived through the World War I period as a child, she must have been keenly aware of the possibility that he might never return to their Bankstown home.

The SS *Orford* in which the 2/1st Battalion embarked was a P & O Liner, and there had been no time to convert her into a troopship.[5] Quarters were well appointed and spacious. The food was also excellent and all ranks enjoyed waiter service at meals. Colonel

Eather was made ship's commandant and as such was responsible to the *Orford*'s captain for the behaviour of the troops and for their administration. Embarked was not only his own battalion but also the 2/1st Field Artillery Regiment. As the *Orford* and other troop transports moved out through the harbour, the railings were lined with soldiers while the harbour shore was crowded with well-wishers.

The 2/1st Field Regiment was also commanded by a lieutenant colonel. When the two colonels met on the wharf, the artillery officer insisted that his troops be allowed to board the ship first because, in the Australian Army, the artillery has corps seniority over the infantry. Eather pretended to consider this proposition for a minute before 'reluctantly' agreeing. The happy artillerymen and their commanding officer proceeded to board, thinking that they had gained a point over the lowly infantry. They were mistaken, however. Eather had discovered in advance that the first troops on board were to be directed to the steerage cabins at the very bottom of the ship. He had been waiting for just this opportunity to get his soldiers the best accommodation possible. The artillerymen soon found this out, but the arrangements could not be changed and thus Eather's troops occupied the well fitted-out first and second class cabins.[6]

On 17 January Eather wrote the first of many letters to his parents:

Dear Mum & Pop,
Just a few lines to let you know that I am feeling as fit as a fiddle & that sea travelling seems to suit me down to the ground. We have had a few patches of pretty rough weather & several of our officers and men have been down with sea sickness. I have been rather fortunate. I have not had the slightest inclination to be ill & have never missed a meal. The meals on board are very good indeed, in fact up to the Orient Lines usual high standard. My quarters are also very comfortable. I have the ship's special suite & have been told that it has been used by some of the big people ... The suite consists of three rooms, cabin, day cabin & bathroom, all beautifully equipped.

We had a wonderful send-off from Sydney. Although everything was supposed to be secret hundreds of people, thousands in fact, turned out to see us off. I did not come down in the train but I believe the whole railway line was lined with waving people who were throwing cigarettes to the troops whenever the train slowed down . . .

Don't forget to write & let me know how you are both doing. I will write as often as I can . . . Don't worry, look after yourselves.

Lots of love,
K<small>EN</small>

The largely uneventful voyage was broken up with additional training. In a letter to his wife—whom he invariably referred to as 'Top'—Eather recorded on 17 January that 'the troops are having the time of their lives'. The 16th Brigade disembarked at Kantara, Egypt, in the second week of April and went by rail to Julis in Palestine where all battalions commenced training with the assistance of British regular soldiers. The 2/1st and the rest of the 16th Brigade were affiliated with the 2nd Battalion of the Black Watch, a famous Scottish regiment. Eather noted to family members several times in later years that 'the training given by the British, and its thoroughness, was indispensable to the 2/1st's later combat effectiveness'.

It was noted by several 2/1st battalion officers in North Africa that the training given by some Australian commanders to their troops was dated, in fact only replicating their experiences in, and the requirements of, the Western Front. Colonel Eather, the only unit commander in the 16th Brigade who had not fought in World War I, introduced markedly different, innovative training methods.[7] Thus, while the others were digging trenches and fortifications, the 2/1st Battalion practised more at mobile warfare, skirmishing, advancing and retreating over the wide expanses. This training accurately foreshadowed the soon to be fought battles of the Western Desert Campaign and may be why Eather's troops would later be selected to play the key role in the AIF's first major action of World War II.

Captain (later Major General) Paul Cullen later noted of the 16th Brigade's preparation and of Eather's part in it:

[Brigadier] Allen, [Lieutenant Colonel George] Wooten and Ken Eather made the 16th Brigade the best trained brigade in the 2nd AIF. [Their training regime] became the pattern for the remainder of the 6th Division and all the other divisions that followed.

In a letter on 17 April, Eather told Adeline:

This camp is getting very comfortable, in fact it feels just like home now. The last three days I have been out with the Unit on a continuous training exercise and to get back again to showers and decent bed is jolly good. The troops are fighting fit: they are brown as can be and are hardening up wonderfully, a twenty mile [32 kilometre] march is child's play now & that's more than could be said while we were in Ingleburn. Of course with their absolute fitness comes high spirits & one never knows what the devil they will get up to next. Generally speaking they are an excellent crowd but there are a few dead eggs among them who cause a lot of bother but they are spotted now & well in hand, a few awards of twenty-eight days detention rather shook them.

In another letter to his mother on 24 May, he noted:

Our chaps are in wonderful trim & will give a good account of themselves if they are called on. In fact they seem eager to get at it. The news of the war in France seems to have made them keener still.

Julis was a tented camp with few luxuries, from which Eather continued to put his troops through a harsh training regime. During this period, one of his soldiers was charged with a fairly serious offence and brought before his commanding officer who had, by this stage, earned a number of nicknames including 'Twenty-eight Days' and 'February' (because that month also has 28 days). Twenty-eight days confined to barracks—the maximum allowable sentence—was a relatively common punishment in the 2/1st.[8]

Warrant Officer Delves, who was present for the charge, cannot recall the offender's misdeed but he and the CO both knew that, although clearly guilty on this occasion, the man was a good soldier. After hearing the evidence which confirmed the soldier's guilt, Eather fined him £3—a considerable sum in those days. The angry soldier responded with, 'You can get f_ _ _ _d', which, after the slightest pause, drew the response '£4'. The soldier again responded in similar vein, which resulted in the fine being further increased, to £5—whereupon the soldier told his CO the same thing a third time.

By now the situation was serious. The errant soldier could not be fined any more heavily, and the next level of penalty would in all probability have resulted in him being sent to a British military prison—a very unpleasant prospect. Instead of doing that, Eather simply told him, 'You can have that last one on me—now get out', and the man was removed before his mouth could cause him any further trouble.

Another of Eather's sergeants, Pat Lawry, later brought one of his own men up before him on a charge. After the matter was heard and sentence pronounced, Sergeant Lawry was called back to the CO's office as Eather thought he seemed unsettled. Asked what was wrong, the sergeant replied that he was worried that his men might think him a bastard for having one of his soldiers charged. Lawry was bluntly told, 'Any sergeant of mine has to be a bastard or he is no good to me . . . now get out!'[9]

Nor did Eather spare his officers, especially where he was unsatisfied with an officer's conduct. In one ugly incident Private Reg Pane recalled that an officer 'was admonished in my presence never to falsely accuse anyone, especially of lower rank, to cover one's shortcomings in honesty and efficiency'.[10] In another incident, a platoon commander who broke water discipline on a desert exercise was removed from the battalion that same day.

The 2/1st Battalion commemorated Anzac Day on 25 April with most of the battalion getting up at 2 am and travelling in trucks to the Australian Section of the Gaza War Cemetery for the dawn service. Other small detachments marked Australia's most significant national event by marching through Tel Aviv and Jerusalem. While he enjoyed visiting Tel Aviv on occasions, Eather, like many Australians, found the hygiene standards and differing cultures in Egypt and Palestine hard to accept.

In a letter to his sister, dated 25 April, Eather wrote:

> Since we have been here I've moved about a lot on various jobs & have seen quite a lot of this strange old land. I've seen a lot of those historical spots mentioned in the bible: Gaza, Jaffa, Jericho, Jerusalem & many others. To be quite candid I was not impressed by what I saw & prefer our own Australia. It may not have the age but it is a jolly sight cleaner . . .

It is strange to be in one of these large towns & be surrounded by people & not be able to understand their speech. The other day I was a member of a party who were guests of the Mayor of Tel Aviv. We all went into town & were shown around & given many pressing invitations to come again. They are a strange race, these Jews. Most of those I have met are very keen on making the country their natural home & in spite of recent land regulations & opposition by the Arabs I think they will do so in the end.

The climate here is very much like our own in Sydney in August. The first few weeks we were here it was as cold as billyoh. I had to wear a jumper all day. Now it has warmed up a lot but is still rather nippy in the evenings. We don't get much rain. I think we have only had half a dozen wet days since we arrived. When it does rain it rains pretty hard. The soil gets very sticky and hangs to one's feet. I've been wearing shorts the past few days. All our troops have been issued with them. It's much cooler.

Except for army cars & trucks and the Jews' buses, there are not many cars here. Most Arabs own either a camel or donkey. There must be thousands upon thousands of donkeys in the country & the poor little beasts are made to carry such huge loads too. They are used for all sorts of work. I've seen an Arab ploughing with a donkey & a camel harnessed into his plough, generally an old wooden affair that would make our home farmers hold their sides with laughter. But they seem to get it done, because there are so many of them probably.

The harvest has just been made, all by hand too with the women working much harder than the men. Around about us barley is the main crop. After this is finished I believe there is not much for the Arab to do until next sowing season comes around . . .

To his father, Eather wrote at the same time:

One Tuesday I went into Jerusalem & spent an hour or so in the old city. By gosh, the place should be condemned. It's foul, stinks like hell and their idea of sanitation is the limit. The main idea is to toss everything out into the narrow, ill lit & smelly streets. I'm afraid I don't want to go into Jerusalem again although the new city is not too bad at all.

Our Good Friday was very quiet. I even went to church, that is we had a church service in the open & I went along. You know I was never that way inclined & after seeing the way they do things in the Holy Land I've even less time for it. The church game in Jerusalem is a big business. It has a funny side too. Each of the big sects: Christians, Coptic Greeks, Jew & Moslem have their own ideas as to the history & one can go along and see several mangers where Christ was born and two or three Mounts of Temptation . . .

In late July, the 2/1st Battalion's commanding officer had a week's leave in Tel Aviv. He later wrote to his mother:

I did a devil of a lot of surfing & sleeping & came back feeling as fit as a fiddle. During my stay in town I rented a furnished three bedroom flat near the beach . . . I used to get up about eight or half past & after my shave & shower used to wander off down to one of the open air cafes on the beach & have breakfast. I generally met some officers there & had my meal with them & swapped news. It was nice & cool in the sea breeze so it would take at least an hour to have breakfast & read the local newspaper, the 'Palestine Post'.

After breakfast I usually went back to the flat & got into my costume & went down to the beach where I'd spend some hours lazing about in deck chairs & having a surf. I'm afraid the beaches in this part of the world do not compare very favourably with our own. Terribly crowded too.

After the battalion had been in North Africa for some time, the 2/1st was allocated a number of timber-framed buildings for use as offices and stores. One of these buildings was divided into four sections with the CO's office at one end, two storerooms in the middle, and an armourers' workshop in the far end. One day, as Eather was working in his office, an armourer working on a rifle failed to carry out a safety check on the weapon and did not notice it was loaded. The rifle discharged and the bullet passed through all four intervening timber walls—exiting through Eather's office wall where he had been stretching and resting his head just a moment before.[11] No doubt the errant soldier at the other building became the object of the CO's wrath and spent 28 days confined to barracks.

A CALL TO ARMS

Following France's surrender, Italian forces began massing on the western border of Egypt. The number of troops available for the obviously imminent Italian offensive was substantially larger than the Commonwealth force in Egypt. However, as events would prove, the Italians were badly equipped, while some formations were irresolutely led and suffered from low morale—conditions that would greatly assist in their eventual defeat.

In the first half of September, the 16th Brigade moved to Helwan, south of Cairo, where training was finalised. Despite having limited time, Eather still managed to pen a line to his parents on 24 September:

> No doubt you already know we have moved down into Egypt & have settled into a new camp. It is a great change after Palestine. In some respects I like it much better, the climate for instance is better, not so humid. Even if it is darned hot during the day generally a cool breeze springs up at night & makes life bearable.
>
> We are training hard still, each week we spend at least three days away from camp in the desert. Lord it is desert too . . . Slept all through an air raid one night in Alexandria. Miss[ed] quite a lot of fire works.
>
> Our fellows go into Cairo quite frequently on leave & have a day in now & again to see the sights. I have only been into town twice since I have been here. [I] much prefer to stay in camp. I am developing into quite a picture fan. We have our camp cinemas. Very comfortable too. It's pleasant to sit in an open air show these cool nights. One can smoke too!
>
> I regret to say I haven't been interested enough to take a trip out to see the Pyramids. I've seen them from a distance, of course, but most of the officers who have been out did not seem very excited about it. Perhaps I will take a trip out one fine day.

After apologising for not writing home often enough, he indirectly warned his parents that he would soon be in action: 'I expect I shall be doing even less writing soon too. This part of the world seems to be becoming much more frequently mentioned in the news.'

Italian forces had crossed the frontier into Egypt earlier on 13 September and by October the 6th Australian Division was concentrated in the Amiriya area south-west of Alexandria. As the final few weeks of inaction slipped by it was clear that it was not just the 2/1st Battalion's enlisted soldiers who were keen to get into battle. In a letter to his parents on 17 November, Eather noted:

> I've not much news for you. Still going strong with our training. They [the 2/1st Battalion] are a pretty good bunch now, ready for anything almost & cracking their necks to have a go at the Dagos who seem to be 'setting' here in Africa. They certainly don't show any inclination to come on . . .
>
> We get a little excitement now & again especially when the moon is up. Some nights we get as many as seven air-raid alarms. Sometimes they don't develop into anything but at the worst we only get a few spent A/A [anti-aircraft] shells whistling around & everybody piles into a slit trench when they hear them coming. I've had several grand stand views of raids on Alexandria but the A/A guns make more din & fuss than bombs.

This letter would be the last occasion Eather would have for some time to complain of there being little news. Two days later he left to spend a month at the Middle East Tactical School. This was an intensive training course designed to ensure that its students were fully conversant with the latest military developments.

Of his time attending this course, the 2/1st battalion's commander told his sister:

> It's some little time since I've written but I've been so darned busy it's difficult finding time for any letter writing at all . . .
>
> I came down [to the school] on the 19th Nov & will not return to my unit until the 21st of this month. By the time I go back I will be, or supposed to be, right up to date with all the latest methods. It's a great change. One hasn't [as] much to worry about as when with the unit but it isn't a holiday by any means. In fact we are worked like the devil.
>
> The hours of work are rather strange & took quite a long time to get used to. We commence work at 8 am each morning & go right through until one or half past. Sometimes the morning is devoted to lectures or sand table exercises & at other times we go out into the

desert along the Suez Road & spend the morning out working on the ground. After lunch there is a break until 6 pm. Although it is termed a break, we are given quite a lot of work to do & spend most of the afternoon on it. At 6 pm the lectures commence again & finish around 8 pm. Dinner is at 8.30 & it's generally well after nine before it's over. The night too far gone by that time to do much so I usually go to bed.

There are a mixed bag of students here, fellows from English, Scottish, New Zealand, Australian & Trans Jordan battalions. They are a very decent crowd & we knock out a fair amount of fun in between times. Wednesday & Saturday afternoons are half holidays but I seldom go out. I have had a run into Cairo two or three times but it's not up to much so I generally muck about at the school getting my notes up to date. One Wed[nesday] I went in & spent the afternoon at the famous Gezira Club which is on an island of the Nile almost in the heart of the city. It's a wonderful place, beautifully kept lawns & greens where one can spend a quiet afternoon...

The living quarters here are very comfortable, so much so that I will be spoiled for my return to the somewhat primitive conditions in camp. I have two rooms nicely furnished...

This morning we spent out on the Ismailia Canal watching some of the Egyptian Army Engineers demonstrate the building of various types of bridges. They are well trained & did a good job. Afterwards we were entertained in the Mess & I met several of their officers who are too pretty to be soldiers but are nice enough.

Having completed his course of instruction Eather arrived back at the 2/1st Battalion just in time to play a pivotal role in Australia's first major land battle of World War II.

3
The North
African Campaign

As you no doubt know by this time, the Battle of Bardia is over, the results are entirely satisfactory from our point of view. My fellows were selected as the spearhead and did a grand job of work. It was a wonderful experience & I felt & still do as proud as punch with my chaps.

Lieutenant Colonel Eather, letter to his father, 13 January 1941

After Indian and British troops decisively defeated an Italian force at Sidi Barrani, the 6th Australian Division relieved the 4th Indian Division and on 12 December 1940 started a move of some 500 kilometres towards the Italian fortress town of Bardia. General Wavell, the British commander, needed to capture Bardia and later Tobruk as his troops advanced into Libya in order to protect his communications from attack and also to assist in the supply of his forces by making use of the port facilities at both locations.

Bardia and Tobruk had well-developed defences and the Italian commanders were expecting an attack. Bardia was surrounded by approximately 28 kilometres of well-planned defences. A substantial anti-tank ditch, minefields and barbed wire protected a perimeter containing two parallel rows of strongly constructed infantry posts. Most of these contained at least one 47 mm gun and several machine-guns. Additional posts were located further to the rear in areas considered vulnerable to attack.

Intensive patrolling of the Italian perimeter at Bardia was carried out in the days and nights preceding the assault, but while these patrols provided detailed information about the defences, they did not reveal the size of the enemy garrison. British plans were based on the belief that only 20 000 Italian troops with 110 artillery pieces would oppose the Australian force in their first major battle of World War II. It was later discovered that the garrison actually contained four infantry divisions and other units comprising about 45 000 troops, and that over 400 artillery pieces and many tanks were available to the defenders. The Australians would have to overcome the enemy's fortifications, strong artillery and a garrison much larger than Intelligence sources estimated. They would be supported in their attack by their own artillery and also by British tanks, artillery and machine-gunners. The Commonwealth air forces and navies would help with bombardments from air and sea. The British 7th Armoured Division, while it would not participate in the actual attack, was to contain any attempted Italian withdrawal towards Tobruk.

Detailed planning and rehearsing took place over several days. On Christmas Eve 1940, the officers of the 2/1st were attending a briefing when the Italians disrupted proceedings by shelling the battalion's positions. During the bombardment, Captain D.R. (Doug) Channell was observed nonchalantly walking through the barrage, even pausing to light a cigarette without taking cover. From the relative safety of his dugout Eather was not impressed and yelled out, 'Run, you damn fool'—sound advice upon which the officer promptly acted.[1] It was an ironic criticism to make, however. On several occasions, in both North Africa and New Guinea, Eather himself was guilty of disregarding heavy artillery fire and striding through it as if it did not exist.

At 4.16 am—well before dawn—on 3 January 1941, the 16th Brigade (with the 2/1st in the lead) advanced quickly and quietly in the pre-battle phase of the assault, then waited for the 'friendly' artillery barrage to open at 5.30 am. The night was so bitterly cold that some of the troops' water bottles froze while they waited.

The 2/1st had been given the vital and dangerous role of spearheading the assault and making the initial breach in the Italian defences in an area south of the Bardia–Tobruk road between posts 46, 47, 48 and 49. After penetrating the perimeter, the 2/1st was to swing left and roll up further Italian posts to widen the gap for the following battalions. To ensure success, Eather had devoted considerable thought to training his infantry—and the attached engineers and pioneers—in the blowing up and cutting through of barbed-wire entanglements.

With the commencement of the barrage the troops attacked. The 2/1st surged ahead with two companies forward and two in immediate support, the engineers and pioneers leading. It was expected that between 5 and 6 per cent of the attackers would become casualties before the wire was breached. The rate of advance was planned at 180 metres per minute to keep pace with the 'creeping barrage', but this proved too fast, and the troops had to stop several times as they waited for the barrage to move forward.[2] As the Australians continued to advance on the Italian perimeter, one of the engineer parties whose task was to blow up the barbed wire was hit by enemy artillery fire. Four soldiers were killed and nine wounded by the detonation which impacted so close to the 2/1st Headquarters party that they were shaken by the blast.[3] The officer leading the engineers, who was to give the order for all the engineer and pioneer detachments to detonate their Bangalore torpedoes, was wounded and unable to carry out his duties. There was confusion among the dazed engineers but Eather, who was advancing with them well forward of his battalion, saw the problem in the half light, took decisive action and ordered an engineer sergeant to immediately detonate his Bangalores in the wire. This was done at 6.08 am. Seeing this, the engineer parties further down the line also detonated their Bangalores, opening gaps in the wire through which the troops poured. The delay had been only three minutes.

After the wire was blown, Eather stood calmly in the gap, with no more lethal weapon than a walking stick and seemingly oblivious to the continuing enemy bombardment and small-arms fire. He directed the troops through the wire and pointed out their objectives to them with comments such as: 'All right chaps, come on! This way.' Many of his soldiers saw him thus and recall his calmness and courage under fire as he encouraged the troops in their and his first fight.

Even later, as the balance of the 16th Brigade moved through the gap, Captain Cullen of the 2/2nd Battalion noted:

> I was leading my company across the anti-tank ditch and the breach in the wire and minefields. I remember Ken standing in the ditch and as I passed him he said 'Good work Paul'. It was very encouraging and very stimulating—as he meant it to be. A true

leader. The Italian artillery shelling was very severe and it was our first action.[4]

The Australian attack, made on a narrow front of only 730 metres, was designed to penetrate the defences at the junction of two sectors of the Italian defences. This was done with the idea of creating as much confusion as possible for the defenders, who initially might be deceived into believing both sectors were under substantial attack by a very large force. In this the plan exceeded all expectations.

After his troops had passed through the wire, Eather was conspicuous in his presence on the battlefield, walking about with his walking stick under his arm, talking to the troops and encouraging them as the battle continued. His forward headquarters had been set up near a Royal Horse Artillery battery but, assuming these guns would come under fire from the well-handled Italian artillery, he moved headquarters to the recently captured Post 46. From here, he and his staff ticked off the various posts as they were captured. Noting that the post next to his own had not been ticked off on the plotting board but that several further along had been, Eather asked one of his Intelligence staff to go over there and ask why the post had not been reported as secured. The soldier had hardly left headquarters when he obtained his answer in the form of several bursts of machine-gun fire flicking up the sand around him.[5] A quickly organised assault soon captured the offending post and it was duly marked off the plotting board.

Once the 2/1st Battalion had made a breach, then widened the gap, the way was open for the rest of the 16th Brigade and the tanks to follow. The 2/2nd Battalion poured through the gap and swung to the right, where it commenced attacking enemy posts, while the 2/3rd Battalion pushed straight ahead to create depth to the Australian bridgehead.

One account of the early fighting graphically recorded that:

> The Australians pressed on towards the first objectives, firing their Brens from the hip at the flashes of machine-guns seen through the thick clouds of dust and smoke being churned up by exploding shells. At many places the Italians fought well, firing until the Australians finished them off with the bayonet.[6]

Despite the initial opposition, it was clear that the 2/1st was meeting all its objectives as the troops continued to capture successive enemy posts. Italian soldiers surrendered in considerable numbers. When it became apparent that they would not be difficult to control, small parties or sometimes single soldiers were used to guide groups of prisoners to the rear. Even despatching single soldiers eventually left battalion numbers seriously depleted. Later the Italians were simply pointed in the right direction and left to make their own way to the rear. Accurate figures were impossible to keep but one source estimated that 10 000 Italian troops surrendered to the 16th Brigade between 12 pm and dusk.

The battle raged throughout the day. Eather made several trips from his headquarters through bullet-swept ground to visit forward platoons and see how they were faring, and to ensure that the operation was proceeding to plan. Some Italian posts surrendered with little or no opposition but others resisted strongly for a time.

Of Bardia and the work of his Bren carrier platoon, Corporal Barry Hennessy noted:

> Having breached the tank trap [anti-tank ditch] we fanned out along the inside of the perimeter, capturing several strongly fortified underground bunkers. As we halted to take stock of the situation, the Colonel came across and got into my carrier directing us to drive to the top of a small rise. There he dismounted and, having moved about fifty yards [45 metres] from the carrier, he stood studying the landscape through his field glasses, completely unworried by the artillery shells which were falling around us. They were much too close for my liking! I was very relieved when he re-entered the carrier and directed us back to where the Unit waited.[7]

That night, when the fighting died down, the 2/1st was over 1800 metres inside the fortress. The troops in the infantry companies got what sleep they could, but the headquarters staff received little rest as they planned and prepared for the following days' action. Eather did not sleep at all.

Fighting resumed the next morning (4 January) and the advance continued for the remainder of the day. The 2/1st pressed forward with the 2/3rd Battalion on its right, capturing enemy posts from within the enemy perimeter. As with the first day's battle, the Italian artillery was well handled and some of the gunners refused to surrender even with the Australian infantry surging into their positions. These brave soldiers, after firing on the Australians over open

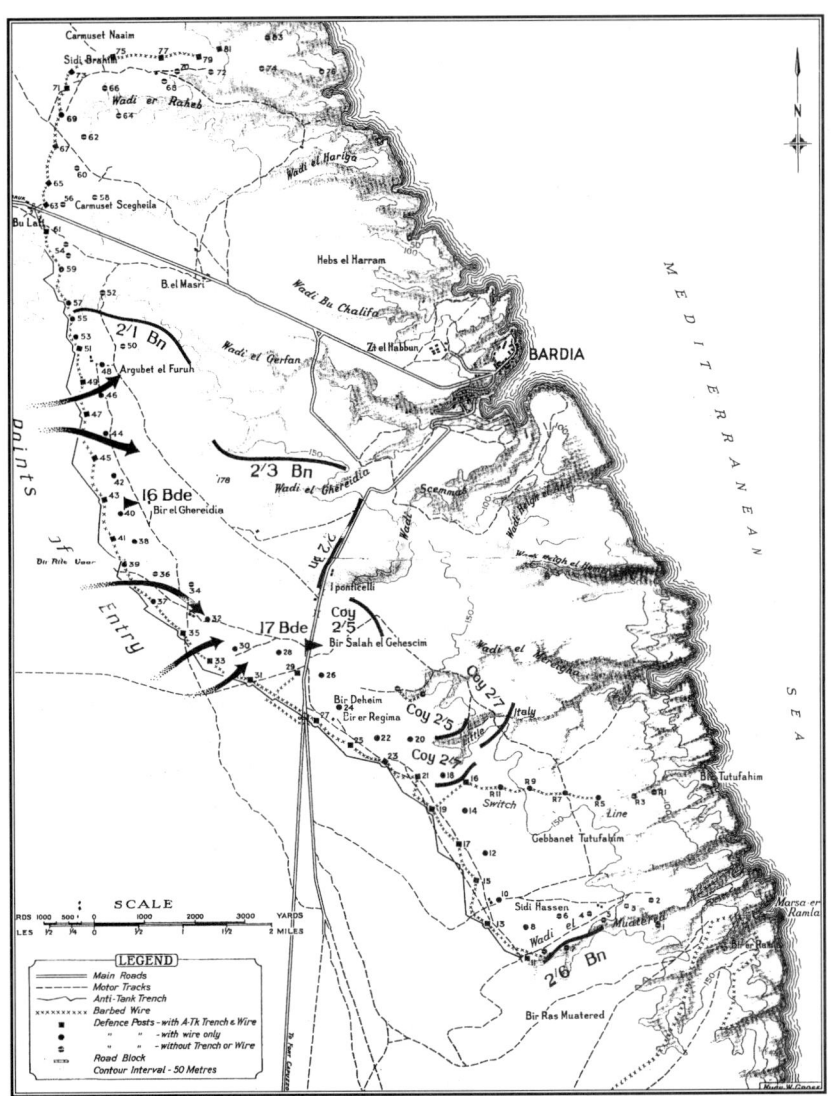

The Battle of Bardia, dusk, 3 January 1941.
Reproduced with the kind permission of the Australian War Memorial

sights and inflicting casualties, were shot down while still serving their guns. Their heroic efforts could not save Bardia, however, and the remnants of the garrison surrendered on 5 January.

Four hundred and twenty Australians were killed or wounded in the attack on Bardia. The 2/1st suffered 54 casualties, a surprisingly small number considering the Battalion had made the dangerous initial breakthrough for the 6th Division. The enemy's losses were, however, extraordinary. In all, around 40 000 Italian troops were captured and the 62nd, 63rd, 64th and 1st Black Shirt Infantry Divisions were all destroyed. Additionally, large quantities of valuable equipment were captured, much of which was later used by the Australians and the British. The booty included 462 artillery pieces of all types, 127 tanks, 708 motor vehicles, food and other supplies.

The assault on Bardia proved that the 2/1st was a first-class battalion within a fine infantry division. It could have been no coincidence that the vital initial penetration role had been allocated to the 2/1st. Clearly, Brigadier Allen selected his finest battalion—although they were all very good indeed—to play the crucial role in

Italian soldiers captured at Bardia.
Photo courtesy of the Australian War Memorial (AWM 004911)

the 6th Division's attack. Eather's innovative and intensive training in mobile warfare in Palestine and Egypt had paid a substantial dividend for the AIF at Bardia. Had the 2/1st's attack failed, the 6th Division's assault would have been seriously impeded. In 1944, Eather would tell the official army historian, Gavin Long, that 'Bardia went like clockwork'.

Eather's decisive action in ordering the blowing of the Italian barbed wire was vital in ensuring that the timing of the AIF's first battle was not thrown into confusion. His presence of mind also ensured that the strong Italian artillery was not presented with the easy target of a concentrated 16th Brigade waiting at the wire. Certainly, his rapid sizing up of the situation and calmness under fire contributed substantially to the relatively small casualties sustained by the 6th Australian Division. Eather was later awarded the Distinguished Service Order for his part in this battle, the citation acknowledging both his leadership and his personal courage in the fighting.

The results of the battle of Bardia were profound. The morale of the Australian troops, having fought and won their first major engagement of the war, skyrocketed. Conversely, the morale of the Italian forces in North Africa plunged. The Italians were now much less likely to attempt an attack on either Egypt or the Suez Canal with the forces remaining to them.

The Italian official history of the battle reveals the full brilliance of this attack and what occurred before it. It noted that for some considerable time there had been disorganisation and disorder within the Bardia garrison.[8] After Bardia was placed in a state of siege, the supply situation became chronic. Over several weeks just two small schooners made port and unloaded cargo. To make matters worse, bombing by the Royal Air Force and naval shelling were very effective, destroying large quantities of rations and equipment as well as reducing the garrison's morale. Stocks of fuel were short. Eventually it became necessary to put the troops on half rations. The Italian Navy and Air Force did virtually nothing to alleviate the ongoing reduction of Bardia.

The Italian history also noted that during the 16th Brigade's initial attack, the assaulting waves moved forward so rapidly that the Italian artillery had trouble locating and tracking them.

Italian sources also confirm that Eather's action in ordering the blowing of the wire not only helped save the 16th Brigade from being caught in destructive fire but ensured the momentum of the attack continued so rapidly the Italians were never able to check the advance. Quite literally, their command system was paralysed by the speed and audacity of the thrust into their positions.

At the site of the 2/1st Battalion's penetration, the 116th Infantry Regiment had been ordered to counter-attack with tank support but, before this could be organised, the Australians had actually surrounded that regiment's headquarters and the commander and his staff were captured. Indeed, by midday, the entire 116th Regiment had been killed or captured.

The Italian Government, desperate to put the best possible face on this defeat, had their propagandists rewrite history and turn the battle around—so that an outnumbered Italian garrison was overwhelmed by a combined force of 250 000 men, 1000 aircraft and the Royal Navy. This propaganda had the unintentional result of further lowering the morale of the smaller and weaker Italian garrison at Tobruk, which was now expecting the arrival of a vast army with massive air and naval support. The Italian propaganda machine would give the Allies an unplanned bonus at Tobruk.

The victory at Bardia had another unintended but profound effect. Hitler, shocked that the Italians could be forced to surrender a substantial fortress after just 55 hours' fighting, would later commit German troops to the North African Campaign. Initially operating in small numbers, the German force would later change the course of the war in this region.

On 13 January, Eather wrote home to his father:

> Well, as you no doubt know by this time, the Battle of Bardia is over, the results are entirely satisfactory from our point of view. My fellows were selected as the spearhead and did a grand job of work. It was a wonderful experience & I felt & still do as proud as punch with my chaps. The way they carried out their difficult job was splendid. At the moment we are sitting out in the desert waiting for the next crack [at the enemy] which I hope won't be long.
>
> I must say it is darn uncomfortable too. Water is a problem and there is tons of dust. I'm dirtier just now than I've ever been in my

life. I'm afraid if I take my socks off I'll take a layer of skin off with them. Thoughts of a bathtub are just like heaven.

He concluded his brief letter, in which he made no comment on his own substantial achievements, with an assurance that he was in good health, claiming that he was 'full of beans and desert dust but I seem to thrive on it'. Unfortunately, this latter comment was far from the truth. During the war Eather was to be hospitalised several times with respiratory problems, including pneumonia, while in later life respiratory illnesses induced by dust inhalation and malaria would severely affect his health.

As soon as the battle was over the 6th Division, using many captured Italian vehicles, advanced westward towards Tobruk. By 8 January, the 16th and 17th Brigades were concentrated in the vicinity of that fortress town. The Australians immediately commenced a rigorous system of patrolling to dominate no-man's-land and test and examine the enemy's defences while the final preparations for the assault were being made. These patrols, which were carried out day and night, sometimes suffered losses from Italian booby traps, artillery and small-arms fire. They did discover, however, that Tobruk's defences were not completed, and that the enemy's positions were not held in the same strength as those at Bardia. As before, the Italian positions were softened up with artillery fire and bombing attacks.

In contrast to the Australian activity, the Italian forces did not make any substantial effort to patrol forward of their positions to gain knowledge of their enemy's strength and intentions. Indeed, one evening, on one of the few occasions when the Italians did anything to oppose the 2/1st Battalion's preparations, an Italian aircraft dropped five bombs near Eather's headquarters. No casualties resulted from this unimpressive effort.

Chester Wilmot, the famous Australian war correspondent, witnessed the attack on Tobruk and described the plan for the seizure of the fortress in his classic *Tobruk 1941*:

> The general plan was for the armoured division in the west and south-west, and the 17th Australian Brigade in the east, to make a demonstration, while the main attack was launched from the south. To soften up the garrison and support these diversions, the Navy

and RAF were to bombard vital areas inside the perimeter during the night immediately preceding the direct assault. Then before dawn, under the cover of a heavy barrage, the 16th Australian Brigade was to seize a small bridgehead on the perimeter about three miles [five kilometres] east of the El Adem Road. With 'I' Tank and artillery support, this brigade was then to roll up the perimeter and overrun the field guns immediately behind it on either side of the bridgehead towards the El Adem Road on the left and the Bardia Road on the right. At the end of this phase, with eight miles [thirteen kilometres] of the perimeter captured, the way would be open for a deep thrust to the junction of the El Adem and Bardia Roads (hereafter called the El Adem Cross-roads) and onwards into the heart of the defences. This deep thrust was to be made by the 19th Australian Brigade, supported by [Major] MacArthur Onslow's [Bren] Carriers and captured tanks, and by strong artillery concentrations.

It was expected that at the end of these two phases the 17th Brigade would have swung in from the east and established itself along the Bardia Road ready to drive north to the sea; the 19th Brigade would be beyond the El Adem Cross-roads, commanding the high ground of the main escarpment and in a position to attack generally west-north-west, while the 16th Brigade—now holding the line of the El Adem Road—could roll up the western perimeter.

(Reproduced with the kind permission of Penguin Books Australia Ltd)

Speed was essential if the enemy were to be prevented from potentially destroying harbour facilities, the valuable water supply and military stores of use to the Allies. The attacking infantry would have the support of their own artillery, sixteen British Matilda tanks of the 7th Royal Tank Regiment, captured Italian tanks operated by the 6th Divisional Cavalry Regiment and machine-gunners of the 1st Northumberland Fusiliers and the 1st Battalion, Cheshire Regiment. The attack commenced in the early hours of 21 January.

On this occasion, however, the 2/3rd Battalion made the initial breach in the defences for the 16th Brigade, allowing the 19th Brigade to follow through. As before, the attack was made on a narrow front at the junction of two of the enemy's defensive sectors, forcing a gap through the Italian 70th Regiment while the remaining troops and tanks fanned out. The 2/1st—again led prominently by Eather—followed the 2/3rd through the breach in the defences. There were some anxious moments for the 2/1st when the Italian field artillery was firing a strong barrage in front of them while coastal defence guns, which had been swung shorewards, landed heavy shells in their rear. Fortunately, the Battalion managed to move forward and out of the most dangerous area during a lull in the barrage. Once inside the perimeter, the 2/1st swung to the east with six Matilda tanks leading them to strike at their objectives. During an advance of 7 kilometres, twenty enemy posts were captured in the next two hours of fighting.[9]

As at Bardia, the Australians advanced so rapidly that the Italians had extreme difficulty in coordinating a workable defence. While some posts resisted for a time, it was noticeable that other seemingly dazed garrisons surrendered after firing just a few shots. The Italian commanders were hamstrung by a lack of infantry for their perimeter. Only the weak 61st Division (six battalions), two other battalions and logistics troops were available to man the posts, with the result that the Tobruk garrison commander, General Petassi Manella, had to rely on his artillery to seal any breaches in his perimeter. It was a strategy that would not work, especially as his garrison was already dispirited over the loss of Bardia and expecting to be assailed by the same vast horde that Rome Radio told them had captured Bardia.

The 2/1st captured its initial objectives either on or ahead of time. On the final objective, Colonel Eather stopped his battalion as planned, but then started taking casualties from artillery fire, so he ordered another advance to the Bardia Road where he again halted. Here too, the troops were shelled, but fortuitously the 2/1st's allotted Forward Artillery Observation Officer eventually found the battalion sheltering along the road. He had been delayed while looking for the unit in its previous position. The young artillery officer introduced himself to Eather who again, as was his wont, was standing in the open observing the shell-bursts around his positions. The artillery officer asked if he could be of assistance. Eather replied, 'Can you see that?' pointing around him to the bursting shells. 'Yes,' replied the officer. 'Well do something about it!' Eather snapped.[10] Unfortunately, the field artillery had been positioned to cover the 2/1st's original objective and the guns were now out of range. The troops had to endure the shelling until the Italian artillerymen were compelled to surrender when other Australians approached their guns.

Of the battle, Corporal Barry Hennessy of the Carrier Platoon recalled:

> We forced our way through the outer perimeter of Tobruk. The Italians were offering only token resistance and, leading my three [Bren] Carriers we raced ahead of the foot soldiers. We came to a large bunker and circled it like red Indians around a wagon train. As we raced around I kept firing short bursts from the Bren. We lined the three carriers up facing the little fort and about 300 Italians poured out begging us not to shoot them. In the meantime an OP of the artillery assumed that the Ities had captured us and fired a few 18 pounders over our heads. We set off for our lines in a hurry followed by a long line of frightened Italians. I felt quite proud when I reported back but was bought back to earth very smartly when the Colonel severely berated me for wasting ammunition! The Colonel was a strict disciplinarian.[11]

Later, the 2/1st Battalion was relieved by other troops, marched back to the site of the perimeter breach, and then commenced an advance north-west as the fighting continued. By evening, the troops were exhausted by the combination of the fighting and the long marches. Next morning the 16th Brigade pushed on towards Tobruk town on a wide front. However, enemy resistance was waning fast. Of this advance, Gavin Long recorded in *To Benghazi*:

> The 2/1st which had moved up from its position in reserve had begun its advance at 8 am deployed over a wide front, as though exercising on an open training ground. A gazelle ran across the front and some men fired at it. Promptly some hundreds of Italians showed themselves 500 yards [460 metres] ahead waving white flags. Some distance past the El Adem road the line reached the edge of a two-miles [3.2 kilometres] wide saucer-like depression on the far rim of which could be seen a line of white flags. Eather and his adjutant, Captain Jackson, who were riding in a carrier with the front line of the battalion, drove forward and found some 3,000 Italians drawn up as if on parade with the officers in front holding

their portmanteaus in their hands. The officers were shaven and wore well-tended uniforms and polished boots. The senior Italian officer looked with disdain at the dusty Eather in a drab greatcoat and over it, concealing the [rank] badges, a leather jerkin and scarf. After the Australians had taken the officers' pistols (the men carried no weapons) Eather sent the prisoners towards Pilastrino with no guards to escort them.

The final remnants of the Tobruk garrison capitulated on 22 January. The seizure of Tobruk just 29 hours after the initial breakthrough had cost the 6th Division 49 killed or died of wounds and 306 wounded. The 2/1st's casualties were 32 killed and wounded. The Australians again acquired a large bounty. Two hundred and eight artillery pieces, 23 medium tanks, 200 trucks and other vehicles, as well as large numbers of machine-guns, rifles, ammunition and other stores were captured. Approximately 27 000 prisoners were taken. Significantly, the port facilities were found largely intact. This would prove vitally important in the following months. Tobruk also contained the only good water supply between Derna and Mersa Matruh, and this valuable resource was also captured intact.

In a minor controversy, British commanders later complained that the Australians had vandalised and damaged captured equipment, including the sights on Italian artillery pieces, rendering many of them useless. The Australian commanders vehemently denied the allegations, insisting that the damage had been done by the Italians themselves to stop usable war matériel falling into enemy hands. In 1944, Gavin Long discussed this issue with Eather, who confirmed that it was the Italians who had damaged their own weapons. Eather further stated that he was the *first* Australian to enter some of the Italian anti-aircraft positions and had found the range-finders, sights and other technical equipment around these weapons smashed or removed. The 2/1st Battalion recovered 42 Italian artillery pieces at Tobruk, *all* of them with either their breech-blocks missing or their sights damaged. Eventually some of the hidden breech-blocks and sights were found, but still only five of these weapons could be made operational before the unit moved on.[12]

The 2/1st was now designated the Tobruk town garrison and its troops deployed to stop looting by both Australian and British troops and by the Arabs who lived nearby in a separate village. Garrison duty was a choice role for the Battalion, and enabled the Australians to enjoy the luxury of sleeping inside buildings and sometimes even in beds! Unfortunately, some of the Arabs were so persistent in their looting that one Australian noted that 'a couple had to be shot' before the rest would cease plundering the town.

The Battalion was keen to move into town and Colonel Eather despatched Warrant Officer Delves on a mission to locate a suitable headquarters. Delves eventually settled on the Albergo Hotel and sent word to Eather, still out on the now silent battlefield. While waiting for his commanding officer to arrive, Delves wandered about the building revelling in its (relative) luxury. Passing a bathroom, he tried some taps but the water to the town had been turned off by the Italians and only a few drops came out. He tried a second bathroom and, to his shock, water gushed into the tub. Quickly finding a plug, Delves filled the tub and enjoyed his first bath in months. This was indeed a luxury after months in the desert where water was in constant short supply. He changed into clean clothes, emptied the black water from the tub and, feeling much refreshed, went to the front door of the hotel to await the CO's arrival.[13]

A short time later, a filthy colonel arrived. As soon as he took in his warrant officer's neat and clean appearance, Eather's eyes narrowed and he said in an accusing voice, 'You've had a bath!' Delves smugly replied, 'Yes sir,' led his commanding officer to the bathroom and proudly pointed to the tub. He turned the tap on, but—just a few drops splashed out, the plumbing banged and groaned and the water flow ceased! Eather gave his chastened warrant officer a withering look and stalked off. Later that afternoon Delves noticed his CO bathing in the sea. He kept out of sight for the rest of the day!

Wally Delves, as Eather's RSM, is in an excellent position to comment on his character. In 2001 he was also the only known surviving member of the 2/1st Battalion headquarters. He commented that Eather was quiet and reserved, and a strict disciplinarian, but nonetheless cared deeply for the welfare of his troops—even if he rarely showed it. He did not drink or swear much and was not even noted for raising his voice. However, all in the battalion were well aware of his forceful character and there were few who would not quail under his piercing stare if their misdeeds came to his attention. Officers were expected to endure the same conditions as the men and all ranks, including the commanding officer, ate exactly the same food—a good incentive for the cooks to do their best!

Delves also remembered that Eather's main relaxation in North Africa was playing bridge at night with his headquarters staff. Wally, who invariably partnered his colonel, noted that while these were enjoyable games, if he played a hand in a less-than-adequate manner and lost, no words of admonishment would be spoken but the piercing brown eyes would focus on him in a withering manner!

After several days of living in 'luxury', Eather decided that the relaxed lifestyle was having an adverse effect on the unit. To Delves, he noted simply 'we are getting soft'. As a result, he moved the Battalion—less one company—back out of town to again live and train in the open.[14]

On 8 February, the Australian Prime Minister, R.G. Menzies, visited Tobruk with General Blamey. The 2/1st provided a smartly turned-out honour guard to mark the occasion and the Prime Minister later had lunch with the town commandant and his officers. Aware of the clout that a prime minister had, Eather decided in advance to make an effort to obtain better rations for his troops. Prior to lunch he warned his officers to ensure that they only gave margarine to the Prime Minister if he asked for butter—even though a captured stock of this luxury item was at that time available. During the meal, as expected, the Prime Minister asked for butter more than once but was always given margarine. Either the ruse worked or by strange coincidence shortly afterwards butter appeared on the ration scale![15]

The 2/1st Battalion later moved on to Mersa Matruh and then Amiriya. At this point Eather developed pneumonia from continued dust inhalation. The illness became very serious and he was transferred to the 8th British General Hospital in Alexandria.

Eather was enraged by his misfortune. From his point of view it could not have come at a worse time. He had already been briefed on the 16th Brigade's forthcoming deployment to Greece and he was very keen to compare the Germans to their Italian allies. Despite his strong protests he was forced into hospital, but with very bad grace indeed. As he later wrote to his sister:

Well here's a devil of a place to be letter writing from—a hospital! I've had a dose of some chest complaint to which nobody has put a name to yet. It started the other day. In fact I believe the blasted rotten trip down did it. You may have gathered from my earlier letters that we had been sitting outside Tobruk after the scrap, waiting for the next thing to turn up. We left & moved to Mersa Matruh & from there to the vicinity of Alex[andria].

I stayed in Matruh for several days & the day I set off, it was a brute, a cold wind blew like the devil & raised such a dust storm one couldn't see two yards [two metres] ahead. I did the trip by car & took all day to do the 180 odd miles [290 kilometres]. The next morning I got an attack of shivers & shakes & stayed in my tent all day. The next morning I wasn't any better & my M.O. wouldn't allow me up and kept harping on a hospital.

I didn't want to go in because something very important was in the wind [the Greek deployment—Eather was taking care not to pass any classified information on to his family] & if I got into hospital lord knows when I would get out again. Anyhow, it was decided I should go into town & lay up in the pub as I hadn't much chance of recovery out in the dusty, windy camp. Accordingly, I was carted into the pub about 5 pm & had a bath and went to bed. The next morning I had half a dozen doctors around me & the pressure was too great. I had to agree to come in and here I am.

I am on the mend but have missed the important thing & can only hope to catch up with it [the 2/1st Battalion in Greece].

With time to fill in, on 25 March Eather penned a letter to his mother from his hospital bed:

I spent a few very miserable nights & days before I recovered enough to sit up & take notice of what goes on about me. Actually, I don't see much. I have a room to myself & since coming in haven't been out of it yet. There is no doubt whatever about it. [The] military medical organisation is by far the most efficient of its kind. It's remarkable the attention one receives. I've had x-rays taken every few days & am fed like a blessed fighting cock . . .

Gen[eral] Sir Iven Mackay dropped in and stayed for half an hour the other day. He came along especially to congrat[ulate] me upon my recent award. Goodness, I don't believe I've told you. A couple of weeks ago my name was among those published as having been awarded some recognition of service during the Libyan Campaign. I had been granted a DSO. So had my two brother CO's [battalion commanders in the 16th Brigade, Lieutenant Colonels] England and Chilton. So you see I've two little bits of ribbon to stick on my manly chest now! . . .

Things over here seem quiet after the clean up in Libya don't they? It will not be very long before the whole of Musso's [Mussolini's] armies in Africa are in the bag [prison] with the rest of 'em. I'll bet he is a sorry cove at the moment & regrets siding with Adolf.

On 6 April, considerably improved in health, he was discharged from hospital on the condition he remained on sick leave, and he was transferred to the AIF Officers' Hostel in Palestine.[16] Of this anticipated change Eather noted to his father: 'It will be a change of scenery & a pleasure to see green fields & orange groves once again. While I was up there in the early days I didn't think much of it but after Libya it will be great.'

Although it was not apparent at the time, this illness was opportune as it almost certainly saved Eather from, at best, becoming a prisoner of war and effectively ending his military career. By the time he had recovered, the disastrous Greek and Crete campaigns had been fought and lost and the 2/1st Battalion all but destroyed.

On Eather's recovery, he took command of the 2/1st survivors at Julis. Of the 800 or so troops he had trained and led so proudly through the streets of Sydney and then at Bardia and Tobruk, just 70—around two platoons—remained. The loss of virtually his whole battalion is known to have played very heavily on Eather's mind. He often wondered whether, if he had been with his troops, he might somehow have got them out of Crete.[17]

It must be said that the highly disciplined and well-trained 2/1st played a pivotal role in the battle for Crete. They inflicted severe losses upon elite German airborne forces before exhausting their ammunition and, cut off from other Allied forces, were compelled to surrender. Their epic defence was due in a great measure to Eather's thorough and relentless training over a long period, backed up by their recent combat experience against the Italians at Bardia and Tobruk. Indeed, the German airborne forces were so severely mauled by the Australian and New Zealand troops in this campaign that they did not participate in another major airborne action for the remainder of the war.

By 31 May the 2/1st comprised just five officers and 91 other ranks. Some of the unit's original officers were returned, other 16th Brigade units contributed troops and the not so badly wounded rejoined over time. Fresh reinforcements untested in battle were absorbed and gradually the 2/1st was built up to full strength. In all, about one-third of the re-formed battalion had previously been in combat. With a view to making the unit battleworthy in the shortest possible time, Eather drove his troops very hard indeed, and he was no easier on himself. Often his working day extended from before dawn until well into the evening as he supervised training, administered the unit and sought replacement equipment, as virtually everything had been lost in Greece and Crete.[18]

Following the promotion of Brigadier Allen and his appointment to command the 7th Division in Syria, Lieutenant Colonel Eather took temporary command of the 16th Brigade from 18 June to 30 August 1941 and oversaw the entire brigade's training. This was Eather's first brigade command for a sustained period of time, although it appears that he may have informally commanded the 16th Brigade for around two weeks on a previous occasion. While filling this appointment, he was attached to the Middle East Combined Training Centre for a course of instruction.[19]

Upon the arrival of Brigadier A.J. Boase, a pre-war Staff Corps officer, as the 16th Brigade's permanent commander, Eather returned to his battalion.

Of this period, Eather wrote to his parents:

Of course you will know that Tubby [Brigadier Allen] has become a Major General, don't you? At the moment I am administering com'd of his old brigade. This means a considerable amount of extra work & to make matters worse I have had a depleted staff. However, things are running along better now & I'm looking forward to a chance to have a breather. Was very cut up about the old bn [the loss of the 2/1st Battalion] but couldn't afford to spend much time over regrets & now it has been built up almost to normal.

These last few weeks I have been taking numerous trips to the north of Palestine & twice into Syria. Have been away several days at a time. Found it very interesting & a change from camp life which we seem to be settling into once again. On my last trip I called & saw Gen Allen & was fortunate enough to arrive at his HQ while plans for attacking Damour were being made, so had a pretty good idea of what was to happen.

Other correspondence to friends and family in Australia reveal Eather's disappointment that his appointment to the 16th Brigade was not permanent. Certainly he considered that he had demonstrated the skill and ability to warrant a higher command. In response to one friend's letter of congratulation, he wrote with perhaps some embarrassment that his brigade command was only temporary and only hinted why. To his wife, however, he was much more candid and blamed his failure to retain that command as being due to the fact that he was a former Militia officer rather than a member of the Staff Corps, and there may have been some truth in this assertion. His disappointment was to be short-lived, however.

4
Syria: A promotion and a homecoming

We are a little worried over the Eastern situation. It would be shocking if anything happened at home with us over here. We try to convince ourselves that should the Japs start anything the Yanks will keep them too busy to worry our people at home.

Lieutenant Colonel Eather, letter to his father from Syria, 7 December 1941

Although the fighting against the Vichy French in Syria had ended, the 16th Brigade was despatched there as part of the occupation force in October 1941. For the troops the area offered an entirely different perspective. With fighting no longer an immediate prospect, they could enjoy their off-duty hours much more. They enjoyed leave in the capital, Damascus, and seemed to socialise with both the paroled Vichy troops and also the Free French. Sporting competitions were organised while the weather was fine. By December, however, it was bitterly cold and many Australians saw snow for the first time. Indeed, the winter of 1941 was destined to be the coldest in 40 years in that part of the world.

In one letter to his parents during this period, Eather's irritation with Brigadier Boase comes close to the surface:

I often take a quick run into Damascus. Boase, our new Brigadier, seems to think it necessary that I go with him on many occasions.

We have attended a commemoration service in the Greek Church & last night a ball run by the Free French in aid of the Red Cross.

Damascus is an extraordinary place. Many of the troops are being sent in for a three day leave. Lord knows what they will do with themselves. Visit St Paul's Gate and Saladin's Tomb I expect. This tomb business is a queer racket. There are two coffins in the Mosque & the guide carefully explains that one is the old one which the body isn't in and the other is the new one which the body is in! . . .

It will be very cold here during the winter. We are not very far from Mt Hermon, a mountain some 6,000 ft [1828 metres] above sea level. It is usually snow clad . . . In a few weeks I expect snow to fall.

We are camped in a small wadi which contains a grove of trees, the only ones for miles. The other two battalions didn't get a spot anywhere near as nice. We have a small stream running through the camp and my pioneers have rigged up a shower. One can wash off the dust!

Eather also managed to do a little sightseeing; apart from visiting Damascus and other centres where duty took him, he squeezed in a short visit to some Roman ruins several hours' drive from the brigade.

In a letter to his parents, prophetically dated 7 December 1941 (in view of part of its contents and the surprise Japanese attacks on Malaya and Pearl Harbor), Eather wrote:

I am standing up to the very cold weather exceptionally well. And my word is it cold. All pools of water and buckets are frozen in the mornings and on the hills nearby we have a wonderful view of snow capped mountains. We have been getting a fair amount of rain too but everybody is quite snug. Each sleeping tent has been issued with one of those kerosene heaters & and they take the chill off.

We are a little worried over the Eastern situation. It would be shocking if anything happened at home with us over here. We try and convince ourselves that should the Japs start anything the Yanks will keep them too busy to worry our people at home.

Pop, I received a letter yesterday from [Major General] Sir Charles Rosenthal congratulating me upon my promotion. It was so very kind of the old boy to remember me & and I haven't the heart to write and tell him it is all huey. Maybe I won't have to as there are whispers going about that one of our brigade commanders is returning to Australia and I may have a chance. Well it is a long bet and I haven't much faith in the possibility of overcoming the strong

SC [preferential] feeling that exists. Still one never knows and they will have to do something with me sooner or later.

And do something with him they did. Just days before the end of 1941, Eather was told that he had been promoted two ranks, to colonel and temporary brigadier. This unusual step, which was officially promulgated on 12 January 1942, was testimony both to his long and dedicated service in the Militia and to his excellent combat record since joining the AIF. He was appointed to the command of the 25th Infantry Brigade of the 7th Australian Division, which was also in Syria. The 25th Brigade had recently fought the short but bitterly opposed campaign against Vichy French forces, including elite Foreign Legion battalions. The 2/1st Battalion's historian noted that Eather was 'a great commander, he had truly earned his promotion'.[1] The author of the 2/33rd Battalion's history stated that Brigadier Eather came to his new command with the reputation of being 'considered the 6th Division's outstanding CO'. Of his promotion Eather himself recorded that 'best of all, Tubby [Major General Allen] is once again my chief'.

Unfortunately, the pleasure Brigadier Eather may have felt about his promotion was tempered by the general war situation. The situation in South-East Asia had become alarming. Japan's initial successes in Malaya, Hong Kong and the Philippines were followed by a string of other victories that brought the spectre of invasion ever closer to Australia.

Regarding these worrying events, on 14 December 1941 Eather had written to his father:

> What do you think of the little Japs, eh? Little devils are springing off their tails. Well they will receive a good hard crack one of these days. Needless to say I am a little anxious about the war spreading to Aust. It would be terrible to contemplate the ravages of war in Aust. The Lord forbid!

The Australian forces faced their own concerns in Syria. On arrival, Eather found his new command preparing fortifications to stop a possible German attack through Syria into Palestine and on to the Suez Canal, should Turkey give in to German pressure and allow its troops access to that country to launch an attack. So worrying was this threat that Eather committed his brigade to having its sector of defensive works completed within 20 days. This involved intensive work by the troops in bitterly cold weather. Fortunately, the attack they were preparing for did not eventuate and the defences did not need to be used.[2]

Apart from supervising the brigade's work, Eather attended training lectures on a variety of topics including the provision of close air support. Another task that took considerable time was interviewing officer candidates from among the troops and recommending promotions. When evening came, he sometimes had time to socialise with the other officers in their mess and enjoyed games of darts and the occasional movie.

In January 1942, the 25th Brigade moved to Palestine. Eather himself made the trip by car with some of his officers. Waking at 6 am, the group drove all day and into the night. On seeing his driver fall asleep at the wheel, Eather hastily took over and continued on till 1 am. The group slept in the open by their car and completed the journey safely later in the day.[3] On his arrival, Eather organised and closely supervised a period of intensive retraining which was apparently well overdue. Commenting on one battalion exercise, he noted in his diary on 27 January:

> Roll out 0600 hours with Bertram [Lieutenant Colonel G.A. Bertram, Brigade Major of the 25th Brigade]. Inspect forward companies. 'Stand to' very poor.
>
> Battalion is carrying out night withdrawal. Porter [Lieutenant Colonel Selwyn Porter, commanding the 2/31st Battalion] very concerned. Realised Unit not putting up a very good showing.

Dust storms 'blew like hell', which made life uncomfortable at times as well as interfering with training. It was still very cold at night and sometimes during the day. As late as 23 January the 25th Brigade's level of efficiency, and that of a number of officers in particular, still did not meet their new commander's standards.[4]

On 30 January 1942 Eather responded to a letter from his father which had apparently criticised the British over their debacles in Malaya, Hong Kong and elsewhere:

> My word Pop you are very acidy about British leadership including Churchill. He very strange but we here in contact with some of them [British senior commanders] have complete confidence in them & the outcome [of the war] in spite of all the muddles as you call them. Libya, Greece, Crete flops were not all due to bad leadership but to causes which began some years ago. However Pop things are moving steady now and this year will see a vast improvement and next year, who knows, we may be able to spend Christmas together.
>
> I've more or less settled down with my new crowd [the 25th Brigade] & find 'em a grand lot. Have all states represented & as fit a bunch it would be difficult to find. I feel they would love to have a crack at the Japs, who seem to be still maintaining their initial surge southwards.
>
> Am not over concerned with thoughts of possible danger to you all at home yet, it's too far away. Can only hope Gen Wavell will be able to get his whack in before there is any actual danger. When it comes it should be a beauty.

Sadly, General Wavell would never be in a position to deliver the strong blow to the Japanese that Eather had optimistically anticipated. The Japanese continued with their string of victories and there was nothing that Eather or the other AIF commanders could do about it from the Middle East except hope for the best.

Training of the 25th Brigade continued, but the troops had now been placed on standby for embarkation to an undisclosed destination—which they hoped would be Australia—and much of their equipment had to be kept packed and ready to move at short notice.

On 8 February the brigade boarded the *Mount Vernon*, an American transatlantic liner converted to a troopship, and set sail for an undisclosed destination. An artillery regiment and other troops were also on board and Eather was made responsible for all embarked soldiers.

In his diary entry for the day, Eather wrote:

> Go aboard 12.30 . . . Meet captain in his quarters. 4000 odd troops aboard by 6.30 pm . . .

SYRIA: A PROMOTION AND A HOMECOMING

Mount Vernon not as comfortable as old *Orford*. 100 bags of mail on board. 150 nurses were to have come with us but changed at the last minute, thank heavens.

Possibly something of the mounting controversy over where *Mount Vernon*'s troops were destined may have been known to the ship's captain, but Eather knew as little as his troops. On 12 February a surprised Eather was told by the captain that he was ordered to turn about and return to Aden. The following day, after retracing 160 nautical miles of its journey, the vessel anchored. A boat was sent ashore for orders. Eather and some of his officers played poker in his cabin to fill in time while they waited for news. No information could be gathered at Aden but at 11 am Eather received a 'further message from captain to effect he is to proceed to Colombo as previously instructed'. Wasting no time, just fifteen minutes later the ship weighed anchor and put to sea. In his diary on this day, Eather noted that he had been in the Middle East for two years.

From 17 February the *Mount Vernon* entered what were deemed dangerous waters, and it was considered possible that surface raiders, submarines or enemy aircraft could be encountered. Machine-guns were set up and manned on the decks. Lifeboat drills were practised and the troops were required to carry their life jackets, filled water bottles and hats at all times. The latter were to give them protection from the sun if they ended up in the water or in lifeboats. Eather noted that our 'cruiser escort leaves us and we are running for it [alone]'.[5]

The following day Eather was on the bridge with the captain when the *Mount Vernon* anchored at Colombo, Ceylon (now Sri Lanka). The situation in South-East Asia was now very serious. Three days earlier Singapore had surrendered in one of the greatest defeats in the history of the British Empire. Despite this disaster, the *Mount Vernon* was held at Colombo when it had originally been planned to weigh anchor that same evening.

With some disappointment, Eather noted in his diary: 'No orders. Are [we] to proceed in this ship to final destination[?] Where is it to be? Perth, Java? Expect to sail about midnight. No leave for anybody.'

The following day he recorded with asperity: 'No news yet. Certain to be here tomorrow. Allow some senior officers to go ashore ... Delay seems criminal to waste so much time here.' Eather's comments reflected the desire of his troops to get into a position where they would be able to halt the Japanese advance before the enemy could directly threaten Australia. On the day he wrote these lines, Timor was invaded and Darwin was bombed for the first of what would be 64 occasions.

What Eather did not know was that the 'criminal' delay being imposed on his troops at Colombo was due to British Prime Minister Churchill and American President Roosevelt attempting to force Australian Prime Minister John Curtin into diverting the 7th Division to Burma—this was despite the obvious threat to Australia.

There had even been some thought that the 7th Division would be deployed in southern Sumatra while the 6th Division operated in central Java. In the event, the Japanese advance was so rapid that the Australian divisions would not have had time to become effective before the capture of those locations. After previously indicating his desire to have the AIF returned to Australia, on 17 February Prime Minister Curtin had made a definite statement to Churchill to this effect. He also requested the early release of the 9th Division, then still in North Africa. Roosevelt offered to send two divisions of inexperienced American soldiers to Australia in place of the AIF troops who would go to Burma. Churchill and Roosevelt contended this would save on both time and shipping space and would leave Australia secure.

On Friday 20 February, perhaps reluctantly, Eather allowed the troops in the *Mount Vernon* to take shore leave for the day. He went ashore himself, hired a car and travelled to various parts of the island with some of his officers, including Lieutenant Colonel Porter. While Eather and his group enjoyed their day, that night in his diary he noted that there was still no news of a sailing date and that the troops' behaviour ashore had been 'very bad'.

It was not just the enlisted soldiers whose behaviour had disappointed their brigadier. Captain M.L. Roberts, then a young lieutenant with the 2/33rd Battalion, noted:

> Eventually, we were given a days leave and the group of officers with whom I shared the day dutifully [returned to the] to ship at the

appropriate hour. After dark, all of them decided to go ashore again but I had a screaming headache and went to bed. They were all caught and next morning were paraded to the Brig en masse. What a roasting they received before they were dismissed. As an observer of proceedings, happily, I was able to see the twinkle in the eye of the Brig as the officers marched off. Here was the no-nonsense commander, using common sense and diplomacy, and at the same time establishing his authority, who knew when to take a lenient view. Later, a significant number of officers were to discover that from time to time, the Brig himself liked to play and when he did, woe betide any who declined to join in the fun.[6]

Churchill, assuming that he would be able to browbeat Curtin into submission, and without waiting for his agreement or advising the Australian Government, actually diverted some of the returning troopships towards Burma. After several exchanges, on 19 February Curtin held the day and the troops were directed to Australia.

After spending six days in port at Colombo, the *Mount Vernon* finally set sail for Australia, stopping briefly at Fremantle and docking in Adelaide on 10 March. Here the 25th Brigade disembarked and moved to Woodside camp by train. During the journey, civilians lined the railway tracks and waved and cheered the troops as they went by.[7] It was a touching welcome home for the first substantial contingent of Middle East veterans to return to defend Australia against the Japanese.

Eather himself was up at 6.30 am. After breakfast, he farewelled *Mount Vernon*'s captain and senior officers, going ashore at 8.30 and setting off for Woodside. On arrival, his staff set to work establishing their headquarters. Almost immediately he received a message to attend a conference at Lieutenant General Mackay's headquarters. It was a 'grand drive through Australian country' and the 'call of magpies [was a] welcome sound'.[8]

The next day was spent touring his units, planning training regimes and dealing with problems associated with moving into Woodside. Eather also managed to get a phone call through to his wife Adeline and daughter Isobel and noted that it 'was delightful to hear them again'. This day started at 7 am and finished at 1.30 am the following morning.

The war situation in the South Pacific was extremely grave by this time, and while he allowed some leave, Brigadier Eather immediately instituted an intensive and rigorous training program suited to operations on the Australian mainland. On 19 March a 27 kilometre route march was completed. Many more were to follow, as were regular night exercises. The day after this first 'hardening' route march, Eather addressed his brigade and it was noted by one of his new battalion's historians that he was 'a soldier of rather strong words, he stressed the need for physical fitness for the coming operations against the Japanese'. These were prophetic words—it is unlikely that Eather himself fully understood how physically taxing those next operations would be.

While at Woodside, Eather was reunited with his wife for a time when Adeline travelled from Sydney and booked into a nearby guesthouse. It was the first time they had seen each other in over two years. Their time together was limited, however, due to the intensive training program being undertaken. Eather worked very long hours, seven days a week, as he prepared his troops to face a possible Japanese invasion. His children did not come to South Australia. It seems that his young son was at boarding school in country New South Wales while Isobel had remained in Sydney in the care of an aunt. A full family reunion was some way off yet.

During this period Eather became deeply concerned over what he believed was the limited ability of one of his battalion commanders and had him relieved of his command, having previously noted that this officer's performance had not improved over time. The officer's fate was apparently sealed when, during an exercise, Eather organised an unexpected attack on his unit to see how he would cope. Apparently he did not do well enough. There was no time for sentimentality when the 25th Brigade might soon be in action against a large Japanese force. Eathers' diary recorded the event: 'Spent the whole A.M. thinking about sacking ―― and finally decided to recommend him going. See ―― and tell him I am recommending he be relieved of his command. Took it pretty hard.'

On one occasion a ceremonial guard was mounted at Woodside for a visit by the Minister for the Army, Frank Forde. Unfortunately, the Minister arrived very late and instead of immediately inspecting the troops went to the mess to eat lunch, leaving them standing on parade. After lunch, Forde eventually inspected the troops. Once he had completed his business at Woodside, Forde boarded the train, only to be pelted with a shower of tomatoes by resentful soldiers, much to the embarrassment of their brigadier.[9] Australian troops had never been inclined to show much respect for authority figures. This was not the only occasion when Brigadier Eather's troops would publicly vent their disapproval of persons of note.

In late April, the 7th Division moved to Casino in northern New South Wales. At this time Eather received his first substantial home leave, allowing him to spend several days in Sydney during which he was reunited with his daughter, his parents and other family members. Just weeks later, the 7th Division received orders to deploy around Caboolture in southern Queensland. There the troops continued to train, also preparing defensive positions north of Brisbane from which it was intended to fight the Japanese should they attempt a landing.

This was a busy period for Eather. He carried out extensive reconnaissance of the coastline and possible areas of operations. He also liaised with the local Volunteer Defence Corps and Militia units with whom his troops would cooperate in the event of a Japanese landing. He pushed himself and his officers hard as they prepared to fight the Japanese.[10]

Another cause for concern was the problem of troops taking absence without leave. Returning to Australia after years of overseas service, the troops had naturally looked forward to spending time with their families—but little time was available for this in the face of the brigade's need to be ready for action. Some soldiers took the time to which they felt they were entitled. By 21 March, 104 were absent without leave. Nine days later the total had exploded to 263.[11]

The first experienced AIF reinforcement to reach Australia from the Middle East, the 25th Brigade soon found itself milked of many of its officers and NCOs, who were posted to the Militia to provide a leavening of experienced leaders in these untried units. While these transfers greatly assisted the development of the Militia, Eather became deeply worried that the numbers were too great and that the fighting capacity of his command was being markedly reduced. One of those transferred was Lieutenant Colonel Porter, who was promoted and given command of the Militia 30th Brigade. The two officers would soon meet again in controversial circumstances.

While juggling with these and many other problems, Eather organised rented accommodation in Brisbane for Adeline and his son Ken so he could spend some time with them. Isobel again had to remain in Sydney. Unfortunately, Eather could rarely be with Adeline and his son once they arrived. Often, the best he could do was to visit one or two nights a week. Cut off from her friends and family in Sydney and knowing very few people in Brisbane, Adeline began a very lonely and unhappy stay.[12] The toll imposed on the wives and children of soldiers could be very harsh. Adeline and her children were no different and paid a heavy price during the war.

Although Eather did not see his family often, he did enjoy the very limited time he spent with his son in Brisbane. Of his now teenage son, he wrote to his parents in early August:

> Ken is a card. He bought a fishing line & sits hours on the jetty below the flat fishing. I believe the poor kid has only caught one flathead but when he took it off the hook it flapped about so violently that it fell back into the water before he could pounce on it. He was very crestfallen about it but still goes on fishing ... At the moment he is busy working on me. Each time I call in at the flat he brings the talk round to fishing excursions in the bay. As sure as a die, he'll have me hanging over the side of a boat yet.

The war situation continued to deteriorate, with the Japanese seemingly unbeatable. In March, Lae and Salamaua on the New Guinea mainland were occupied, while on 9 April the American garrison at Bataan capitulated. On 6 May, Corregidor surrendered, thus completing the final capture of the Philippines. Weeks later, Japanese midget submarines raided Sydney Harbour and Newcastle; Sydney was shelled by submarines, and Allied shipping came under submarine attack along Australia's east coast. Darwin, Broome and Wyndham were all attacked by enemy aircraft.

From Queensland, the 7th Division's 18th and 21st Brigades embarked for Milne Bay and Port Moresby in New Guinea in the first days of August and an early opportunity to face the Japanese, leaving the disgruntled troops of the 25th Brigade behind. Those 7th Division units not deployed to New Guinea were placed under Eather's command. However, in the first days of August, the 25th Brigade's senior officers were warned that the brigade would soon embark for Milne Bay.

Of this momentous occasion, Eather wrote in his diary: 'We are off to have a lash at New Guinea within a few days. Disguising it as a move to Mackay for special training.' A few days later there was still no word on the 25th Brigade's departure date and Eather was becoming worried: 'Hope to goodness we are not left [behind].'

While Eather was impatiently waiting the brigade's final movement orders, he spent a day with General Edwin Harding, who was commanding the American 32nd Division. The two officers discussed 'ideas on jungle warfare'. Eather agreed to provide written notes to Harding on proposed jungle warfare tactics. These were completed on 17 August and delivered to his American counterpart.[13] Whatever thoughts he was able to impart, they were not enough to save the American's career. Harding was later relieved of his command when his ill-trained National Guard troops (the equivalent of Australian Militia) failed to perform adequately at Buna.

On the night of 17 August Eather watched with a critical eye as the 2/31st Battalion practised beach assault exercises in the dark. It was a long day. He was up at 7 am and did not get any sleep till lunchtime the following day.

One aspect of Eather's training regime well demonstrates its gruelling nature and the preparation he gave the brigade in anticipation of what the troops would soon face. A platoon of the 2/33rd Battalion won a £30 prize for the best performance in a route-marching competition. Those tough soldiers marched a staggering 67 kilometres in fourteen hours, with just two soldiers falling out. The prize should have been awarded by General Allen, but as he was already in New Guinea, Eather made the presentation himself.[14]

It is interesting to note that, while the 25th Brigade had been well prepared to fight the Japanese, this training related to a war to be fought on the Australian mainland. It would not adequately prepare the soldiers for battle in the mountainous terrain, dense jungle and harsh climate they would soon encounter in New

Guinea. Information on jungle fighting and Japanese tactics gleaned in Malaya had been received, but would prove of limited relevance in later fighting.

Emphasising that the development of military skills was not only advanced by training, Eather ensured that the troops participated in sporting activities to help boost physical fitness and team spirit while at the same time providing relaxation and entertainment. Thus, even when the time for active service was imminent, on 23 August the 25th Brigade held an inter-battalion sports afternoon.

In the last days of August, the 25th Brigade finally embarked from Brisbane in a small convoy that included three troopships, its destination Milne Bay. As he prepared to board the small steamer *Katoomba*, Brigadier Eather was given a briefing on the situation at Milne Bay by General Blamey, the Commander of Allied Land Forces in the South-West Pacific.[15] After setting sail, however, the brigade's destination was changed to Port Moresby. As the ship weighed anchor, Eather could see his rented flat in the distance and his wife and son on the verandah waving farewell. It was a heart-wrenching moment for them all.

As the ships sailed north, apart from routine administration there was little to do except enjoy the voyage. The small size of the ships precluded any training. On Friday 4 September Eather was 'on deck watching islands of Whitsunday slip by. Weather still remains beautiful but beginning to warm up. Spent whole AM on deck'.

The convoy was held off Townsville for some days. During this time, one of the troopships was involved in a collision with another vessel, which necessitated the transfer of the troops from the damaged ship into the remaining two. Conditions were very cramped when the convoy sailed for Port Moresby.

The convoy arrived at Port Moresby on 9 September. *Katoomba* anchored by 10 am and Eather immediately went ashore to confer with Major General Allen.[16] Troops were disembarked immediately and without delay moved into defensive positions forward of Port Moresby towards the hills. The situation was clearly very serious and there was no time to waste as the Japanese continued to force the 21st Brigade back towards Port Moresby. The newly arrived Australians were shocked by the defeatist attitudes displayed by fellow Australians in the area and came to scornfully know the largely

SYRIA: A PROMOTION AND A HOMECOMING

Brigadier Eather (third from left in the front row) and his staff officers disembark from the *Katoomba*. They would shortly go into action against the Japanese.

Photo courtesy of the Australian War Memorial (AWM 026704A)

Militia garrison at Port Moresby as the 'mice of Moresby'—a play on the AIF's famous nickname, the Rats of Tobruk.

Eather wrote of the day's activities:

> Up 0500. On bridge 0600. Sight land 0730. Have cup of tea with mate. Breakfast 0800. Anchor 0900. Move in closer 1000. Message from shore. Ferry alongside by 1030. Disembark . . . Car meets me at wharf & drives me out to see Tubby. Get the 'picture' from him & have lunch then drive out to camp site 24 miles out from Moresby in hills. 33Bn in by evening. Meal with my staff at a Maj Rutherford's mess on bank of creek. Return to camp 1900hrs. Buttrose down, move one of his company's forward as a 'block'. Spend evening going through reports with [Major] Larkin. Turn in 1030 pm. Drop a short line to Top. [Brigadier] Potts has been relieved of his command, temp, by Porter.

Little did he realise that in a few short days his own command abilities would come under intense political and military scrutiny from General Douglas MacArthur, Supreme Commander of Allied Forces in the South Pacific, and General Blamey, his commander of Allied Land Forces. Like the hapless Potts before him, Eather's military career would come perilously close to being ruined on the Kokoda Track.

5
Imita Ridge and
the last line of defence

'There won't be any withdrawal from the Imita position, Ken. You'll die there if necessary. You understand that?'
'Yes, I understand that.'
Conversation between Major General Allen and Brigadier Eather on agreeing to allow the 25th Brigade to withdraw to Imita Ridge, 8.35 am, 16 September 1942[1]

By the time the 25th Brigade disembarked at Port Moresby, the situation in New Guinea was critical. Despite a heroic and desperate defence by the vastly outnumbered and ill-equipped 39th (Militia) Battalion, the Japanese had advanced over much of the Kokoda Track and were closing on their objective of Port Moresby. From here, they intended isolating Australia from outside supply by means of bombing attacks on coastal centres and naval operations. The capture of Port Moresby would also provide a convenient jumping-off point for either a limited lodgement or full-scale invasion of the Australian mainland. The Australian commanders did not know that the Japanese Army was opposed to an invasion, due to a lack of available troops and the logistical effort that would be involved in maintaining them on the Australian mainland. Nonetheless, had the Australians not offered stout resistance on the Kokoda Track it is possible that the Japanese—masters of improvisation and the art of applying constant pressure on their enemies—could have reassessed their position and decided on some form of landing on Australian soil.

Even the commitment of Brigadier Arnold Potts's elite 21st Brigade and other Militia troops had failed to arrest the rapidly deteriorating military situation. Fed forward to meet the Japanese in company-sized groups (due to the inability to supply larger numbers), the efforts of these experienced and well-trained soldiers could only slow down the larger Japanese force. After a number of battles the 21st Brigade, while inflicting serious casualties and forcing delays on the increasingly supply-starved Japanese, was itself gravely weakened. Although the Americans would later suffer much heavier casualties in the island-hopping campaign towards Japan, the capture of most of the Kokoda Track with the virtual destruction of the 21st Brigade was the last major strategic victory the Japanese achieved on land in the Pacific.

On 3 September Brigadier Potts received some good news, when Major General Allen guardedly informed him of the impending arrival of the 25th Brigade: 'Expect to have Ken for dinner approximately 6 September.'

Although the 21st Brigade and 39th Battalion had fought magnificently, General Blamey, under pressure from the Australian Government and General MacArthur, searched for a scapegoat. It was important that Blamey cover up the fact that he (and MacArthur) had failed to develop an effective supply system to support large-scale operations in the Owen Stanley Range and check the early Japanese advance. Despite his brigade's inflicting punishing losses on the Japanese and critically delaying their advance, Brigadier Potts was to be that scapegoat.

On 10 September Potts was ordered back to Headquarters to explain the deteriorating situation on the Kokoda Track. He was replaced by Brigadier Selwyn Porter. Like Potts, Porter was well able to read the tactical situation. In Potts's absence, his instructions were to hold the Japanese and retake ground if possible, pending the arrival of reinforcements. These instructions were impossible to carry out, and Porter's first action was to order yet another withdrawal to a position just north of Ioribaiwa Ridge. By 12 September the amalgamated 2/14th and 2/16th Battalions (around 300 strong, all that was left of the 21st Brigade), the 3rd Militia Battalion, the 2/1st Pioneer Battalion and a small patrol of commandos from the 2/6th Independent Company were in the Ioribaiwa area, awaiting reinforcement and eventual relief.

These dramatic events were unfolding as the 25th Brigade was preparing to move up from Port Moresby through Ower's Corner

IMITA RIDGE AND THE LAST LINE OF DEFENCE

and over Imita Ridge to link up with the troops at Ioribaiwa. The 25th Brigade had only just arrived at Port Moresby, and Brigadier Eather and his men quickly prepared for battle. Their conspicuous khaki uniforms were hurriedly dyed jungle green and long American canvas gaiters, ammunition and rations were issued. Surprisingly, Eather's troops were the first Australians to wear jungle green in New Guinea.

Quickly grasping the gravity of the situation, Eather ordered his troops into the mountains and the prospect of early action. In the early morning of 9 September, the advance guard of the 2/33rd moved forward, followed by the main body of that battalion as well as the 2/31st Battalion on 11 September.[2] By 12 September the 2/25th Battalion was also on the move. The 25th Brigade travelled by truck to the end of the road, after which the unacclimatised troops (an important factor when fighting in a debilitating tropical climate) began their first significant challenge—the infamous climb into the Owen Stanleys via the 'Golden Stairs' (some 2000 roughly placed steps) up the first razorback to the top of Imita Ridge.

Brigade Headquarters set out from Port Moresby on the morning of 11 September.[3] Brigadiers Eather and Potts met briefly on the track as Eather was going forward and Potts was returning to report at Port Moresby. With the two officers having separate sets of orders and Eather going forward to face an advancing Japanese force, there was little time for more than the briefest of words to pass between them. This was a pity, as there is no doubt that Potts could have passed on much valuable information to Eather as he prepared to fight his first jungle action.

Eather was allocated an indigenous carrier named Mena to look after most of his equipment during the march. Mena's assistance during the harsh times that followed was a godsend to Eather as he did not have to worry about his kit and was free to plan the major actions without distraction. At the end of each very long and exhausting day, without fail Mena would have a rudimentary camp ready. A close bond of friendship would develop between the two men.[4]

The trek was a sobering experience. Aside from coping with the jungle and tropical weather, the troops had to contend with the terrain. In its beginning stages the Kokoda Track rose 365 metres in the first 5 kilometres, then dropped 490 metres, followed by a rise of 1220 metres in the next 7 kilometres. Recording the experience in his diary, Eather wrote that it was a 'muddy, slippery, narrow track, very steep steps. Has been work of wonders to have supplied Potts & others along this track'.

Little did the 25th Brigade's commander realise that there was nothing in the way of 'wonders' to describe the failed supply system that had 'supported' the troops thus far in the campaign. Indeed, it was the failure of that supply system which was largely responsible for the precarious situation he was about to face. When the lead troops of the 25th Brigade arrived at the rear of Brigadier Porter's defensive positions at Ioribaiwa, they made contact with some demoralised Australian stragglers. Many of these soldiers carried neither weapons nor equipment. This did not augur well.

The situation confronting Eather when he arrived at Ioribaiwa on the afternoon of 14 September and took command of the combined force was a difficult one. The Japanese, continuing to advance in large numbers, were attacking the ridge up one side as his troops were approaching it from the other and attempting to deploy. The situation was critical, as Ioribaiwa was one of the last defendable positions before Port Moresby. Events were being closely scrutinised by General MacArthur and General Blamey—both were concerned, and not without reason.

For the troops of the 25th Brigade, their arrival at Ioribaiwa gave them their first taste of combat in jungle conditions. There is no doubt that for a time they were disorientated. Apart from the difficulty of moving and fighting in jungle conditions, and on top of the arduous and debilitating climb over the mountain, battle in the tropics was even more appalling than in North Africa. Flies swarmed on the dead, and it was common to see bodies moving within hours of death from the sea of maggots that infested them. After just a day or two, corpses would bloat with gases and sometimes explode. Being detailed to bury the dead was a very trying duty. The overpowering stench seemed to physically attach itself to those handling the dead and could not be washed off. It was not uncommon for bodies to fall apart when they were picked up for burial.

Recalling the first hours of the fight, Private 'Doc' Waters of the 2/25th Battalion wrote:

IMITA RIDGE AND THE LAST LINE OF DEFENCE

> I was in A Company HQ... Our HQ position was on the safe side of the ridge. My first impression was of Drover Dick [Captain Marson, the officer commanding A Company of the 2/25th Battalion] standing right on top of the feature with Colonel Withy and Brigadier Eather. These three officers were evidently evaluating the whole position. Their calm demeanour would lead one to think that it was no more than taking part in manoeuvres. It must have been an inspiration to all though to see their leaders so boldly placing themselves in full view of the enemy. Almost from the moment we reached the top of the ridge, casualties were occurring.[5]

Concern over the aggressive Japanese attacks was compounded by the knowledge that Eather commanded the last body of reliable and well-trained troops in a position to halt the Japanese advance. If his men failed or were lost, only the poorly trained Militia and base troops at Port Moresby remained.

The orders received at Port Moresby instructed Eather to attack and drive the Japanese back. In accordance with these orders, he had intended as his first objective to launch a flanking attack on the Japanese confronting him at Ioribaiwa, push them back and capture Nauro (around 7 kilometres forward by air, but much further along the tracks which the ground troops were forced to use). His 2/33rd Battalion was to assault through positions held by the 3rd Battalion on the right. The 2/31st Battalion would swing through on the left flank while the 2/25th Battalion would attack up the centre of the Ioribaiwa positions, through the surviving 21st Brigade troops, to hold the Japanese in place while the flanking moves were made. While this appeared a sound plan, it did not unfold as intended.

On 14 September, the 2/31st had advanced in heavy rain to outflank the Japanese along a razorback just a few metres wide at the top with very steep slopes. The terrain made flank moves extremely time consuming and difficult and, in any event, the Japanese had occupied a position in the 2/31st Battalion's path. Skilfully employing mortars, machine-guns and snipers, they defied all attempts to eject them. The Australian troops became disorientated in the thick jungle and were lost for a time, resulting in little progress forward. Had there been time to make a reconnaissance of the area, this movement might not have been attempted. Similarly, the 2/33rd Battalion's attack over a mountain covered by thick jungle had little chance of success. These troops also withdrew and were counter-attacked by the Japanese. Knowing that his plan had been checked, Eather halted the operation to allow re-assessment of his options.[6]

In the early afternoon of 15 September, in the midst of the general fighting taking place, the Japanese achieved an unexpected success. A platoon of the 3rd Battalion on the high ground above Ioribaiwa village was pushed out of its position by a determined Japanese offensive patrol, which then occupied the area. Subsequently, the remainder of the company to which the platoon belonged withdrew. It was later disclosed that the militiamen had not had their weapons nearby while digging entrenchments, and that their sentries were not alert. Caught by surprise without weapons, they could offer no opposition to the Japanese and fled. This was a significant failure and one which would have major ramifications. The Japanese had also managed to work their way behind elements of the 2/31st Battalion.

Eather's right flank had now been penetrated by an enemy force which could not be dislodged, and potentially the Japanese could move fresh troops through the gap. In all likelihood, this incident seriously coloured his opinion of the fighting ability and capabilities of the 3rd Battalion. His wariness of Militia troops would already have been heightened due to the 53rd Battalion's failure in the earlier fighting. There had also been criticism—mostly unjustified—of the conduct of the 39th Battalion. It remains to be said that this failure by the 3rd Battalion was an isolated one. In subsequent fighting, the unit would repeatedly distinguish itself.

The situation was becoming confused and it was difficult to know exactly what was happening. The inadequate map issued to Eather showed only one peak where the 3rd Battalion platoon had been dislodged. In reality there were two peaks, and the Japanese were now occupying the higher one, wedged between troops of the 3rd and the 2/31st Battalions. Neither group could safely fire on the enemy without risk of hitting their comrades. A counter-attack failed to dislodge the Japanese, who were far more experienced in jungle warfare than their Australian counterparts.

Interestingly, a writer of the 3rd Battalion's history, in covering the 1942 fighting denies that there was any Japanese penetration between the two battalions, and considers that the recording of this

IMITA RIDGE AND THE LAST LINE OF DEFENCE

in the official war diaries was due to the poor maps available. He suggests that Eather really did not know exactly where his battalions were in the rugged, jungle-clad terrain.[7] As the 25th Brigade's battalions were being engaged even as they were trying to move into position, and there had been no time available for reconnaissance, this suggestion cannot be entirely discounted.

In Eric Bergerud's history, *Touched With Fire*, Sergeant Bill Crooks of the 2/33rd Battalion recalled the fighting:

> This was a time of great confusion with three of our battalions trying to retreat [author's note: a misconception—the 21st Brigade was trying to hold its positions] and our Brigade trying to move into position. The Japs were attacking full blast . . . We saw the Japs advancing through the jungle and up the right flank of the ridge our Brigade was assembling on. There were hundreds of them, green uniformed and covered in branch-vine camouflage, moving in two or three single files . . .

From his rough and ready headquarters at Ioribaiwa—a piece of 'canvas stretched over a boulder in a sea of mud'—on the evening of 15 September, Brigadier Eather told Major General Allen by telephone that it would 'take me all my time to stabilise the position for the present'. Fighting continued that night. By the next morning, the Japanese—with some justification—felt they were in a winning position and continued to exploit their earlier successes. The hard-pressed 21st Brigade soldiers, still unfortunately located in the foremost position on the battlefield, were lashed with fire from mortars and mountain guns to which they could not reply and which caused more casualties. Their positions were also probed by aggressive Japanese patrols. Though these worn-out troops continued to hold their ground, Brigadier Porter was concerned that, mentally and physically, they would not be able to take much more of the Japanese fire. The battalion doctor had already reported several cases of nervous and physical collapse. More could be expected soon if the troops remained in the line.

Some 21st Brigade veterans and recent writers have bitterly attacked Brigadier Porter's assessment of the 21st Brigade's remaining powers of endurance. Those criticisms, however, are tainted by bias against Porter, who had been ordered forward to take over from their beloved Brigadier Potts when that gallant officer was unjustly relieved of his command. Porter was not seen to be one of them—and indeed he was not. He was therefore eminently suited to make a dispassionate and unbiased judgment—untinged by misplaced loyalty to the troops' reputation—on just how much more they could take. Having fought a bitter campaign against overwhelming numbers of better-equipped Japanese for several weeks, in appalling mountain terrain, on inadequate rations and suffering terrible battle casualties, it is inconceivable that the battered remnants of the 21st Brigade were not near the end of their powers of endurance. Undeniably they were elite troops from an elite division, but there is a limit to what any troops, no matter how good, can endure. Brigadier Porter had served previously in Syria and Australia with Eather, and there can be little doubt that he advised Eather—now the commander of the whole force—that his AIF troops were nearly finished as a fighting force. It was his obligation and duty to provide the force commander with an honest appraisal, no matter how unpalatable, particularly as Eather was not in a position to make the assessment himself due to the lack of time and the critical battle situation.

The combined factors of effective Japanese attacks supported by artillery, the 25th Brigade's lack of jungle warfare experience, misfortune, and a disappointing failure by the 3rd Battalion platoon to maintain proper security, ensured that the 25th Brigade's offensive operations could not succeed. On the contrary, the Japanese seemed to have the upper hand. Attempts to dislodge the enemy from their newly won positions failed and casualties were suffered in the process. By now, all of Eather's battalions had been committed to the action or were holding important ground, and he had no other troops available as a reserve. Simply put, the Japanese were likely to keep the initiative unless the Australian commander could devise a solution in short order.

Additionally, Eather must now have had serious doubts—even if in retrospect those doubts were not fully justified—about the ability and remaining endurance of a significant portion of his force, namely the untested 3rd Battalion and the remnants of the 21st Brigade. Determined to regain the initiative without committing his force by simply reacting to Japanese actions, on the morning of 16 September Eather

IMITA RIDGE AND THE LAST LINE OF DEFENCE

came to his controversial decision to withdraw to a firm base at Imita Ridge from where he could re-launch his stalled attack.

In seeking and receiving General Allen's agreement before putting the withdrawal into effect, Brigadier Eather made the following observation to Divisional Headquarters: 'Enemy feeling whole front and flanks. Do not consider can hold him here. Request permission to withdraw to Imita Ridge if necessary. Porter concurs.'

Commenting on his decision to withdraw, in more recent times Eather noted that 'Imita was a much more decisively defensive position [than Ioribaiwa which] was a hopeless bloody thing ... I did not allow them [the Japanese] to probe [my positions]. It was always my policy to obtain and retain control of no man's land'.⁸

American historian Lida Mayo, in *Bloody Buna*, recorded that:

Brigadier Eather, usually imperturbable, was shaken by the situation [at Ioribaiwa] and asked for permission to withdraw. 'I want

Imita Ridge (centre foreground) with Ioribaiwa Ridge behind. Taken from Ower's Corner.

Photo courtesy of the Australian War Memorial (AWM 061958)

your permission to withdraw chief. I know what I am doing. I must have a firm base for the start of my offensive and it doesn't exist here.' Allen granted Eather's request but bluntly stated, 'There won't be any withdrawal from the Imita position, Ken. You'll die there if necessary.'

Lieutenant General Rowell—an able and experienced commander—supported Brigadier Eather's and Major General Allen's decision, but prophetically commented to Allen at the time, 'Our heads will be in the basket over this, Tubby.'

While Rowell reluctantly agreed with Eather's request to withdraw, he was concerned about the situation. To Major General Allen he stated:

> Stress [to Eather] the fact that however many troops the enemy has they must all have walked from Buna. We are now so far back that any further withdrawal is out of question and Eather must fight it out at all costs. I am playing for time until 16 Inf Bde arrives.

Nonetheless, Rowell clearly retained confidence in his new forward commander. Around this time, he commented to Major General Clowes at Milne Bay that 'I've got a lot of faith in Eather'.

Naturally, however, Rowell implemented other prudent defensive measures in case Imita Ridge, which was just 42 kilometres from Port Moresby, should fall. The 14th (Militia) Brigade was moved forward to Hombrom Bluff, where it could attempt to block any Japanese breakthrough, and the base troops at Port Moresby were put on alert. The Americans made plans to demolish heavy equipment and evacuate their aircraft and technical staff to Australia.

Discussing this difficult decision and its extraordinary ramifications in *Crisis of Command*, David Horner has written:

> As Eather and the 25th Brigade moved forward to take over from Porter, [General] Berryman told [General] Sutherland [one of MacArthur's senior staff officers] that he knew Eather to be a fine soldier who could be trusted to do the right thing. The first thing that Eather did was to withdraw from Ioribaiwa to Imita Ridge, about twenty-five air miles [40 kilometres] from Port Moresby and

this, after Berryman's confident statement, caused the Americans to have grave fears. General Kenney told Berryman that if the Japanese reached the Goldie River, just over the Imita Ridge, then he would pull all his aircraft out of New Guinea. The confused events, which culminated in Australia's most important command crisis of the war, were now moving inexorably to their climax.

However, Eather had no intention of leaving the battlefield free for the enemy to continue their advance unhindered. The 2/33rd Battalion's companies were all left in ambush positions between Ioribaiwa and Imita and forbidden to move back until they had engaged the Japanese.[9] The clear intention was that any further Japanese advance would be harried by the 2/33rd Battalion while his other troops moved back unmolested and prepared their new positions for the expected pitched battle. On 16 September an advancing Japanese patrol entered one ambush and lost an estimated 50 killed before the Australians withdrew without loss. While the 2/33rd delayed any Japanese follow-up, the rest of the brigade, lacking entrenching tools or any engineering equipment at all, dug in on Imita Ridge as best they could, using their helmets as shovels and bayonets as picks.

On his return to Port Moresby, Lieutenant General Rowell interviewed Brigadier Potts and asked for his views on the chances of the Japanese pushing the 25th Brigade off Imita Ridge, thus paving the way for the loss of Port Moresby. Potts's response was emphatic: 'None. Unlike Ioribaiwa, there's not room for deployment. There's only one approach, along a narrow track. The range is precipitous anyhow.'[10]

Potts was entirely correct. Both he and Eather had very recently scaled Imita Ridge from both sides and were in an excellent position to judge its natural defences. In his diary, Eather very briefly described the climb from Ioribaiwa to Imita: 'Track very rough and steep. Passes along razor backs . . .' Indeed, the track was so precipitous that the withdrawing troops were forced at times to crawl on hands and knees. In certain places, when they rested or tried to sleep, the soldiers had to hold onto the men above them to avoid falling down the ridge.

At Imita, Eather's 2600 troops faced an estimated 5000 Japanese, but it was now highly unlikely that the 25th Brigade could be pushed out of their new positions, regardless of how many troops the Japanese could mass against them. Reinforcing the importance of holding Imita Ridge were General Allen's orders to the 25th Brigade—Imita was to be held at all costs; Eather and his command would die there if necessary.

Of the withdrawal, Private Waters wrote:

> Late in the afternoon came the word to evacuate the position. We were to pull back to another high feature called Imita Ridge. This position was to be held to the last man . . .
>
> Then the trek began . . . On the apex of Ioribaiwa Ridge was a clearing which evidently had been a native village. As there appeared to be only one track from one side of the ridge to the other, all traffic had to pass over this clearing which was a bald spot among the jungle . . . This was undoubtedly the place where many casualties occurred [from artillery fire].[11]

Before the troops commenced their punishing day-long trek, stocks of equipment and food that could not be removed to Imita Ridge in time were either destroyed or (for what could not be destroyed in time) booby trapped to deny them to the enemy.

Lieutenant General Rowell and General Blamey, who had gone to Port Moresby on 15 September to review the situation, both seemed to have accepted that everything was still under control. General MacArthur was not impressed, however.

Eather's diary entry for 16 September does not indicate that he ever intended to remain at Ioribaiwa if General Allen agreed to his withdrawal request. Rather, it seems he acted on that permission immediately. He was clearly confident that his decision was the right one, apparently feeling that nothing was to be gained in remaining at Ioribaiwa any longer and that the only way to gain the initiative was to break contact with the aggressive Japanese forces pressing his own troops. The withdrawal was complete by late on the morning of 17 September.

In hindsight, his decision to withdraw must have been difficult. His original orders had been to advance not withdraw. Brigadier Potts, a competent commander who had been unable to hold the Japanese through circumstances not of his making, had been recalled to Port Moresby to a future that must have seemed uncertain to the 25th Brigade's commander. Eather was treading perilously close to the same ground, yet he knew that this was the right course of action and was determined to pursue it, regardless of the potential cost to himself.

General Allen clearly had not wanted the withdrawal to proceed, if at all possible. However, he took the view that it was up to the front-line commander to make the final decision, as he was the one actually in the fighting and therefore in the best position to understand the unfolding situation. This was a sound principle of command demonstrated by a sound military commander. It compared starkly to General MacArthur's style of leadership. MacArthur had not yet set foot in New Guinea. He remained unforgivably ignorant of the conditions in which the campaign was being fought but this did not stop him issuing orders which were impractical or even impossible to implement.

The order to withdraw was not overly popular with the troops. Some of the 25th Brigade, depending on their location, had not been under fire at all; indeed, the complaint that many had not seen a Japanese soldier was common. Among the exhausted 21st Brigade survivors, the reaction was bitter. These soldiers had faced the Japanese for several weeks and in the process had inflicted—and suffered—extremely heavy casualties. At Ioribaiwa, they held forward positions on the battlefield while the fresh 25th Brigade was initially located behind them. They simply could not believe that with an entire fresh brigade available, as well as a battalion each of the Militia and Pioneers, that any further withdrawal was necessary. The 25th Brigade had suffered less than a hundred casualties in the fighting which, if no other factors were taken into consideration, was hardly excessive and by itself did not offer a reason to withdraw.

Nonetheless, the decision to withdraw was logical. Apart from achieving the desired effect of making a clean break from the Japanese and gaining freedom of movement, by withdrawing Eather moved back to a firm and secure base of considerable natural strength from which to operate. At Imita Ridge the Australians were able, for the first time, to make use of an additional advantage that the Japanese had constantly exploited—artillery support. The field guns of the 14th Field Regiment had been dragged over extremely rough terrain to Ower's Corner where they commenced bombarding Japanese positions. Most importantly, the withdrawal had stretched the extended Japanese supply line even further. We now know that the Japanese had been ordered not to advance to Imita Ridge due to their parlous supply position. This order, however, might have been ignored by forward commanders had they been able to smash the 25th Brigade at Ioribaiwa.

What of the Japanese force that was causing so much trouble? Commanded by Major General Horii Tomitaro, the South Seas Force of 13 000 troops had previously participated in the invasions of Guam and Rabaul. At Tol Plantation at Rabaul they had massacred many of the surrendered Australian garrison. Other Japanese troops of the 41st Regiment, who reinforced the South Seas Force in New Guinea, had fought and defeated Australian, Indian and British forces in Malaya and Singapore. The South Seas Force was a highly trained, well-equipped, experienced and ruthless foe, not used to taking backward steps.

An important outside influence affecting the conduct of Japanese and Allied operations in New Guinea was the simultaneous operation in the Solomon Islands. Guadalcanal was over 1000 kilometres from Port Moresby, but the operations being conducted there by the Japanese were inextricably linked to those in New Guinea and were controlled by the same Japanese headquarters at Rabaul. Both areas diverted troops and resources which could be used in the other.

Despite the recent Australian victory at Milne Bay, in late September the military situation remained tense. Fighting at Guadalcanal continued with no clear victor in sight. The Japanese failure at the Battle of the Coral Sea did not guarantee that they would not attempt a future seaborne invasion of Port Moresby. After General Blamey returned to Australia, he made a radio broadcast to the Australian people on 16 September, in which he stated that he was confident that the commanders and troops in New Guinea were in control of the situation and that there was little chance of Port Moresby falling to a landward attack. The following day he addressed the Advisory War Council in similar terms. Unfortunately, Blamey did not tell the Government that the 25th Brigade had just withdrawn to Imita Ridge. This was a dangerous omission and

IMITA RIDGE AND THE LAST LINE OF DEFENCE

one which General MacArthur would have no inhibitions about sharing with a profoundly shocked Australian Prime Minister.

On the evening of 17 September, MacArthur spoke to Prime Minister Curtin, telling him of the withdrawal and saying that he was extremely worried about the situation in New Guinea. MacArthur also complained that the Australians were inefficient and had been forced back by a much smaller Japanese force. Eather's fighting withdrawal had precipitated a political crisis. Apart from being untrue, MacArthur's comments were an ironic criticism from a commander whose 131 000 troops had been forced to retreat, yield virtually all the Philippines and eventually surrender to a Japanese force substantially smaller than his own. Nonetheless, MacArthur held the inexperienced Australian Prime Minister under his control. At the American's suggestion, Curtin ordered General Blamey back to Port Moresby to take personal control of operations. Blamey knew his presence was not at all necessary. He was apparently to be used as an 'on the spot' scapegoat in the event of Port Moresby falling to the Japanese.[12] If it did not fall, MacArthur, the supreme Allied commander who controlled and censored all media coverage in the South-West Pacific, would still be able to take credit for this victory. Curtin was later to concede that his ordering of Blamey to New Guinea was a serious mistake.

Japanese battle casualties in capturing Ioribaiwa are not known but appear to have been substantial. They had halted temporarily at Ioribaiwa to regroup while waiting for supplies and reinforcements to sustain them on their last thrust to Port Moresby. While waiting, other orders—most unwelcome and delayed several days in their transmission—were received, ordering the shocked South Seas Force to withdraw across the Owen Stanleys to Buna. The Japanese headquarters at Rabaul had changed its mind as it tried to control two campaigns simultaneously. Guadalcanal was now to take priority and receive reinforcements and supplies, and this made the South Seas Force's withdrawal imperative. After the Americans had been eliminated, it was then planned to cross the Owen Stanleys once more and finally capture Port Moresby. The Japanese had also become aware that General MacArthur was planning an amphibious assault on Buna, which now had to be reinforced urgently to guard against that possibility. Rather than divert reinforcements from Gaudalcanal, Major General Horii's troops were to reinforce Buna. General Horii was enraged by his new orders and is recorded in Lida Mayo's history as saying to his staff, 'I'm not going back [to Buna], not a step', while some of Horii's officers urged a 'desperate, single-handed thrust into Port Moresby'. Even had Horii chosen to disregard these orders in favour of a final thrust against Port Moresby, Eather's withdrawal to Imita Ridge ensured that any further Japanese attack would almost certainly meet with disaster.

Once back at Imita, Brigadier Eather ordered an extensive offensive patrol program to begin so that his troops could gain information on Japanese intentions, and ambush them, which would also allow the soldiers to gain experience in the jungle without the immediate pressure of fighting a major battle. By these means, over several days, the 25th Brigade gained both a good knowledge of the terrain and confidence in operating in the jungle. There was still no indication of a Japanese withdrawal in the reports coming back to Brigade Headquarters from these patrols.[13] However, the Japanese were soon on the move back, screened by a determined rearguard.

How did Eather himself see the Ioribaiwa/Imita controversy as it unfolded? His private diary contains entries covering the 25th Brigade's first contact with the Japanese right through to his subsequent decision to withdraw; there is no evidence of panic or of his being 'shaken', as recorded in Lida Mayo's history. Indeed, it seems that far from being shaken, Eather made a careful assessment of the situation and acted in his usual calm, pragmatic and unflappable manner. Had he been as perturbed by the situation as Mayo suggests, it is unlikely that he would have taken the time to continue writing his daily diary to the same level of detail (if at all) during these dangerous days. Not only did he continue diarising events, there is also no appreciable difference in his handwriting on the pages that deal with the Imita controversy. Indeed, on both 14 and 18 September, Eather made time to write letters and send cables to Adeline. These were hardly the actions of a shaken man.

New evidence on the dramatic 'You'll die at Imita' conversation between Allen and Eather puts the situation in an entirely different light. It seems that this conversation has become distorted over the years in its re-telling. In the mid-1970s, Eather's stepson Owen asked him about this dramatic conversation. Eather laughed and recounted the following interchange:

> Allen: 'You'll die where you stand [at Imita].'
> Eather: 'Don't you worry Tubby, the only people who will die there will be the Japs.'[14]

Eather's absolute confidence in the outcome and the correctness of his decision to withdraw is patently obvious. Similarly, when Dr G.A. Vernon called at his Ioribaiwa headquarters, the doctor was taken aback to be asked: 'How do you think we ought to reward the [native] carriers after the war?' This was certainly a forward-thinking question and one that indicated that Eather was highly confident about the ultimate success of the campaign.[15]

Of these events Eather himself recorded in his diary:

Monday 14 September
... sound of mortar fire forward ... Track very rough and steep. Passes along razor backs. Crosses numbers of creeks. Arrive at Porter's show [headquarters] 1500. Meet Kairo [sic; Lieutenant Colonel Caro commanding the 2/16th Battalion] and [Lieutenant Colonel] Cameron [commanding the 3rd Battalion]. Established HQs. 31 Battalion contact enemy almost at once. Doesn't seem to be able to make much headway. Lots of noise all day.

Tuesday 15 September
Spent very uncomfortable night. Up 0530. Shooting and mortars. [Lieutenant Colonel] Dunbar [commanding the 2/31st Battalion] still held up trying to outflank Japs. Towards 1400 hours Jap attacks on right. Send [Lieutenant Colonel] Withy [commanding the 2/25th Battalion] with two companies out from centre and one of [Lieutenant Colonel] Buttrose [commanding the 2/33rd Battalion] companies from right. Withy makes contact. Buttrose doesn't. Gunfight goes on all afternoon until dusk then quietens. May pinch him [the Japanese] out during night. Nothing much else doing.

Wednesday 16 September
Up 0530 to sound of fire. An attack on centre front and left flank. Buttrose and Dunbar do not seem to be able to make much headway. Enemy penetration on right front. Not dislodged. Wire to Tubby [Major General Allen] for permission to move back to next position. Get answer agreeing. Commence to move 1130 hours. Manage to get 'em all away. Alf does the rearguard. Bob killed this afternoon . . . Porter and [Major] Larkin move back to recce next pos. Heavy rain makes going very hard. Have to bivouac on track side with Beresford and Towns. Wet through.

Thursday 17 September
On move at first light. Very hard going indeed. Make it [to Imita Ridge] by 0800. Meet Porter and Larkin. [Colonel] Spry [7th Division Headquarters]. Recce possy [position] all day. Mena turns up with my gear. Good boy. Speak to Tubby on phone. Receive direct orders [to hold Imita Ridge at all costs]. Also good news on other moves. Hold conference COs 1400 hours to tee up occupation. Rain begins 1600 hours. Buttrose reports reasonable success. Send patrols forward to locate enemy.

Friday 18 September
Up at 0530. No contact yet. Evidently [enemy] has not followed up. Send out several offensive patrols during the day and other protective ones.

On 19 September Brigadier Porter and his staff left Imita Ridge to reorganise the remnants of the 21st Brigade further back. The enemy's failure to follow up made for a quiet day as the troops strengthened their already strong defensive position. Still apparently unaware that his decision had precipitated a major panic among the American command and Australian politicians, Eather noted in his diary at Imita that the 'Troops dirty, ragged but in very good heart' and also that 'Tubby sends me up a couple cans of beer and cigarettes. Very welcome. Beer received from US General Willoughby'.

By 20 September, with the lack of enemy offensive activity more evident, Eather decided to advance and recapture Ioribaiwa Ridge.[16] When this action commenced on 22 September with the

2/25th Battalion, it was done in a methodical and careful manner. Eather clearly did not want his men to be ambushed by parties of Japanese, nor did he want his troops exhausted by the difficult terrain. He intended to keep the initiative in his hands rather than be reacting to the enemy, as had been the situation so recently. During the day, Australian artillery began ranging on Japanese positions. Eather noted, however, that ranging these guns was 'most difficult because of heavy timber'.

Patrols continued to probe forward in the succeeding days, noting that the enemy were active on Ioribaiwa Ridge and that they still held the steps at the base of the ridge. On 24 September both the Australian 25-pounders and Japanese mountain guns were active for a time.[17] That same day saw the first political casualty resulting from Eather's withdrawal. Lieutenant General Rowell, commander of New Guinea Force, was relieved of his command by General Blamey. Rowell, distraught at the implied lack of faith in his ability, had not fully cooperated with Blamey since his senior's forced arrival in New Guinea. Blamey then took personal control of operations pending his appointment of Lieutenant General 'Ned' Herring to command New Guinea Force.

The same day that Rowell was sacked, General Allen came forward to Eather's headquarters:

> Tubby turns up 1330hours. Take him to lookout & discuss outline of my plan. Return to HQ 1630. Rain commences 1700. Very heavy. Eases about 2000hours. Have a spot [drink] or two with Tubby & discuss various subjects . . . Tubby brought whisky, lime juice & cigarettes.[18]

Although Brigadier Eather and General Allen were soon to be criticised for not advancing fast enough, indications were that the Japanese still planned to make a fight for Ioribaiwa, even though they did little or no patrolling forward of their main positions.[19] Little did the Australians realise that they were coming up only against a rearguard, albeit of well-trained and highly disciplined troops, whose leaders had no intention of giving ground easily. At 5.30 on the morning of 25 September, B Company of the 2/25th launched an assault on the old battalion and brigade headquarters'

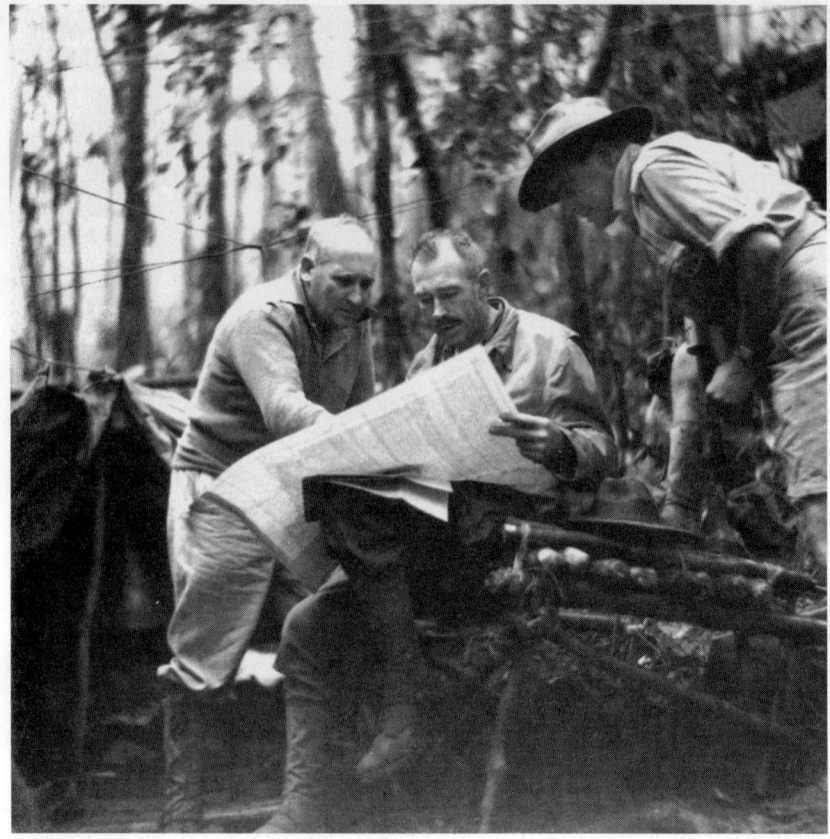

Major General 'Tubby' Allen (left) and Brigadier Eather in a forward position prepare their attack on the Japanese, September 1942.

Photo courtesy of the Australian War Memorial (AWM 026750)

positions near Ioribaiwa but withdrew after losing several wounded and coming under mortar fire. The next day, the same troops again probed the enemy positions but came under light and medium machine-gun fire, as well as artillery fire.

On the evening of 26 September Eather, having ordered both the 2/31st and 2/33rd Battalions to join the 2/25th's advance, noted in his diary:

> Things moving very well. Jap on the defensive. Does no patrolling whatever that we can discover ... Tubby rings me at 2200 hours. Seems pleased with way things are shaping up.

IMITA RIDGE AND THE LAST LINE OF DEFENCE

The Japanese were still in position the following day, but by mid-afternoon on 28 September Ioribaiwa was reoccupied by Australian troops. There was no opposition, the last of the Japanese having withdrawn the previous evening. The following day the 3rd Battalion and Brigade Headquarters moved forward to Ioribaiwa. Eather recorded that it was a:

> Frightful trudge up and down hills . . . Sent patrols forward to find Jap. Seems to have gone back past Nauro in a hurry. Left a good deal of stuff here . . . Very tiring on men. After such a march must have a day['s] rest.[20]

Brigadier Eather's controversial decision to move back to a firm base and a more easily defended position had been vindicated. The immediate threat to Port Moresby had been removed. Now the 25th Brigade and other troops would pursue and harry their enemy as they recaptured the Kokoda Track. No longer would they be dancing to the Japanese tune. It was now Australian plans and actions that would dictate what would occur in the following battles, and the Japanese commanders would not regain the initiative.

No matter how exhausted Eather's troops were, however, allowing them to rest at Ioribaiwa was, politically, a mistake. General Douglas MacArthur's political imperatives would ensure that the advance along the Kokoda Track would be criticised as much as had been the withdrawal.

It is interesting to speculate on the ramifications for Australia had the Japanese managed to capture Port Moresby—even assuming that the Japanese Army continued to veto a full-scale invasion of Australia (which seems likely due to their soon-to-be flagging fortunes at Guadalcanal). From the well-developed airfield system at Port Moresby, the Japanese could have mounted heavy bomber attacks over eastern Australia as far south as Townsville. Their flying boats would have had the capacity to make lighter raids even further to Brisbane. To complement these actions, it is likely that they would have intensified submarine operations along the east coast. Even the small-scale operations mounted in 1942–43 had a massive impact, disrupting maritime trade and forcing the introduction of convoys. Allied air and naval forces, diverted from the main theatre of action, proved largely ineffective in combating these submarines, none of which were sunk (excluding the midget submarines destroyed in Sydney Harbour). The Japanese, however, destroyed eighteen Allied vessels and damaged a further eight. The loss of life in some of these sinkings was very heavy.

The Japanese might also have supplemented air and submarine operations with anti-shipping raids and shore bombardments by cruisers. They may even have considered using some of their surviving aircraft carriers to devastating effect against industrial and population centres. Australia did not have the capacity to readily resist any of these eventualities. It is clear that the Japanese would have caused Australia great material damage as well as many service and civilian casualties, as they did so successfully over the north-west of the continent. All this, and perhaps more, could have happened had the AIF and Militia been defeated at Ioribaiwa/Imita. The debt that all Australians owe those gallant troops and their commanders is all the greater for that.

6

Taking the offensive
on the Kokoda Track

Tubby shows me messages from TAB written in complete ignorance of local conditions. Grumbling about slowness of advance & tactical handling of troops. MacArthur had a word to say on the same lines. Pity one of them did not come and see.

Brigadier Eather, diary entry on the Kokoda Track, 21 October 1942

After the 25th Brigade occupied Ioribaiwa, patrols were pushed forward in an attempt to locate the enemy. On 29 September one such patrol discovered that the Japanese had abandoned Nauro.

The advance of Brigadier Eather's troops was not fast, the diabolical terrain and an inability to supply the forward troops proving to be limiting factors. General Allen would soon voice his concerns about the small number of supply-dropping aircraft and the insufficient number of indigenous carriers available to support his force. On the other hand General Blamey, under pressure from General MacArthur, showed scant regard for the situation confronting the forward troops and was soon harassing Allen to move faster.

On 30 September, Eather noted in his diary, with surprise, and the beginnings of disgust, that the Japanese had not bothered to bury the Australian dead at Ioribaiwa, as was custom for the side occupying the ground after a battle had been concluded.[1] He would find this to be just the first of many differences. Indeed, he would quickly develop a revulsion for the Japanese that would grow as the war continued and last for many years afterwards. He also noted that General Allen called him on this day and advised that the commander-in-chief was 'very pleased with way things are going'.[2] This may have been the first occasion on which Allen either hid or twisted the truth from his brigade commander. It is now clear that although the higher commanders made little effort to understand the terrain the troops were fighting over, not to mention the serious supply problems for which they themselves were ultimately responsible, they were definitely not happy with the rate of progress. Communications were very bad and it took a long time for information from the forward troops to get back to Brigade Headquarters. Eather found this very frustrating, particularly when his soldiers were in contact with the enemy.[3]

The advance continued and by 2 October the leading troops were approaching Efogi, a long hard trip from Menari and nearly 1400 metres above sea level. Here they came upon the site of a major battle between the Japanese and the 21st Brigade where the skeletons of many Australians and Japanese were in evidence. Some of the dead were found still holding their weapons in firing positions. Ominously, a number of corpses were found lying on stretchers—wounded Australians that the Japanese had killed after capture. The dead of both sides were buried before the troops moved on. Apart from a few stragglers, the Japanese had still not been contacted at this point. During the day Eather was again told that General Blamey was happy with the progress being made.[4] That night in his diary Eather noted that he saw his first live Japanese—a prisoner.

On 3 October Eather recorded that there was great difficulty in obtaining sufficient indigenous people to carry supplies for the brigade. He also tried to talk to 'Tubby' Allen by phone, but the line was so bad he had to arrange to have messages relayed between the two commanders. This was a most tedious and unsatisfactory method of communication. On a happier note, he received two letters from his wife that he read avidly. No matter how bad the military situation, Eather always found the time to write to Adeline at least once a week. For her part, Adeline had maintained a close correspondence with her husband since he went overseas in 1940. The following day, Eather enjoyed a 'bath' in a nearby creek, and managed to write back to Adeline, despite moving his headquarters forward to the fringes of Nauro. Some aerial supply-drops for his troops took place as the advance continued, but the quantity of supplies received was much less than that required. Eather's headquarters was also visited by a number of war correspondents and photographers covering the momentous events then unfolding.[5]

Brigadier Lloyd's 16th Brigade was moving along the Kokoda Track behind the 25th Brigade to reinforce the Australian offensive, and Eather first met Lloyd and his staff when they caught up with him on 5 October. Over the next few days the 25th Brigade received air-dropped supplies, but Eather noted that there was considerable danger of the troops being hit by falling loads. In fact, one soldier was very severely injured and later died. Communications remained most unsatisfactory. Again he had to have a relayed conversation with Allen which was very difficult to understand.[6] By this time he was thinking that General Allen might be getting 'restless about slowness of adv[ance]', a suspicion that was indeed correct. Allen was soon to be placed under immense pressure by Blamey who in turn was being pressured by MacArthur. If Eather was aware of the situation, he could only have been confused by a signal from Blamey, received on 8 October, offering congratulations at the occupation of Nauro.

Despite their badgering of General Allen, neither MacArthur or Blamey saw fit to alleviate the logistics problems plaguing Eather's advance by providing more supply-dropping aircraft. On 9 October the air force was to have dropped supplies for the 25th Brigade at Efogi North, but the promised aircraft failed to materialise. Eather had to threaten to stop the advance and withdraw his forward troops before he received an assurance that air drops would occur the following day.[7] His plight and understandable threats to withdraw his troops inadvertently put General Allen under more pressure as he tried to persuade his ignorant senior commanders of the 7th Division's needs. On this day Eather managed to have a wash, put clean clothes on and shave, basics which were considered luxuries during the campaign in New Guinea.

Notwithstanding Eather's reputation as a disciplinarian, Captain M.L. Roberts of the 2/33rd Battalion recalled of his brigade commander in this fighting:

> During the early actions across the Owen Stanleys he showed the utmost concern for the welfare of the troops who were fighting under extreme duress because of acute food and ammunition shortages. He did everything humanly possible to keep casualties to a

minimum even though he was at times unfairly hounded by higher command. He encouraged rather than drove his battalions when he understood just how they were suffering.[8]

The 25th Brigade re-established contact with the Japanese on 8 October in the Templeton's Crossing area, and a major battle ensued. The Australians attacked over several days but, while they made some gains, the Japanese were not ejected from their main positions. The Japanese had selected Templeton's Crossing with great care and it was a major delaying position. On 13 October, Eather wrote that 'the Jap is digging his toes in and is hard to move'. Air attacks and mortar shoots seemed to have little effect. Bitter fighting continued. Eather requested air strikes on several occasions to help neutralise enemy opposition.[9]

As this fighting was occurring, Brigade Headquarters was moving forward behind the infantry battalions. Of that movement Eather wrote:

> Very stiff climb out of Menari. Track very bad & stinks of death. Lots of gear strewn about. Rains like hell from 1530 hrs. Arrive at Efogi 1800. Wet through . . . Find shelter in old native hut with a couple dozen sick, wounded & stragglers.

Next day he noted, 'track in shocking condition. Slush & mud'. It was also extremely cold at night at this altitude and the troops and their commander, who had few warm clothes, shivered through the nights. Their misery was made worse as it rained most afternoons, leaving the soldiers wet as darkness fell and the temperature went down.

On October 15th, Eather recorded that the 2/31st Battalion had come across 'some of our dead with arms missing and large piece [of] flesh cut from thigh. Parcel of flesh found in Jap position'.[10] This was probably the first indication he received that the enemy was resorting to cannibalism to survive. The incident redoubled his rapidly developing hatred of the Japanese.

On 17 October Eather wrote in his diary of the fight around Templeton's Crossing:

> Very active in forward area. Japs using mortars and a [mountain] gun. Two companies from Cameron [the 3rd Battalion] did a

splendid job. Got in behind, dug in and then attacked rear. Thirty Japs killed ... no loss to attackers.

By now many soldiers had been evacuated due to the effects of tropical diseases. Supply problems continued to hamper operations. Fortunately, Myola had by now been occupied and with its extensive dry lake-beds high in the mountains, air-dropping of stores increased and became more organised.

Fighting continued to rage in the Templeton's Crossing area on 19 October, even as the relief of the 25th Brigade by the 16th Brigade was occurring, and the Japanese commenced a strong counter-attack.[11] Of this event, Eather wrote in his diary that shortly after daybreak:

> Jap attacks Cameron [3rd Battalion] but beaten off. Edgar [the 2/2nd Battalion of the 16th Brigade] in position on right. Flank attacks throughout AM. All beaten off. Two companies of Withy [2/25th Battalion] return. Lost two men. Tubby rings early to find out what noise about. Evidently he can hear it. Carry out mortar shoot. Barrel explodes killing three of crew ... Shoot very effective but stirs him up. His searching replies [from mountain guns] come pretty close. Cameron attacks during afternoon. Hell of a din. Although [the 3rd Battalion] clears Jap from spur cannot hold it. Lloyd and Cullen [commanding the 2/1st Battalion] arrive. Cook up plan for tomorrow. Rain from 1600 all night.

With the exception of the 3rd Battalion, the 25th Brigade was relieved by the 16th Brigade on 20 October after participating in another day's fighting. In the relatively short time it had been in action, Eather's force had already lost nearly 1000 troops—four-fifths of them to tropical illnesses. Having noted the effectiveness of the Japanese mountain gun batteries, Eather thought it was a 'pity our people could not give us some kind of light gun'.[12]

On the night of 18 October, Eather made time to pen a quick letter to his mother. He described the conditions his troops fought under and also his failure to recognise much of Port Moresby from when he lived there as a child. Although the way in which the indigenous carriers are referred to is unpalatable by today's standards, his affection and admiration for their vital work is very evident:

Dear Mother,

Just a few lines to let you know all is well & that I haven't forgotten you. Have been very busy indeed ever since arriving in this part of the world. Am afraid my opinion of NG is a very poor one although under different conditions it might not be too bad. At the moment I am well inland & up some 7000 feet [2130 metres] on a mountain. Not at all hot, rather chilly in fact & we have plenty of rain. No water shortage here! Am feeling very fit indeed, must be all the climbing I'm doing for once one leaves the coastal area its climb up or down the whole time . . .

Pop enquires if Port [Moresby] is the same. Only saw it as I passed through the day I landed & to me it looked an entirely strange place. The old BP building on the corner was the only landmark I recognised.

See plenty of 'boys'. 'Boongs' our chaps call 'em. They do most of our carrying for us & to see a team of 'em bringing out a stretcher case over these very rough tracks is something worth seeing. They are most careful with the load & and try to give the poor chaps as easy a carry as possible. They do not mind the noise of firing very much provided they have somebody to go with 'em . . .

Thanks for the envelope, Pop. Supplies are very low indeed. If one was to carry a supply the gummed edges all stick down. Regret to tell you I am not wearing my 'woollies'. In fact haven't worn 'undies' for weeks and weeks. My last set got too stiff for me to bend in comfort so I chucked 'em away. Am also being delightfully dirty! My last 'bath' was four days ago & it looks as if my next is about four days hence . . .

Will write again when the chance presents itself.

Your loving son
Ken

After the 25th Brigade had been relieved and the 16th Brigade had taken up the pursuit, Eather moved back and reported to the 7th Division's Headquarters. Arriving at around 6 pm on 21 October, he had dinner with his divisional commander. Afterwards, 'Tubby' Allen finally told his good friend the full extent of MacArthur's and Blamey's attacks on the 7th Division's work and on Allen in particular.[13] Eather was appalled and wrote that night:

> Tubby shows me messages from TAB [General Blamey] written in complete ignorance of local conditions. Grumbling about slowness of advance & tactical handling of troops. MacA[rthur] had a word to say on the same lines. Pity one of them did not come and see.

On 24 October the 25th Brigade, after the briefest of rests, began moving forward again but supply problems still impeded the advance. In the rear, the badgering Allen was receiving from Blamey about the pace of forward movement may have caused tension between the two friends. The pressure upon Allen was enormous. On 26 October Eather sent all his indigenous carriers and 200 soldiers back to Myola to carry supplies forward to the brigade. In a footnote to his diary entry this day Eather wrote: 'Learn Potts has gone to Darwin & Ian [Ivan] Dougherty taking over his brigade.'

Still dissatisfied with the rate of advance—now being led by the 16th Brigade—and the seemingly low number of battle casualties sustained by the forward troops, Blamey acted. General Allen was advised on 27 October that he would be relieved of his command and replaced by Major General George Vasey. Noting this sad event in his diary, Eather recorded:

> Tubby rang me. He is going back [to Port Moresby]. Geo Vasey taking over today! He does not know what it is all about, promised to write & let me know. Says we could not do more than we are doing at the moment.

At the end of this entry Eather later penned some additional news: 'Receive note from Tubby. Recalled because of "health"! Darn shame.' The next day he recorded that: 'Tubby flies out today. Will miss him. Haven't much faith in Geo (Crete).'

Eather's mention of Crete refers to the cutting off and eventual capture of his beloved 2/1st Battalion at Retimo airfield while it was under Vasey's command. Eather, somewhat unfairly, may also have held Vasey responsible for the less than successful evacuation of Australian forces from Crete. So much for Brigadier Potts only being relieved temporarily. After Allen's departure as well, Eather could have little doubt about the cost of perceived failure.

General Allen's removal had come at the end of a string of increasingly acrimonious signals between Blamey and Allen. In these signals—in which the full extent of the attacks on Allen and his commanders was hidden from Eather until afterwards—Blamey displayed an inexcusable lack of knowledge of the terrain being fought over as well of the logistics problems for which ultimately he and MacArthur were responsible. At the very heart of these bitter exchanges was Eather's, and later Brigadier Lloyd's, handling of their troops and the two brigadiers' tactical ability.

11 October   Blamey to Allen:
Your order definitely to push on with sufficient force and capture Kokoda. You have been furnished with supplies as you requested and ample appears to be available [author's note: this was not true; very large quantities of the airdropped supplies—sometimes up to 90 per cent of each load—were never recovered from the jungle or kunai patches]. In view of lack of serious opposition your advance appears much too slow. You will press enemy with vigour. If you are feeling strain personally relief will be arranged. Please be frank about this . . .

12 *October*   Allen to Blamey:
My outline plan . . . is to capture Kokoda as soon as possible. Apparently it has been misunderstood. Nothing is being left undone in order to carry out your wishes and my brigade commanders have already been instructed accordingly. The most serious opposition to rapid advance is terrain. The second is maintenance of supplies through lack of native carriers. Reserve supplies have not repeat not been adequate up to 11 Oct. Until information of recoveries today am unable to say whether they are yet adequate. Rate of advance does not entirely depend on air droppings. Equal in importance is our ability to carry forward and maintain our advanced troops. Notwithstanding that men carry with them up to five days' rations maintenance forward of dropping place is still necessary. This country is much tougher than any previous theatre and cannot be appreciated until seen. From all reports the worst is north of Myola. The vigour with which we press the enemy is dependent on the physical endurance of the men and the availability of supplies. Our

men have pressed so far with vigour consistent with keeping them fit to fight. With regard to my personal physical fitness I am not repeat not feeling the strain. I never felt fitter nor able to think straighter. I however feel somewhat disappointed on behalf of all ranks that you are dissatisfied with the very fine effort they have made.

17 October   Blamey to Allen:
General MacArthur considers quote extremely light casualties indicate no serious effort yet being made to displace enemy unquote. You will attack with energy and all possible speed at each point of resistance. Essential that Kokoda airfield be taken at earliest. [It is] Apparent enemy gaining time by delaying you with inferior strength.

17 October   Allen to Blamey:
25 Bde has been attacking all day and enemy is now counter-attacking. Will advise when situation clarifies. Serious efforts have been made to dispose of enemy and energetic steps have been taken at each point of resistance. This action will continue. Battle casualties since contact with enemy are killed offrs [officers] 5 ors [other ranks] 45 wounded offrs 10 ors 123 but I respectfully submit that the success of this campaign cannot be judged by casualties alone. Lloyd's 16th Brigade starts move forward 18 Oct to continue pressure. Until dropping ground further north is established possibly Alola there is no alternative once Lloyd's brigade is forward but to base Eather on Myola and Efogi North. In short with the carriers available I can only maintain three battalions forward in contact with enemy. Respectfully suggest you defer judgement until you receive [Lieutenant Colonel] Minogue's [staff officer from New Guinea Force Headquarters who was moving up to the forward area] report or until a more senior staff officer can come forward and discuss situation with me. The severity of the conditions under which the troops are operating is emphasised by the fact that the net wastage by sickness alone in 25 Bde is offrs 24 ors 706 and 16 Bde offrs 1 ors 38.

21 October   Blamey to Allen:
During last five days you have made practically no advance against a weaker enemy. Bulk of your forces have been defensively located in rear although enemy has shown no capacity to advance. Your attacks for most part appear to have been conducted by single battalions or even companies on narrow front. Enemy lack of enterprise makes clear he has not repeat not sufficient strength to attack in force. You should consider acting with greater boldness and employ wide encircling movement to destroy enemy in view of fact that complete infantry brigade in reserve is available to act against hostile counter-offensive.

You must realise time is now of great importance. 128 US [Regiment] already has elements at Pongani. Capture Kokoda aerodrome and onward move to cooperate with 128 before Buna is vital portion of plan.

21 October   Blamey to Allen (again):
The following message has been received from General MacArthur. Quote. Operations reports show that progress on the trail is NOT repeat NOT satisfactory. The tactical handling of our troops in my opinion is faulty. With forces superior to the enemy we are bringing to bear in actual combat only a small fraction of available strength enabling the enemy at the point of actual combat to oppose us with apparently comparable forces. Every extra day of delay complicates the problem and will probably result ultimately in greater casualties than a decisive stroke made in full force. Our supply situation and the condition of the troops certainly compares favourably with those of the enemy [author's note: this was certainly true; the Japanese were starving and those of the 7th Division had very little to eat; this of course was not what MacArthur actually meant] and weather conditions are neutral. It is essential to the entire New Guinea operation that the Kokoda airfield be secured promptly. Unquote.

To this message a disgusted Allen drafted a curt and bitter response: 'If you think you can do any better come up and bloody try', but he was talked out of sending this and instead sent the following on 22 October:

TAKING THE OFFENSIVE ON THE KOKODA TRACK

I was singularly hurt to receive General MacArthur's signal of 21st Oct since I feel the difficulties of operations in this country are still not fully realised. This country does not lend itself to quick or wide encircling movements. In addition owing to shortage of carriers I have been confined to one line of advance. As is already known to Commander New Guinea Force my available carriers forward of Myola are far below requirements. There is one line of advance which I would certainly have used had I the necessary carriers and that was the Alola–Seregina–Kagi. However, under the circumstances it was quite out of the question. I have complete confidence in my brigade commanders and troops and feel that they could not have done better. It was never my wish to have a brigade defensively in rear but the supply situation owing carrier shortage has enforced it. I fully appreciate the major plan and therefore that time is most essential. All my force are doing their level best to push on. I am confident that the capture of the high ground at Eora Creek our entry into Kokoda and beyond will not long be delayed provided Alola is utilised as a dropping place. It is pointed out however that the track between Alola and Myola is the roughest and most precipitous throughout the complete route.

26 October   Blamey to Allen:
Your [signal] of 22 Oct does NOT confute any part of General MacArthur's criticism in his message sent to you on 21st. Since then progress has been negligible against an enemy much fewer in number. Although delay has continued over several days attacks continue with small forces. Your difficulties are very great but enemy has similar. In view of your superior strength energy and force on the part of all commanders should overcome the enemy speedily. In spite of your superior strength enemy appears to delay advance at will. Essential that forward commanders should control situation and NOT allow situation to control them. Delay in seizing Kokoda may cost us unique opportunity of driving enemy out of New Guinea.

26 October   Allen to Blamey:
One. Every effort is being made to overcome opposition as quickly as possible. Present delay has and is causing me considerable concern

in view of its probable effect upon your general plan. Jap however is most tenacious and fighting extremely well. His positions are excellent well dug in and difficult to detect. I feel it will be necessary to dig him out of present positions since his actions to date indicate that a threat to his rear will not necessarily force him to retire. I have already arranged for 2/31 Bn to assist 16 Bde 27 Oct but it must be realised it would take 36 hours to get into position. Owing to precipitous slopes movement in this particular area is extremely difficult and a mile [2.5 kilometres] may take up to a day to traverse. I had hoped that 16 Bde would have been able to clear enemy position today. Two. As I feel that a wrong impression may have been created by our sitreps [situation reports] I must stress that throughout the advance a brigade has always been employed against the enemy but up to the present this has been the maximum owing to supply situation. Three. Jap tactical position at present is extremely strong and together with the terrain is the most formidable up to date. No accurate estimate can be given of Jap strength except that commander 2/3 Bn reports at least one battalion opposes him alone. You may rest assured that I and my brigade commanders are doing everything possible to speed the advance.

27 October   Blamey to Allen:
Consider that you have had sufficiently prolonged tour of duty in forward area. General Vasey will arrive Myola by air morning 28 October. On arrival you will hand over command to him and return to Port Moresby for tour of duty in this area. Will arrange air transport from Myola forenoon 29 October if this convenient to you.

27 October   Allen to Blamey:
It is regretted that it has been found necessary to relieve me at this juncture especially since the situation is improving daily and I feel that the worst is now behind us. I must add that I feel as fit as I did when I left the Base Area [Port Moresby] and I would have preferred to have remained here until my troops had also been relieved.

After Vasey took command of the 7th Division he did not change the previous divisional commander's plans to capture Kokoda—proof enough that Allen had been a political casualty and that his plans were sound. The 16th Brigade would advance towards Alola and hence to Oivi while the 25th Brigade would move forward over the mountain ridges and take Kokoda with its vital airfield. It was then intended that any Japanese attempting to escape from Kokoda would be caught by the 16th Brigade at Oivi and trapped.

As the 25th Brigade moved forward, they suffered severely from cold and exposure due to the high altitude and lack of warm clothes and blankets. The lack of food and poor quality of that available was another problem that inhibited the rate of progress. On 31 October, although air-dropping occurred, Eather noted that the supply situation was very grim. He also wrote that night that:

> Tubby has flown back to Aust to see MacArthur. Hope he gives him a true picture. Rest of Div Adv HQ arrives during afternoon. Establish near me. Rations very short. Planes dropped this AM. Only 800 rations collected. Cameron [3rd Battalion] comes under command 25 Brigade again. Vasey arrives 1800. Knocked up & sick. Kokoda or bust now. No rations.

This was Vasey's first meeting with Eather. When he realised Vasey was nearby, Eather brewed him a mug of sweet tea to help him recover from his arduous climb to the 25th Brigade Headquarters but Vasey was so ill that, much to his embarrassment, he vomited the drink almost immediately. Vasey must have been very unsure of his reception by Eather who bitterly resented General Allen's dismissal. For the first couple of days Vasey addressed Eather very formally as 'Brigadier' before the pair became more comfortable in each other's presence, after which he simply called him 'Ken'.[14]

Sergeant Bill Crooks of the 2/33rd Battalion noted as the advance continued that the jungle was so dense that most of the natural light was blocked out. At night it was so bitterly cold that the troops wore scavenged sacks, previously used to hold the supplies dropped to them, as coats. In places, the stench emanating from the rotting bodies of dead Australian and Japanese soldiers, buried in shallow graves near the track, was overwhelming. The surreal, dim, dank environment, combined with their debilitated physical condition, had a corrosive effect on the mental state of the troops, some of whom broke down under the strain.

On Sunday 1 November Eather recorded:

> Up 0500. Glorious to watch the sunrise. Remarkably little rain last few days. Grand to be in an open patch . . . GOC seems to think our advance going as fast as can be expected . . . Leave for Isurava at 0920. War correspondent tags along . . . Establish new HQ north of Isurava 1200 . . . Not a ration in Alola & none dropped today. Vasey can now see for himself.[15]

Depressingly, as Eather moved up the track, he often came across the graves of his former soldiers and officers of the 2/1st Battalion, which was fighting as part of the 16th Brigade. Some of the dead were his close friends, and often the first indication he received of their deaths was seeing their graves.[16]

Mindful of the need to sustain morale and to mark achievements that were gained under such adverse circumstances, on the morning of 2 November Brigadier Eather sent the following message to all those under his command:

> Expect to occupy Kokoda today. Congratulations to all ranks on a fine effort under adverse conditions. Continuance of campaign in this spirit will result in complete defeat and destruction of enemy. Signal has been received from divisional commander congratulating all ranks on their efforts.[17]

Eather had expected to fight for possession of Kokoda but, happily, patrols found it abandoned by the enemy and the village was occupied that morning as forecast. Efforts to repair the all-important airfield were immediately effected so that supplies could be flown in. The supply situation was by now chronic and Eather wrote in his diary that while there were plenty of mosquitoes at Kokoda village, his troops had eaten the very last of their rations for breakfast that morning. Fortunately, from 9 am onwards the air force was able to drop supplies and, once the airfield was repaired, supplies were landed directly. On 3 November a flag-raising ceremony was held outside Eather's headquarters when General Vasey arrived at Kokoda. Privately to Eather, the new divisional commander expressed his view that he was satisfied with the 25th Brigade's progress, but that he was unhappy with the 16th Brigade.[18]

The Australian flag is raised in front of Brigadier Eather's headquarters at Kokoda, 3 November 1942.

Photo courtesy of the Australian War Memorial (AWM 013572)

At Kokoda, other administrative matters were completed. Not happy with the performance of one of his battalion commanders, Eather had the officer interviewed before Major General Vasey. After this interview, the two senior officers agreed that the officer concerned should be relieved of his command and returned to Australia.[19] Previously, Eather had removed a battalion commander with whom he was unhappy without the prominent involvement of his divisional commander. That he felt it necessary to involve Vasey in the matter may reflect that, at this stage, Eather himself was still unsure where he stood with him.

On 5 November Lieutenant General Herring, the GOC of New Guinea Force, and seven senior US Army officers flew into Kokoda. The 25th Brigade's commander entertained these 'fortunate' visitors 'with a mug of tea'. Presumably, this was all that the supply system could manage. That night, with no great certainty, Eather wrote that Herring thought that he and his brigade had done well.

The capture of Kokoda and its strategically vital airfield meant different things to different people. For the humble foot soldier, Private Waters noted:

> Kokoda. Let history record all the razza-mattaz that went on when this goal was secured. To us in the Unit it meant a short space of time to recoup our strength and clean up somewhat, write letters and not much more.[20]

However, the *Canberra Times* reported to the Australian population on 4 November:

> Kokoda in our hands affords a geographic measurement of Australian achievement since the change from defensive to offensive in the New Guinea area beginning with the storming of Ioribaiwa Ridge at the end of September. This advance over forty miles [64 kilometres] of the worst mountain and jungle country in which fighting has yet taken place on any front, is a military achievement adding to the renown of the Australians as fighters . . .

General Vasey had arrived just in time to make the final preparations for what would prove to be the climactic engagement of the Kokoda campaign—the battle of Oivi–Gorari. The plan was for the 16th Brigade to press forward to Oivi where it would attack the strong Japanese positions on the high ground in that area, holding the enemy in position. The 25th Brigade, with the 2/1st Battalion under command, would make use of its commander's preference for avoiding frontal assaults. Consequently, the battalions would strike at the enemy by way of a most difficult flanking attack, ending up behind the Japanese forward positions with the hoped-for result of cutting off the enemy from both escape and reinforcement. It was clear that the Japanese intended a major battle to occur here on the ground of their own choosing. However, they did not appear to be fully prepared for other plans the Australian commanders had made for them.

Eather's record of the final day's planning and activities on 6 November belies the momentous events which were about to unfold:

TAKING THE OFFENSIVE ON THE KOKODA TRACK

Up at 0700. Finish [letter number] twenty-three to Top. Rain gone. Planes landing from 0815. Issue warning order to units to be prepared to move 0630 tomorrow. Take bath in river. Many parcels in but none for me yet. Geo Vasey comes down at 1530 & discusses my role [in forthcoming attack]. Have afternoon tea battalion commanders. Marson appointed lieutenant colonel & Jim Miller also. Hold conference of Battalion commanders re move tomorrow. Malcom [Eather's personal carrier who had replaced Mena earlier in the campaign] presented with medal. Rain from 1800. Visit Geo Vasey at 1900. Discuss move tomorrow. Lloyd [16th Brigade] still held up at Oivi. I am to clear up Oivi area then secure bridgehead. Have a couple of gins with Geo presents me with fresh egg! Heard Tubby is Base Area Commander Moresby [a backwater command]. God! 2/1st Battalion to come under [my] command tomorrow.

On 7 November, in an eleven-hour march through harsh terrain, the 25th Brigade moved out of Kokoda in pouring rain, many of the troops sick and straggling. Eather's plan was for the 2/31st Battalion to seize Gorari while the 2/25th and 2/33rd Battalions would strike the Japanese positions at Oivi from the rear—while they were still being engaged and held in position by the 16th Brigade from the front. The 2/1st Battalion would capture the Ilimo area, further to the rear of Gorari, thus providing further obstacles to any retreating Japanese, as well as sending strong fighting patrols towards both Gorari and Wairopi. The latter was the key crossing point for the fast flowing Kumusi River—a natural barrier to any retreating Japanese and an important area to seize if the Australians were to cross the river themselves and capture the enemy beachheads in the Gona, Buna and Sanananda areas. It was Eather's hope that the Japanese mountain guns which had caused so much trouble in the fighting in both directions on the Kokoda Track would be captured or destroyed in the forthcoming battle, before the Japanese once again could get them to safety.[21] Significantly, two of his three battalion commanders had only just been appointed to their commands and this would be the first major action they would fight as senior officers. The battle would prove a severe test of both Eather's judgment and the new commanders' abilities.

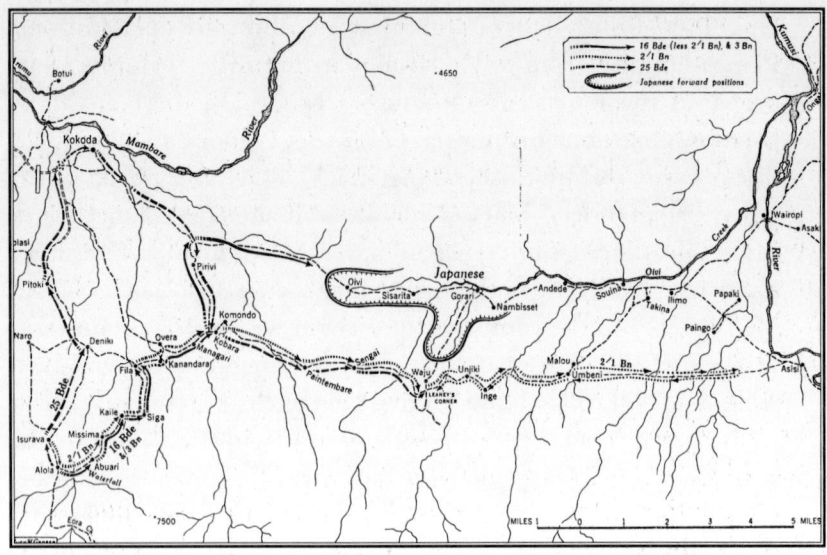

The approach to Oivi–Gorari, 31 October 1942 to 8 November 1942. This map shows clearly the Japanese dispositions and the depth of Brigadier Eather's deep flanking attack which so surprised the Japanese and which was so pivotal to the outcome of the battle.

Reproduced with the kind permission of the Australian War Memorial

The plan was a bold one. If the battle was successful, the Japanese force might well be destroyed and the way left open for ending the campaign in New Guinea. Despite the terrain, by nightfall the 25th Brigade had reached a position west of Leaney's Corner where the troops camped for the night.

The following morning, 8 November, the attack commenced in earnest. Elements of the 2/1st Battalion were already in contact with the Japanese, and the 2/31st Battalion began its flanking attack but met rigorous opposition from Japanese in prepared positions. The 2/31st Battalion had to capture its objectives before the 2/25th and 2/33rd could commence their own assaults against the rear of the enemy's Oivi positions. By 3 pm they were astride the Japanese approach tracks. To assist the 2/31st in its endeavours, Brigadier Eather ordered the 2/25th Battalion to make an even deeper flanking move so that it could pass the 2/31st then come in at the back of the

TAKING THE OFFENSIVE ON THE KOKODA TRACK

Japanese positions to sandwich and trap them between both battalions. The weather did not help, Eather noting that it 'rains like hell' from 5 pm and all through the night.[22]

Next day, the 2/1st and 2/33rd Battalions were ordered to swing past the 2/31st and 2/25th Battalions, still heavily engaged but taking some ground in the dense jungle, and to cut the track close to Gorari. Savage fighting continued and for some hours the 2/33rd was subjected to severe shelling from a mountain gun. Allied air attacks assisted and by 10.30 am the 2/31st Battalion was astride the Gorari track, at times fighting hand to hand with the Japanese.[23] One company of the 2/33rd captured Gorari village during the day but was forced out by a counter-attack. The company reorganised, attacked again and held their objective.

During this bitter and confused fighting, Eather remained confident of the eventual outcome, despite the strong opposition encountered. When one of his battalion commanders became alarmed about the number of Australian casualties, Eather told him that 'you can't expect to run into a hornets' nest without being stung'.

Eather recorded the fighting on 9 November thus:

> Push fwd through AM with Cullen [2/1st Battalion] and Marson [2/25th Battalion]. Japs pushed back 600 yards [550 metres]. Send Buttrose [2/33rd Battalion] and Cullen around right flank to secure Gorari. Buttrose contacts enemy and chases him away towards

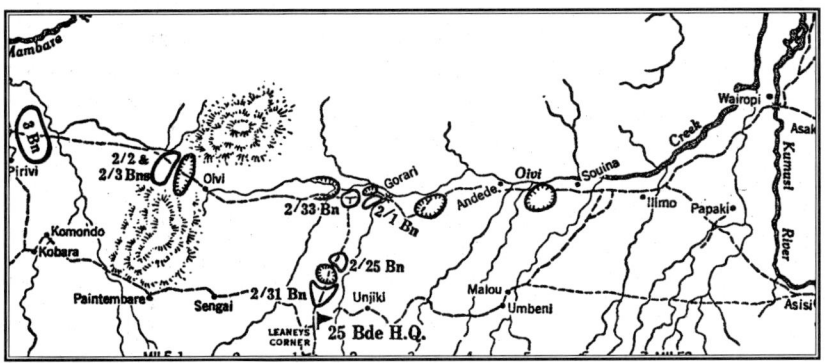

The situation at Oivi–Gorari, nightfall, 9 November 1942.

Reproduced with the kind permission of the Australian War Memorial

Cullen who does likewise. Marson mounts an attack at 1800. Took one POW today. Inflicted many casualties upon enemy. A few [sustained by] ourselves. Both Cullen and Marson reach objectives . . . Both meet with plenty enemy. Miller [2/31st Battalion] and Marson continue to squeeze.[24]

The situation was rapidly turning against the Japanese. Where they could, they began to break back towards the Kumusi River. Others were trapped between large groups of Australian troops. The 2/1st and 2/33rd Battalions in particular were involved in bitter fighting on 10 November as Japanese soldiers tried to escape through their positions. Japanese casualties on this day were very heavy but the 25th Brigade's losses were also mounting and Eather was becoming concerned about his own casualty levels and the low fighting strength of his battalions.[25] That evening, to make matters more difficult, the Japanese at Oivi finally withdrew from their forward positions and attempted to escape through the 25th Brigade, which had now severed their communications. Rather than surrender, most of the Japanese launched suicidal attacks straight through the Australian perimeters in which many were killed, some in hand-to-hand fighting.

During the day Eather also discovered from a Japanese prisoner that 'many more Jap troops in area than supposed . . . Many Jap casualties and, sad to say, many of ours. Am very concerned about strength of units'. Despite the larger than expected number of enemy troops encountered, the Japanese were being systematically destroyed by the 25th Brigade. Not surprisingly, Eather had not had the time to pen a letter to Adeline and noted this with some disappointment in his diary.

Late in the morning of 11 November, Eather's headquarters was established at Gorari and those Japanese who had escaped the trap abandoned much of their equipment as they fled. Machine-guns, rifles, food and equipment were all recovered, as were the prized Japanese mountain guns. Twenty or so enemy horses were found here and Eather kept a black mare for himself, naming it, rather irreverently, Tojo.[26] Later, more horses, along with conscripted people from Rabaul and a few Japanese, were captured. In the early hours of the morning there had been some anxious moments when a report was received that large numbers of Japanese were approaching the area occupied by Brigade Headquarters. No attack eventuated and Eather's management of the complex battle continued unhindered. The 2/25th and 2/31st Battalions had previously launched major attacks to 'clear up [the] whole thing'.

For all their well-known ruthlessness in war, in their own fashion the Japanese could sometimes respect their foes. During the desperate fighting around Gorari, Padre Don Redding and several troops were burying a soldier from the 2/31st Battalion in a clearing when the Australians became aware of a platoon of twenty well-armed Japanese nearby in the jungle, watching. The padre concluded that the enemy would have opened fire already had they desired to, and calmly completed the burial service and left unmolested with his men.[27] This apparent display of chivalry is all the more remarkable as the battle of Oivi–Gorari was one of the decisive engagements on the New Guinea mainland and the Japanese had the most to lose if they did not ruthlessly pursue it to the end.

An incident at Gorari revealed that the Australians could act in as brutal a manner as the Japanese. As the battle reached its conclusion a number of Japanese medical personnel—that is, those who are to be accorded the very highest degree of protection by the rules of war—put their hands up and surrendered. For many Australians

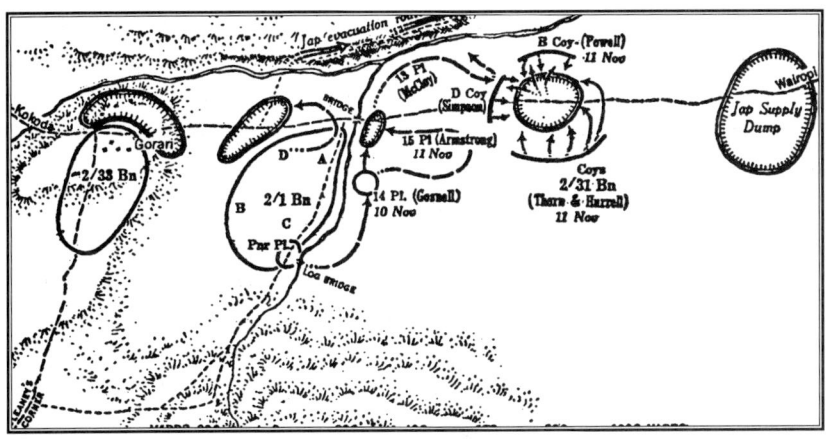

Gorari, 10–11 November 1942.
Reproduced with the kind permission of the Australian War Memorial

this would be the only time they actually saw Japanese soldiers voluntarily surrender. Unfortunately, when a junior officer from the 2/33rd Battalion heard of the surrender he located the prisoners and shot them all. It has been recorded that 'headquarters' staff, either from the battalion itself or from 25th Brigade Headquarters, came forward to investigate this incident but that none of the witnesses was prepared to speak as they were all too frightened of the officer who committed the murders—some considered him insane. The officer escaped punishment then but later in the war was cashiered from the Army for stabbing an Australian soldier. This individual was a prewar regular officer who had earlier been decorated for gallantry.[28]

Not all the Japanese at Gorari ended up like the surrendered medical personnel. Sergeant Moriki Masaru of the 144th Regiment was so badly wounded that he was captured alive—much to his horror and shame. He was carried across the mountains back to Kokoda so that he could be flown out for proper medical treatment. Sergeant Moriki was stunned when his guard protected him from resentful soldiers and indigenous people who wanted to take revenge on him.[29] At one stage he was carried on the back of an Australian soldier over difficult parts of the trail. At Kokoda he found a few other Japanese wounded—all being cared for in the same manner as the Australian casualties. Moriki would later refer to the Australians who fought on the Kokoda Track as 'true samurai'—perhaps the greatest compliment that the Japanese could give to any foe.

By the morning of 12 November the battle was all but over, and the pursuit continued to the Kumusi River, slowed down only by the occasional Japanese straggler. An estimated 600 enemy were killed in the fighting while many others drowned trying to cross the flooded Kumusi. Major General Horii and some of his staff officers were among those lost in this fashion. The South Seas Force had been decisively beaten. The way to the final elimination of the Japanese presence in New Guinea was open.

When Eather himself later reached the banks of the Kumusi he was confronted by a sight which, for him, confirmed his recently found view that the Japanese were a rabid and unfathomable race. Some Japanese soldiers, unable to cross over before the Australians reached them and scorning surrender, quickly made nooses, tied them to branches overhanging the river and hanged themselves, the

These six soldiers from the 2/33rd Battalion have just buried eleven Japanese soldiers (the grave is marked by the helmets of the dead Japanese) after the battle of Gorari. The Japanese generally did not bother to give Australian dead the dignity of a burial on battlefields they occupied. Of interest is the extremely thick jungle and the soldiers' shocked expressions, typical of those who have just survived intense combat. Also notable is that only one soldier in the group has a rifle. Four of the others have Thompson submachine-guns and the last, a Bren light machine-gun. The ready availability of submachine-guns greatly assisted the Australians in close quarters jungle fighting.

Photo courtesy of the Australian War Memorial (AWM 013645)

fast current dragging against their partially submerged bodies to hasten their agonising deaths.

In *Touched With Fire* American historian Eric Bergerud made the following assessment of the Battle of Oivi–Gorari:

At Oivi–Gorari the Australians had used in the fierce New Guinea jungle the techniques pioneered by the Japanese in Malaya. The AIF inflicted a massive defeat on crack Japanese troops at small cost to themselves. Rarely would the Japanese fight Australian troops in open battle in the future. When they did, the result was defeat.

> ... if I were to pick one place where the war turned irrevocably against the Japanese Army, it was at Oivi–Gorari ...

The 25th Brigade, under the calm and uncompromising leadership of Brigadier Eather, had played the decisive role in this crushing victory. Lieutenant Colonel Cullen, who commanded the 2/1st Battalion at Gorari, would later comment:

> Ken Eather's plan succeeded and by pushing the 2/1st Battalion onwards while his brigade blasted and destroyed the Jap flanking positions was successful—a very bold move. At the time I admired his calm, thoughtful presence and his total command of the situation which gave the four battalion commanders he had under his command the confidence they needed to be so successful in the action.[30]

7
Gona: A fight to the last man

During the night Miller sends back urgently for ammo. Haven't any. Sent orders to Miller to withdraw. He was in sight of ocean too! Captain Thorn killed. Rained all night and morning ... I am sitting tight until I get some supplies. [Major] Larkin has the fever. Mine much better. Enemy does not follow Miller. Rain all day. Still no [supply] dropping ... Looks as if we will be very, very hungry.

Brigadier Eather's private diary entry, Gona, 20 November 1942

The Kumusi—a large fast-flowing river—was a difficult obstacle. Initially, only one damaged flying fox was available for crossing it, but soon others were in operation. The engineers also constructed precarious wire and sapling bridges, enabling the troops to cross at a greater rate. An abandoned Japanese boat was also pressed into service.[1]

Once over the Kumusi, the 25th Brigade took up the pursuit of the Japanese and headed towards Gona, while the 16th Brigade struck out for the Sanananda area. American troops, recently flown to New Guinea, attempted to besiege nearby Buna. The Kokoda campaign was over and a new, equally vicious one was about to begin. The terrain in which the Australians would now fight differed markedly from that previously encountered. The mountains were behind them but the jungle remained. They would now live and fight in highly malarious, stinking and leech-infested coastal swamps and patches of kunai grass over two metres high. Temperatures in the kunai could soar to 50° Celsius—high enough to bring on heatstroke and occasionally kill.

Eather and his brigade headquarters crossed the Kumusi on 15th November. Of the crossing and pursuit he wrote:

Up [at] daybreak. Commence to move units over river. Slow job. George Vasey poking about. Get whole of Buttrose [2/33rd Battalion] over by 11 O'clock. Miller [2/31st Battalion] gets over by noon. Cameron [3rd Battalion] went out to take over from him . . . Go over myself at 1230. Move forward. Pass enemy hospital area. Plenty of graves. No tobacco issue. Darn shame. After three hour tramp select HQ area in old village site. Rained like the devil. Wet through . . . Took POW today. Sent him back.[2]

On 16 November Eather recorded:

Up early. On move at 0830 hours. Very hot. Track shows very little improvement. Pass several dump areas. Buttrose who is leading collects a few Jap stragglers. Arrive Awala about noon, my limit for today fixed by Division. Could have made more ground. Have asked to be allowed to go on tomorrow . . . Many men falling out sick, a type of fever. Have repeatedly asked for anti-malarial stuff but never received any.

The Australians continued to push forward, moving through Wairopi and Jumbora and finding only Japanese stragglers on the way. Continuing supply difficulties forced a halt in the advance and the 2/33rd prepared a dropping ground for the American and Australian transport aircraft. By now Eather was totally disgusted with the supply situation. Almost daily he complained to Divisional Headquarters about the failure to supply his soldiers.[3] On the approach to Gona his logistics staff were reduced to taking food, ammunition and other supplies from the units under his command and giving them to the most forward. When these were relieved at the front, the supplies were redistributed so that their replacements had some ammunition and essential stores even if the rest did not.

As they advanced, the Australians made use of handcarts, bicycles and other equipment hastily discarded by the enemy. They found quantities of rice and biscuits which they gratefully used to supplement their own meagre rations. By nightfall on 17 November the 25th Brigade was about 'eight miles [13 kilometres] ahead of line laid down for today [by General Vasey]'.[4] Presumably, Eather was forcing the pace and exceeding his orders in an attempt to catch the

GONA: A FIGHT TO THE LAST MAN

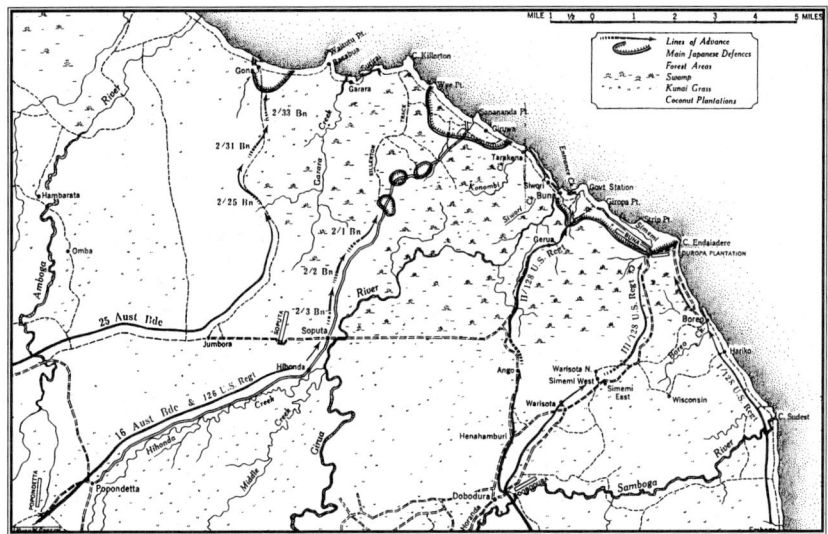

The Australian and American advance on Gona, Buna and Sanananda, 16–21 November 1942.

Reproduced with the kind permission of the Australian War Memorial

Japanese before they could consolidate their defences. Perhaps he also hoped to beat the American 32nd Division, which had been flown to the area from Australia and had not yet participated in any fighting. Most certainly he wanted to conclude the campaign before his troops became incapable of further offensive effort, and before his tenuous supply line failed completely. In his diary on 18 November he noted that he hoped to reach Gona the following day. Ominously, he also recorded that the mosquitoes were 'very bad' and that many soldiers, including Lieutenant Colonel Marson, were falling ill. He himself was feeling 'a bit off'.

During this period, one evening as he slept Eather was half-wakened by a noise outside his shelter. Bleary-eyed, he saw the silhouette of what he thought was a Japanese soldier about to throw a grenade at him. Quickly snatching up his revolver, Eather fired a shot—and to his horror heard an animal bellow waking the nearby troops, who prepared to repel an enemy attack. Next morning it was discovered that he had shot one of the captured Japanese mules (happily, only through the ear) which had been grazing close by.[5]

Notwithstanding the critical lack of supplies, on the evening of 18 November Eather ordered that one company patrol towards Gona the next morning to locate the Japanese. It would prove to be a fateful decision. Virtually nothing was known of enemy dispositions or intentions and, to make matters worse, maps of the area were inaccurate. Unfortunately, just a day or two before, no less than 1000 Japanese reinforcements had been landed at nearby Buna and more were to be sent in the future. This vital information, known to General MacArthur's headquarters due to the high level of 'Ultra' signals intelligence available to them, was not passed on to the forward commanders.[6] What *was* known at brigade level was that they had been starved of supplies, ammunition and reinforcements for a protracted period, and there was no indication that this situation would change in the immediate future. So sick and weak were the troops of the 2/33rd Battalion that the whole unit had to be scoured to find 60 reasonably 'fit' soldiers to make up the patrol.

On the morning of 19 November, this patrol moved out, and making good progress, came within 1200 metres of the sea. No opposition had been encountered. A small party of scouts was then sent further forward, covered by the rest of the troops. These soldiers came under heavy fire. The 2/31st Battalion had been moving up behind the patrol and immediately attacked. The fighting was intense but the battalion pressed on and, in part, actually reached Gona village. The firefight rapidly depleted the battalion's ammunition stocks and the battalion commander, Lieutenant Colonel Jim Miller, made a resupply request to Brigade Headquarters, but unfortunately no ammunition was left to send forward.[7] Eather had to make the painful decision to withdraw the troops so that they would not be counter-attacked without means to defend themselves. At the cost of 32 killed or wounded—including all four company commanders—the attack achieved little except to warn the enemy of the arrival of the Australians and consume much of the 25th Brigade's dwindling stock of ammunition.

The anguish of the troops and their commander brought about by these circumstances is easy to imagine. Had sufficient ammunition been available it is possible that Gona could have been held and the campaign ended sooner with far less casualties. Eather had gambled on an early rush that would seize and hold Gona before the enemy realised what was happening. The gamble failed.

A number of veterans who participated in this attack believe they could have held on had reinforcements been sent to them. While reinforcements may have been useful, it was actually ammunition that was the decisive issue and, as has been seen, there was none to send. In contrast, many of the Japanese who opposed Eather's troops had only just arrived from Rabaul and had ample ammunition. They were also physically fit and well fed.

As his soldiers could now do nothing further, Eather had no choice but to call a halt to operations until supplies were air-dropped to the brigade. Unfortunately, the delay necessary to allow this also enabled the Japanese to strengthen their defences in anticipation of further attacks, which they now knew were imminent. The Gona area was defended by between 800 and 1000 soldiers under the command of Lieutenant Colonel Yoshinobu Tomita and comprised survivors and reinforcements of the 41st and 144th Regiments and base troops. Significantly, although the Japanese who had fought on the Kokoda Track had not had time to recover from their debilitating experience, and the support troops were not as well trained in combat duties as the infantry, they were able to mount a strong—indeed, fanatical—resistance when fighting from well-prepared positions.

It is interesting to reflect on what Eather was told to expect in the way of opposition at Gona. Although General MacArthur and General Headquarters knew about the recent landing of fresh reinforcements, Eather was led to believe that he was only facing around 250 sick defenders, when in reality there were substantially more, many of whom were fit and healthy. Under the circumstances, it is not surprising that his attack was made with just part of his brigade, or that he subsequently remained confident in his ability to crush the small pocket of resistance he was told faced him. This misinformation clearly affected his operational tactics and planning. Eather was also told that the Japanese were withdrawing, when the reality was that they had no such intention and in fact were being reinforced and fully intended to stoutly resist the Australians.

On the night of 18 November, seemingly more concerned about the lack of support from his own side than opposition from the enemy, Eather angrily recorded in his diary:

... waiting for [air] dropping. Bastards! Short of everything. Good deal of noise from direction Buna ... in contact with [the Japanese] on outskirts of Gona. Not serious. Should clean up tomorrow. Muddiest track ever. [My] fever fairly high. Take couple aspros. Ask Peter for Quinine. Rain stops 1700 for awhile.

This passage is the most emotive entry in Eather's entire dairy and reveals a great deal about how he felt. Even the difficulties he faced at Ioribaiwa, Templeton's Crossing or Gorari did not draw a similar annotation.

Feeling that his supply needs were either being misunderstood or ignored, Eather took strong action and sent Lieutenant Colonel Miller back to 7th Division Headquarters with a very blunt message for General Vasey: 'I am sitting tight until I get some supplies.'[8] Eather was taking a significant risk in doing this. Unlike his last divisional commander, he hardly knew Vasey and could not foresee how he would react to his ultimatum. Fortunately, Vasey was sympathetic.

Back in Australia there were numerous aircraft in training units and uncommitted operational squadrons—Hudsons, Beauforts and impressed civilian transport aircraft—which could have been used to supply the troops at this critical time; however, few were made available and then only when the campaign was drawing to a close. Likewise, the Americans did little to provide sufficient transport aircraft or divert bombers to this vital task. The price for this failure would be very high indeed.

Despite the scandalous failure of the supply system, Eather remained confident of an early victory.[9] In this he was very wrong. The failure of the attack on 19 November was to have terrible consequences. Although Eather did not know it, this new campaign would be a race against time. The ailing Australians would have to eliminate the Japanese before they received enough reinforcements to enable them to go on the offensive again.

Eather's difficulties were many. The greatly under-strength 25th Brigade was in poor physical condition even before it had reached Gona. Nor did his command possess the generally accepted numerical advantage to attack fortified positions. Three attackers to each defender was the usual ratio regarded as necessary for a good chance of success. With just 1000 troops left before any fighting had started, Eather's command hardly outnumbered the Japanese force. His greatest difficulty was, however, the misinformation he had received, and would continue to receive, on enemy troop strengths and their intentions. Essentially, his tactics reflected the intelligence he continued to receive, that there were few defenders and that the enemy was attempting a withdrawal. Eather did receive one small reinforcement before reaching Gona. 'Chaforce', a group of the fitter 21st Brigade survivors who were meant to operate in a commando role, arrived. The commando work did not eventuate and the 'Chaforce' troops were split up and joined each of the 25th Brigade battalions.

On 21 November 7th Division Headquarters—clearly passing on information from MacArthur—again advised that the Japanese were withdrawing from Gona and that General MacArthur required an immediate attack that was to be driven through, regardless of losses.[10] With little time available for reconnaissance or planning, Eather now had to organise another attack to fit in with MacArthur's orders. Air support was available, but the defences were difficult to locate and so strong that they often required direct hits to destroy them.

David Horner, General Vasey's biographer, suggests that MacArthur was badgering his Australian field commanders not just because he was aware of Japanese reinforcement plans, but also because he was keen to win his own campaign before his hated US Navy rivals achieved victory at Guadalcanal. In view of what is known of MacArthur's extreme vanity and legendary self-promotion, this suggestion would seem to be entirely in keeping with the American's flawed character.

The following afternoon (22 November), as darkness was falling, the 25th Brigade launched the attack demanded by MacArthur. Some supplies had been received on 21 November. Had they not arrived, it is interesting to wonder whether Eather would have refused to attack. The assault was made from the south, and with two battalions forward and one in reserve. In this fight the Australian infantry, despite being met by withering fire as soon as they began to advance, actually reached some of the Japanese positions but could not hold onto them. The attack was only partially successful. The 2/31st held onto about 50 metres of ground but at the cost of nearly 70 casualties.

Of this action, the 2/31st Battalion's war diary recorded:

> At zero [hour] the men rose and were immediately met by most intense fire from front and right flank, they cheered and yelled as they advanced and returned a heavy barrage of automatic fire. They reached the Jap pits, but were not strong enough to continue as they were enfiladed from both flanks . . .
>
> The attack died down but the enemy continued an intense fire. Remnants of A, B & HQ Companies were organised with E Company, and formed the central portion of a small perimeter backed by the swamp. We lined this perimeter and track we had made along edge of swamp and waited. The Jap did not counter attack and E Company began getting all the wounded they could find, this was done under intense fire. A request for stretcher-bearers saw the 2/25th Battalion rush up two parties of thirty. Meanwhile the perimeter dug in desperately, and by morning had a position they could reasonably expect to hold. The wounded were attended by stretcher bearers and RAPs attached to Companies. Fifteen stretcher cases still remained at dawn. Jap picked away all night giving us no rest . . .

While this battle was in progress, a supply drop took place. As the brigade had not been advised, and with its troops in action, almost all the supplies were lost in thick vegetation.[11] Angry soldiers even saw some of their urgently needed stores landing behind Japanese lines. Eather was enraged, and in his diary that evening noted that his battalion commanders were becoming despondent and that resistance had been 'very stubborn'. He also recorded that Japanese barge activity had again been heard from the Japanese-held beach.

In the 25th Brigade Association's newsletter Captain Bruce Robertson, the 2/31st Battalion's Intelligence Officer, has since stated:

> we did not capture Gona that day because it was beyond the capacity of any infantry battalion even at full strength, unaided by supporting arms, particularly artillery batteries and heavy mortars, with targets properly zeroed in . . .
>
> There was a continuous trench system in the centre, plus a continuous trench system on the beach. There was a screen of slit

trenches facing the direct approach up the Gona–Kokoda road. There were forty-one MG posts plus thirteen strong posts. Being sited on almost flat ground the machine guns could inter-lock their fire and develop their beaten zones to a far more effective capacity than in the undulatory jungle which quickly absorbed their cones of fire. The ... defensive system occupied perhaps 400 yards [360 metres] roughly square, but the Japs reached out all over the Kunai and the scrub far more so than in the jungle. Forward of the prepared system, the Japs maintained standing patrols, tree snipers and listening posts.

In my opinion any attack had to be deliberate—the standing patrols and tree snipers had to be driven in, so that the direction of the attack could be concealed. The enfilading strong posts and machine guns had to be neutralised at least until the first wave reached the weapon pits. Then there had to be depth in the assault—more waves to push in past the lines of weapon pits.

Robertson's comments are entirely valid. The simple fact was that the sick and weakened 25th Brigade was unequal to the task of seizing Gona without substantial supporting fire from heavy weapons and fresh troops to back them up. Neither was available. Time also mitigated against detailed planning. General MacArthur well knew that any delays would give the Japanese further opportunity to reinforce their garrison. The attacks on Gona and Buna had to be pushed through despite the lack of preparation and the weakened state of the troops.

So desperate was MacArthur to see the Japanese eliminated before they could be further reinforced that, when Lieutenant General Eichelberger later relieved General Harding and took command of the US 32nd Division at Buna, Eichelberger was told to take any necessary steps to get the troops fighting: 'Put sergeants in charge of battalions and corporals in charge of companies—anyone who will fight. Time is of the essence *the Jap may land reinforcements any night*' [author's emphasis]. Finally Eichelberger was instructed by his desperate commander to 'take Buna, or not come back alive'. MacArthur's panicky orders reflect his well-founded fears that the Japanese bridgeheads needed to be captured quickly, despite the difficulties involved. It is a tragedy that he did not trust his Australian commanders sufficiently to tell them the truth (that Gona was being reinforced and that the Japanese had no intention of withdrawing), as he later told Eichelberger. MacArthur certainly would have attained better results had he done so.

Gona's swampy coastal environment was officially classed as an hyperendemic area for malaria transmission. A number of factors helped make the disease more seriously felt among the Australians. Their debilitated condition after the arduous Kokoda campaign was the prime factor. Another was the continuing parlous state of supply. Mosquito nets and repellent creams were virtually non-existent while the uniforms of many soldiers were torn and ragged, leaving them more susceptible to mosquito bites.

The officially acknowledged malarial infection rate during the Buna–Gona–Sanananda campaign rose to a staggering 48 cases per 1000 personnel per week by January 1943. This extrapolated to 2496 infections for each 1000 troops over one year—that is, malarial infection was universal. Everyone had it, and if soldiers were in the area long enough they would be reinfected.

No other disease caused anywhere near the same concern as malaria, but others were also serious. Scrub typhus, a mite-borne disease, was extremely dangerous if contracted, with an overall fatality rate of 9 per cent. Lieutenant Colonel Jim Miller, the commanding officer of the 2/31st Battalion, died after contracting this frightening illness at Gona. Other diseases and illnesses such as dengue fever, dysentery and tropical ulcers all claimed casualties. These were all exacerbated by the intense heat. Some soldiers also developed 'swamp sores' from living and fighting in these squalid conditions.

The Japanese were no better off, trapped in their bridgehead. Most of their troops were also suffering from malaria and a range of other tropical illnesses and some were malnourished—the daily ration could be as low as half a cup of cooked rice. Sometimes the forward troops received no food at all. They were able to make such a determined defence at Gona for the simple reason that they did not have to attack but only to hold their positions. The stench of their decomposing dead, who in some cases were used as firing steps or parapets, was so appalling that some Japanese were observed fighting from their bunkers in gas masks.

GONA: A FIGHT TO THE LAST MAN

At 4.30 in the morning on Monday, 23 November, the 25th Brigade launched another attack. The 2/25th moved forward and struck at enemy positions to the west along the shore, with the 2/31st providing supporting fire, including a 76mm mortar shoot. Thirty minutes later, the 2/33rd also attacked. Both assaults failed. In just a few days, the 25th Brigade had suffered 200 casualties for little gain, and many more soldiers were now afflicted with malaria and other illnesses.

Brigadier Eather's diary entry for this day is instructive about the issues confronting both him and the 25th Brigade:

> Up pretty nearly all night trying to find out details re Jap barges. Shot donkey [presumably for food]. Marson [2/25th Battalion] moves forward 0430. Passes Miller [2/31st Battalion] at 0600. Am afraid Miller has suffered heavy casualties. Carry out 3" mortar shoot. Marson's attack now timed for 0820 hours. Commences 10 minutes late. Makes slow headway with casualties. Capture 4 natives escaped from Jap at Gona. They say plenty dead. Few left alive. Some Japs landed last night & went east to Gerua [sic; Giruwa]. Pass it [this intelligence] on to [Colonel] Spry. Ring from [Lieutenant Colonel] Cameron [3rd Battalion] will be here in four hours. Marson attack held. He also loses men. Speak to Vasey re air support tomorrow. Order Marson and Miller back out [of] close contact. Cameron turns up. Fit him in on Buttrose's [2/33rd Battalion] left flank. Bright moonlight night. Report from Marson. Landing barges and ship [at Gona].

The comments from liberated indigenous people to the effect that few Japanese were left alive, combined with the previously received misinformation that the Japanese were withdrawing, must have heartened Eather and led him to think that his attacks were having a serious impact on the enemy. He clearly believed that if he continued to push he would soon break through their defences. The Japanese barge and shipping activity was also construed as evacuation attempts. Under the circumstances this was an understandable misinterpretation.

The following afternoon Eather ordered a change of tactics. Fighting patrols went forward covered by mortar fire and by bombing and strafing from the air. An air attack scheduled for 9 am was one hour late and the results, according to Eather, so poor that a protest was made to 7th Division Headquarters.[12] In response, he received an assurance of extra heavy support between 12 and 2 pm. The aircraft finally arrived at 2 pm but while some bombs landed in the target area, most impacted too far to the east to be of use.

At a conference at Brigade Headquarters on 24 November it was decided that the 25th Brigade's AIF troops were now too weak and few in number to make any serious inroads against the Japanese. They would for now hold their positions and harass the enemy with fighting patrols, artillery fire, mortar shoots and air attacks.

At 4 pm on 25 November, however, the 3rd Battalion attacked from the south-west, supported by four newly arrived artillery pieces, mortar and machine-gun fire. Although the 3rd Battalion had only recently been re-allocated to the 25th Brigade and was considered 'fresh', the troops were hardly rested at all and with less than 200 soldiers available to it, it was far closer in strength to a company than a battalion in strength. The troops managed to enter the Japanese positions but, unsupported by additional infantry, could not hold them and they were withdrawn under heavy covering fire.

That evening enemy barges were again landing at Gona and Eather, still believing General Headquarter's fictional intelligence assessments, wrote in his diary that the enemy seemed to be evacuating the area. Artillery fire was used in an attempt to interfere with enemy activity on the beach. Eather received instructions from General Vasey that he was now to contain the Japanese rather than attempt to eliminate them. He changed his units' dispositions slightly to fit his new role. The 3rd Battalion 'moved to east to protect flank'.[13] Just where the 3rd Battalion moved is now open to conjecture, for it would soon have unfortunate results for the incoming 21st Brigade.

During the afternoon of 26 November the Japanese attacked part of the 2/33rd Battalion in their perimeter positions, but was also engaged by troops of the 2/25th Battalion and withdrew. This was particularly fortunate for, had they closed with the Australians, they might well have realised the weakness of Eather's force. Eather must have been particularly concerned about this attack and the possibility that more might occur in the future.

However, assistance was finally on the way and Eather penned in his diary on 27 November:

Up daybreak. Cloudy and overcast. Little activity during [the] night. Spend AM discussing plans with [Brigadier] Ian D[Ivan Dougherty]. One of his shows [battalions] should be in my rear tonight. Jap patrols fairly active during day but ours also. Ten enemy killed and one POW. Geo Vasey arrives 1300. Hold conference re attack. Hope it comes soon, have many fever cases. Geo leaves 1430 hrs. Enemy planes over during afternoon. Dropped bombs near [Colonel] Chas Spry. Later learn Ian Vickery killed in MDS . . . Very humid. Very quiet. Jap very inactive except odd patrols and stragglers who we are collecting. No activity during night except a barge or two.

Eather's diary entry regarding Major Vickery's death refers to an incident when an Australian field hospital was deliberately strafed by Japanese aircraft, killing and wounding many patients and staff. This appalling breach of the Geneva Conventions and the accepted rules of war was yet another incident which intensified Eather's hatred of the Japanese.

From Saturday 28 November, responsibility for operations at Gona passed to the 21st Brigade. However, the 25th Brigade was to remain and assist the newly arrived troops' efforts to reduce the enemy positions. Curiously, neither brigadier was put in overall charge. During the morning, Eather and Brigadier Dougherty met and 'cooked up' a plan for an attack the following day.[14] 25th Brigade patrols had been active and from the information they supplied it was concluded that 'the Jap seems to have thinned out considerably . . . I doubt if he will be able to do his stuff tomorrow'. Liberator and Flying Fortress heavy bombers would strike the defences for two hours, which were also to be strafed by fighters. Mortar and artillery fire was to batter the Japanese positions for good measure.

Describing the combined action, Eather recorded:

Up 0600. Fine, clear. Will be hot day . . . Air action commences 0945 hours. Not very accurate but most on target. One plane crashes in flames. Dougherty's attack goes in but a little on the late side.

Cameron [3rd Battalion] gets a platoon into edge of village. Capture a Jap captain, holed [wounded] but will live. By 1600 hours . . . the attacking [2/27th] Battalion decides to call a halt.[15]

Over the next few days, the 21st Brigade mounted a strong series of attacks against Gona. The 3rd Battalion was to support the 2/27th Battalion in these operations but, due to critical errors, did not participate in the fighting. It now appears that the Militia battalion was not in the position stated by either its commanding officer or by Brigadier Eather. Significantly, Lieutenant Colonel Cameron had earlier protested that his role in this operation would be extremely difficult to execute in view of the terrain in which his men were located. His objections were overruled. The 2/27th's attack failed and casualties were heavy. Afterwards there was some criticism of the 25th Brigade's planning.

Eather's diary entry for this fighting indicates that he was not aware that the 3rd Battalion was in the wrong position or that it had not supported the 2/27th Battalion. Indeed, he blamed the ultimate failure of this operation on poor planning by the 21st Brigade, suggesting that the Australians who gained their objectives were driven out by friendly artillery fire. His diary entry also indicates that he was not happy to be working with the 2/27th Battalion's commander, but he did not elaborate on the reason why.

Eather's assessment of why this operation failed is suspect. Despite close planning and liaison between the 21st and 25th Brigades, neither formation became aware that the 3rd Battalion was not physically located where even its own commander believed it to be. While this situation was undoubtedly due in part to the poor maps available and the poor physical condition of the commanders, ultimately blame for the error must rest with 25th Brigade's Headquarters and its commander.

In retrospect, Eather would have done better had he heeded Lieutenant Colonel Cameron's protest. Cameron was an able and experienced AIF commander, although it must be said that Cameron himself must also accept some responsibility for not realising that his battalion was in the wrong position.

During this period, on 30 November, a Japanese Zero fighter pilot located Eather's headquarters.[16] The Zero circled several times at 700 metres before flying off without attacking. Of the event, Eather wrote in an offhand manner that the Japanese pilot was 'having a good look. Will probably return with friends'. Happily, his prediction was not fulfilled and an attack did not occur.

On 2 December, the relief of Eather's exhausted and worn-out troops was to have been effected. In the morning, however, most unwelcome news was received from General Vasey. The 7th Division's commander advised Eather that the Japanese had landed reinforcements the previous evening and would do so again that night and on the following evening.[17] Clearly, General MacArthur was finally providing accurate 'Ultra' intelligence data to his forward commanders. It is ironic that it was only as the 25th Brigade was planning on leaving the front line that Eather was told the truth, for by then he was unable to use this information to his advantage. After receiving this new intelligence, General Vasey quickly changed plans. The 25th Brigade, with additional battalions under Eather's command, was left at Gona, while Brigadier Dougherty was to take a force and attack the Japanese at nearby Sanananda.

Eather recorded the day's events in his diary:

Up daybreak. Plenty of flares during the night & air activity: all ours. Heavy artillery shoots. First of Porter's [30th Brigade] arrive this AM. Had arranged to relieve some of mine. Vasey turned up 1130. Changed ideas. Information that Jap is to land reinforcements last night, tonight & tomorrow. Dougherty takes over Honner [39th Battalion from Porter's 30th Brigade] & is to move east [to Sanananda]. I take balance [of the 21st Brigade] & with own troops am to contain Gona. Little activity during afternoon.

General Vasey, gravely concerned about the losses being sustained at Gona, had changed his plans, deciding to simply hold the Japanese there and attack the enemy forces at Sanananda instead, where he clearly hoped for a quicker result. Brigadier Dougherty was to command the force moving out. Unfortunately, the following day, the faint track his troops were following petered out into scrub and swamp. This forced the abandonment of Vasey's short-lived plan and on the night of 3 December Dougherty's troops were ordered back to Gona.

When Eather heard this, he was relieved. He had had little confidence in the mission Dougherty had been unexpectedly set, referring to it in his diary as a 'wild goose chase'. Dougherty's troops were back in the area at 11 am on 4 December and the relief of the 25th Brigade (including the 3rd Battalion) was immediately initiated; the remnants of the 25th Brigade moved back into reserve. Brigadier Dougherty took formal command of the Gona forces at 4 pm on 4 December and Eather left an hour later. 'Leave Ian [Brigadier Ivan Dougherty] my tent and tent flys. Strange feeling now strain eased off', he recorded that night.[18]

At this time the Japanese were being contained in an area of less than 300 square metres and had little freedom of movement. Over a period of 85 days, the 25th Brigade had walked and fought from the south-east coast of New Guinea to just a few hundred metres short of the north coast, across some of the most rugged and hostile terrain in the world. For the duration of the campaign, the supply system was entirely inadequate and virtually no reinforcements were sent forward.

It would be up to the 21st and 30th Brigades to eventually complete the capture of Gona. The Mission Station itself finally fell on 9 December, but fighting in the area did not cease for another ten days. In the process of finally eradicating the Gona garrison, the relieving troops suffered many battle and sickness casualties. Several hundred dead Japanese soldiers were counted around the Gona defences and many others had previously been killed. Very few Japanese surrendered.

Of the scene at Gona after its capture, one 21st Brigade diarist made the following observations:

> Gona village and beach were a shambles with dead Japs and Australians everywhere. Apparently the enemy had made no attempt to bury the dead, some of whom had obviously been lying out [in the open] for days. The stench was terrific. The Japs had put up a very stubborn resistance. They still had plenty of ammunition, medical stores, and rice, although a large quantity of rice was green with mould. In one dugout rice had been stacked on enemy dead. More Japs had died lying on the rice and ammunition had been stacked on them again.[19]

GONA: A FIGHT TO THE LAST MAN

Japanese dead at Gona, December 1942.

Photo courtesy of the Australian War Memorial (AWM 013877)

After Gona was taken, American and Australian forces concentrated on the reduction of nearby Buna and Sanananda. Construction of airfields in the area commenced and these would soon play an important role in the neutralisation of the major Japanese base at Rabaul.

In the battles around Buna, Gona and Sanananda, the Japanese lost perhaps 13 000 of the 20 000 troops they committed. The Australians and Americans also suffered heavily, with over 8500 battle casualties and another 27 000 medical casualties—mainly to malaria.

Having being relieved at the front, Eather's next battle was to get his troops flown back to Port Moresby. While waiting, the troops were given defensive roles in the area. Eather drew up plans for the defence of Popondetta and its airfield.[20] A Japanese paratroop attack was considered possible, although his troops' physical and mental condition meant that they would have had little chance of repelling such an attack. Eather was also debriefed by senior officers of New Guinea Force Headquarters, including Lieutenant General Herring who had moved over from Port Moresby.

At this time it seems that there was some disagreement between Blamey and Herring on the employment of reinforcements coming to New Guinea. Unable to change Blamey's mind himself, Herring enlisted the support of Eather, who noted:

> Ned Herring is in quandary re use of George W[ootten's 18th Brigade]. C-in-C wants to use him on coast with tanks. Herring thinks not possible & decides to send me down to C-in-C as an LO [liaison officer]. Fix it with Vasey . . . Leave by plane from Popondetta at 1605. Ned comes down to see me off. Go in his Wirraway. Grand trip, my very first one. Arrive airstrip Moresby area 1645 . . . Met by Brig Edwards. C-in-C out for a walk. Awful fuss. Ray Broadbent, Tom White, Milford, Tom Porter & others cannot do enough for me. Berryman arrived from mainland this afternoon too. Had a hair cut, shower & Edwards gave me a clean shirt & new pants. See C-in-C and put Ned's ideas to him. Won't listen! [Blamey] asks me to stay night. Is sending me home on leave. C-in-C at dinner told me at dinner Ned's request will be agreed to.[21]

Subsequently Brigadier Wootten's 2/9th Battalion and supporting tanks attacked near Cape Endaiadere, to the east of Buna. Getting the tanks into the area of operations was immensely difficult, and many of them were destroyed in the unsuitable terrain. Infantry losses were also heavy but the operation was ultimately successful.

While at Port Moresby, Eather also had the opportunity to catch up with his good friend and former commander, Major General Allen, who was still in the area. His pleasure at seeing his friend again was dampened somewhat by the manner in which Allen was being treated by some of his peers. It seems that Allen and Herring were on poor terms, hardly surprising in view of the way Allen had been removed from his command, not to mention the circumstances in which Herring had been appointed. Of the meeting he later wrote:

> Meet dear old Tubby. Very glad to get back with him. One knows where one is with him. Arrange to have my kit brought down from base area. Spend morning chatting over things generally. See file of messages [Blamey's and MacArthur's attacks on the 7th Division].[22]

Before their return to Australia, the remnants of the 25th Brigade—now just 400 soldiers—were addressed by General Blamey. He congratulated the troops on their extraordinary efforts in both the Kokoda campaign and at Gona.

To the troops he said in part:

> I am frequently asked how the new AIF measured up to the old AIF. I say never was the original AIF asked to perform so difficult a task that you have accomplished so splendidly. This is not the first time I have addressed you but it is by far the most memorable. I bring you from the Prime Minister, the thanks of the nation for what you have done. You deserve, and have, the highest praise of the nation. Your deeds will remain to your eternal credit. In doing what you did, you set a standard for yourselves, for the rest of the AIF, and the rest of the Australian Army that will be difficult to live up to.[23]

This was high and well-deserved praise indeed for the troops and their commander who had played such a pivotal role in blunting the Japanese threat to Australia.

General Blamey's promise of an early leave in Australia resulted in Eather leaving New Guinea before many of his soldiers. At 4 am on 13 December his aircraft took off and headed south. On board were some unusual travelling companions: an American general, other Allied soldiers of various ranks and the wounded Japanese captain Eather's soldiers had taken at Gona on 29 November. Eather recorded that it was a 'grand morning for flying'. The aircraft landed at Cairns and then at Townsville. Poor weather then intervened, and the aircraft diverted to Maryborough as it could not get into Brisbane.

Eather noted with excitement in his diary that he would be surprising Adeline when he arrived unannounced in Sydney the next day.[24]

Awake at 4 am the following morning (Monday 14 December), Eather found his plans subjected to a series of misfortunes. First, take-off was delayed an hour by bad weather. The aircraft eventually took off and managed a landing in Brisbane, despite more bad weather, but engine trouble then terminated the flight. He managed to book a berth on an interstate train and arrived in Sydney at 9.30 am the next day. He immediately went to his house but no one was home, and it was not till later in the day that Eather was finally reunited with Adeline and Isobel. Sadly, he was still quite ill from his time in New Guinea and had little time to enjoy his homecoming. Even before reaching Sydney he was suffering from the symptoms of malaria. He ignored the symptoms of his illness as long as possible, but on 14 January he was admitted to the 2/2nd Australian General Hospital. Relapses afflicted him well into 1943.[25]

At this point it is worth reflecting on the problems and failures associated with the Gona campaign. While some recent commentators have disparaged the performance of the Australian commanders—including Eather—in the reduction of the Japanese positions at Gona,[26] the 25th Brigade had clearly performed a valuable role even if it had been unable to fully capture its objective. For some weeks as the brigade wasted away, its remnants had besieged and attacked strong fortifications, gaining ground despite significant handicaps that included a failed logistic system, a lack of supporting forces and reinforcements and, above all, misleading Intelligence information. They had inflicted casualties on the Japanese and had kept them under pressure for a protracted period. The Japanese had only been able to launch one significant counterattack against the 25th Brigade and that had been defeated.

An interesting view of the 25th Brigade and its commander is offered by Lieutenant Colonel Frank Sublet in his work *From Kokoda to the Sea*. Sublet was a competent infantryman who was appointed a liaison officer from the 21st Brigade. For a time he was based at Eather's headquarters. He noted:

> The unreliability of the Army supply system had sapped the energy and will of the men of the 25th Brigade, most of whom, from the

brigadier down, suffered pangs of hunger, gastric disorders and fever. The unit and brigade war diaries make daily references to their disabilities, and these feelings of deprivation may have borne some responsibility for an emphasis displayed towards a defensive outlook and greater concern for security, than for offensive action and concentration of force. Eather consistently under-estimated the strength and resolution of the enemy, and except for the 2/31st Battalion attacks, operations smacked of a 'penny packet' approach. In several Australian attacks the initial momentum had carried the troops up to the enemy positions, only to find themselves under withering fire from the rear or flank positions which could not be pin pointed. Since these hidden posts could not be silenced because there were no follow up troops, the assault waves became too vulnerable, and having lost leaders and Bren gunners, who had become special targets to the hidden snipers, had to withdraw over the same killing ground which had invited them into the assault in the first place.

Lieutenant Colonel Sublet's observations have some merit. It is highly unlikely that following the rigours of the arduous Kokoda campaign that the 25th Brigade's senior officers, and the brigadier himself, were able to perform at either peak physical or mental capacity. While directing the fighting at Gona, Eather—like all his troops—was sick and hungry. Almost certainly his poor physical condition and general exhaustion contributed to a lower than usual level of planning during the operations.

Criticism that Eather had 'consistently under-estimated the strength and resolution of the enemy' is however, misdirected. Incorrect information which suggested that the Japanese were withdrawing was passed on to him on a number of occasions. These intelligence assessments were further 'verified' by escaped indigenous people who reported that many Japanese were dead and few remained.[27] Eather could hardly be held accountable for acting in good faith on information passed on to him. That this information may have been deliberately incorrect would have been inconceivable to him.

While Colonel Sublet has been somewhat dismissive of the 25th Brigade's 'defensive outlook', realistically, precautions had to be taken to guard against enemy attacks from within the Gona bridgehead and from potential break-outs from Buna or Sanananda.

Potentially, the Japanese could also have used the large numbers of barges available to them to land on the outside of the Australian perimeter defences and attack from the rear with additional forces from Rabaul. This security requirement, combined with the fact that the 25th Brigade was at such low strength, meant that there were never enough troops in the area for either defence or attack. Nonetheless the two roles had to be constantly weighed up. It must also be remembered that the 25th Brigade and its commander had recently played the pivotal role in the battle at Oivi–Gorari. In that fight, once the Japanese had been cut off, many of them had engaged in massed charges and infiltration attempts through the 25th Brigade's positions. These tactics had little chance of success but had the potential to inflict many casualties. After that recent lesson it was clear that considerable care had to be taken in containing the Japanese.

Lieutenant Colonel Sublet also noted that when both the 21st and 25th Brigades were at Gona, neither Eather nor Dougherty was in overall command of the total force. He has suggested that this was an opportune time for Eather to be relieved for a rest and for the efforts of both Brigades to be controlled by one officer. This is a valid point. Although Eather was the senior commander and knew the ground situation better than Dougherty, he was clearly ill and tired. General Vasey had previously offered him a break from the front to recuperate but Eather declined until his troops could also be relieved.

Apart from being an affront to his style of leadership, which entailed sharing the same hazards and conditions as his troops, there may have been another reason why Eather refused an early relief. Brigadier Potts, Major General Allen and Lieutenant General Rowell had all recently been relieved of their commands on various pretexts. Eather may have thought that accepting Vasey's well-intentioned offer could have resulted in a similar fate. If he felt it was necessary Vasey should have insisted on Eather's relief, but of course this was Vasey's responsibility. Vasey would also have been cognisant of the fact that Gona represented Brigadier Dougherty's very first jungle battle and that Eather was the more experienced commander. Regardless, he should have appointed one officer or the other to overall command. It is interesting to note that Vasey himself was worried about being relieved for health reasons during this period.

Lieutenant Colonel Honner, commander of the 39th Battalion

and a highly respected soldier, believed that Gona could have fallen earlier and with fewer casualties had a more concealed approach through to the heart of the enemy's defences in the 3rd Battalion's sector been utilised. This was the tactic by which the defences were eventually over-run. He noted that earlier failed assaults had involved frontal attacks over shorter stretches of ground but these, being without much cover, had little chance of success. Other officers have echoed these sentiments. In view of the eventual success attained this way, the logic of this statement would seem to be irrefutable. It is not known why Eather did not organise attacks in this area. He seems to have been unaware of the potential advantages of this avenue of approach. It is also not known whether any of his battalion commanders suggested attacking here. What is known is that Eather disliked making frontal attacks and avoided them whenever possible. He was also known to be a careful planner. It seems likely that, weakened by malaria and hunger, and under constant pressure to launch attacks, he had neither the strength or time to personally visit most of the positions his troops were holding to see the ground over which they were fighting. Certainly his diary does not record any visits to his forward troops of his battalion commander's headquarters in this period.

It is interesting to note that General MacArthur awarded Brigadier Eather the US Distinguished Service Cross for his service in the Kokoda campaign and at Gona. One cannot assume that the high honours bestowed on senior commanders are always deserved. At times, they can be seen as a fairly routine and expected event which does not necessarily reflect any exceptional contribution by the commanders involved. This award is interesting though. MacArthur had previously referred to the Australian commanders on the Kokoda Track as inefficient and complained that they were beaten by smaller forces. Implicit in this criticism was Eather's withdrawal to Imita Ridge. His operations to recapture Kokoda and Gona were also strongly criticised by MacArthur. Yet at the end of these campaigns Eather was awarded the DSC—the very highest medal available to non-American personnel. Despite his constant complaints, clearly MacArthur was pleased with the 25th Brigade commander's operations. If he was not, surely he would have nominated him for a lesser award or, indeed, no award at all.

Of this grim campaign, David Horner recorded in *Crisis of Command*:

> The Buna battles proved to be a test of command and leadership in every respect and at all levels... The reputations of none of the senior commanders remain untarnished... The tactical errors were made because neither MacArthur nor Blamey visited the front early in the campaign. They lacked the knowledge of the ground, the conditions, the state of their own troops and of the enemy...

The fighting at Gona, Buna and Sanananda was undoubtedly the most vicious and difficult the Australians faced in the Pacific War. In the period the 25th Brigade was at Gona the enemy had been forced to hold their positions, had suffered casualties and lost ground, which materially assisted in the final reduction of Gona.

Eather had displayed strong leadership in adverse situations and had made good use of the limited supporting arms available during the siege. His tactics generally involved launching attacks from various directions at different times and supplementing these attacks with fighting patrols and other harassment. His apparent inability to leave his headquarters to see the ground his troops were fighting over was out of character for a commander who regularly made the point of being forward with his troops. It was indeed unfortunate that the 25th Brigade was so under-strength and badly supported that it was not able to fully exploit its successes and capture its objective in the first days of the siege. The fighting at Gona was a particularly frustrating business. Of all the campaigns Eather took part in, this was the only occasion in which he could not achieve an outright victory over his opponents. As such, it can only be seen as the low point of a brilliant military career.

8

The capture of Lae and the Markham and Ramu Valleys Campaign

My word, the Australian after being well trained & disciplined makes a wonderful soldier. I doubt he can be beaten unless things are overwhelmingly against him. Recently I had about 150 men out in front on an offensive patrol. They penetrated into enemy held country, ambushed four parties of Japs killing forty. Lord knows how many were wounded. The usual figure is about double the [number] killed.

Brigadier Eather, in a letter to his father, 1943

In early 1943 the Joint Chiefs of Staff in Washington issued General MacArthur with a directive for 'Operation Cartwheel', a series of assaults which were to isolate and facilitate the eventual reduction and capture of the Japanese fortress at Rabaul.[1] Some of Cartwheel's objectives included the seizure of Lae and the Markham Valley. The capture of these would be the next operation undertaken by the 7th Division, after its rehabilitation following the campaigns in New Guinea.

On 8 July 1943 the 7th Division was warned to prepare for forward movement. Most of Eather's troops were at sea from 20 July and the brigade was concentrated at Port Moresby by 26 July, with the last of the division arriving in mid-August. In late March Eather himself had sailed from Sydney for Port Moresby in the American attack transport USS *Henry T. Allen*, to take part in the detailed planning for the forthcoming important operations.[2]

Elsewhere, the war was finally turning against the Axis. Sicily had been invaded in July, Italy would be invaded in September and would soon be out of the war. The Germans had suffered major reverses in the Soviet Union.

At Port Moresby, the senior officers of the division continued the planning for their next operation and trained their troops in tropical conditions. During this lengthy interlude, Eather had ample time to write to family members. A number of these letters were to his mother, to whom he was particularly close, and the following extracts provide an interesting insight about this period:

21 July
I'm very fit. Have been very busy with exercises & other duties. Have been doing a bit of getting about too including some fairly long trips by air. These fast modern planes are wonderful things. One covers so much ground in such a short time.

I'm just having my camp altered a little. Like you, I think a change is almost as good as a holiday. One change is that my tent is being moved about 200 yards [180 metres] up on to a ledge on a hill side. I've just over heard the chaps who have been told to shift it. When the sergeant pointed out where it was to go one cove said 'what, away up there! What does the silly old —— think he is, a blasted eagle?'

Yesterday afternoon, having little to do I took a run around the Port [Moresby] road sticky beaking. War does alter these places & not for the better either. One hardly recognises them. I tried to pick out a spot where once I was driven into the mangroves in a whaleboat but no trees exist now. In fact the whole character of the place is altered.

2 August
Have once again become used to the climate. Have been doing a little exploring in the last couple of weeks. One can go almost anywhere by jeep these days, vastly different to earlier times. Am camped in a little valley out towards the inlet & we can catch a view of the open sea over the bay. The beauty of the spot is that we enjoy a breeze which blows in from the ocean & keeps things fairly comfortable. I saw that native boy that went with me on the first trip [across the Kokoda Track] & he wants to be in this one but I doubt if it can be arranged. [The fact that Eather's former personal carrier

had volunteered to go in harm's way for no better reason than to be with Eather says a great deal about Eather's character and his relationship with and respect for the indigenous peoples of New Guinea. That respect was clearly reciprocated.] I'm keeping remarkably fit. Haven't felt a touch of fever for over ten weeks.

3 September
I've been fairly busy these last few weeks. We've been doing some solid training & thirty miles [48 kilometres] with a full pack up is not to be sneezed at in this climate even if the march is carried out by night.

I've taken a few plane trips & one had rather an element of excitement, the US Air Force [US Army Air Forces] is doing a splendid job. Has the little yellow beast, as Gen Blamey calls him, just where they want him. The Jap [air force] doesn't like meeting our fighters these days. I had mess the other evening with Gen Blamey and his staff. I know a number of them of old. The 'old man' is in good fettle & anxious to let his troops off the chain. It's almost twelve months ago to the day that we met the Jap at Ioribaiwa & chased him back over the hills. Our chaps and the Yanks seem to have him bottled up around Salamaua this time & no doubt will have to kill 'em all off as they did at Gona and Buna last year. Well I suppose our turn will come one of these days to meet him, the fellows are very fit indeed & and I'm sure anxious to go in & get it cleaned up. The sooner it is done the sooner we will all be able to get home again . . .

No sign of a recurrence of fever, think that last treatment must have killed all the wogs I had in my blood. Am living in a grass thatched roofed hut with open sides, it's much cooler than a tent, but lets any breeze that there is in also the moths and insects. They buzz around at night in dozens. Still it could be much worse (& better too I suppose).

When operations finally commenced, the 7th Division's initial role would be to fly into Nadzab, near the Markham River (32 kilometres by air from Lae) and advance on that town. Meanwhile the 9th Division, in a pincer movement, would capture Lae after making a coastal landing.

In preparation for his brigade's role in the forthcoming campaign, Eather trained his troops very hard in the tropical conditions. Of one four-day exercise which began on 23 August, Captain M.L. Roberts of the 2/33rd Battalion recollected:

> The exercise was through undulating kunai and swamp, in some ways simulating the country between Lae and Nadzab. It was done in heatwave conditions and each soldier was restricted to a water bottle per day, not a drop more. The return journey was twenty-eight miles [48 kilometres] and by then men were starting to drop out through dehydration . . . I was amongst those who fell out before completing the return journey. I was ushered into a medical post under a large tent fly and within hearing a Medical Officer (presumably on Brigade HQ) told the Brig that the exercise should be abandoned as nobody could survive on a single bottle of water in that heat. The Brig refused point blank! The Medical Officer refused to accept responsibility for the health of the troops! Stalemate. Two stuck-out jaws! The exercise went on as planned right up to the end, though a significant number were picked up by vehicles.
>
> A similar, perhaps even more arduous exercise was conducted from Woodside Camp soon after we disembarked from the *Mount Vernon* in April 1942 and became known as 'the palmer stunt'. Both are talked about even to this day. The Brig's stunts apparently were aimed to confront the troops with very difficult conditions some of which were even tougher than those experienced in action. The tougher the exercise the better the troops would cope when it mattered most. This was his training philosophy and he never deviated from it.³

On 4 September 1943 troops from the 9th Division landed on Red Beach, approximately 50 kilometres east of Lae, and proceeded towards that strategically placed town. Meanwhile, American paratroops of the 503rd Parachute Regiment descended on Nadzab without opposition. Engineers were soon hard at work rehabilitating the old Nadzab airfield so that the 7th Division could be flown in. From 7 September, in a process disrupted by bad weather, these troops were flown in by C47 transport aircraft. This would be one of the first large-scale movement of troops into battle by air in the Pacific War. Thanks to the very careful planning at division and brigade level, it would prove to be a very successful operation. There were approximately 11 000 Japanese in the Lae and Salamaua region and the 7th Division's role was to prevent them reinforcing their comrades from Madang via the upper Markham and Ramu Valleys.

The move to Nadzab was marred by a frightful accident. For the 2/33rd Battalion, Port Moresby's Jackson's airfield would be the site of its greatest wartime tragedy. While some of the troops were waiting in trucks by the side of the runway, an American Liberator bomber laden with fuel, bombs and ammunition failed to become airborne and crashed into a group of five vehicles. For those not killed outright by the impact an even crueller fate awaited. Sprayed with burning fuel, many soldiers ran about on fire until their mates could either put them out or until their ammunition and grenades exploded, killing them.

Of this horrific incident, one survivor later recorded:

Men charging around with clothes on fire would suddenly disappear as the grenades and mortar bombs they were carrying went off. Others, rolling on the ground, would give a quick jerk as their bandoliers exploded. We did our pitiful best, all the time with one eye on an unexploded 500 lb [226 kilogram] bomb, while horribly burned men pleaded to be shot...[4]

Fifteen soldiers were killed outright in this incident, another 44 later died of their injuries while 92 were hospitalised—many of them with severe burns.

So well trained were the troops of the 25th Brigade that the shocking nature of this incident hardly affected the continuance of the operation to move the brigade forward, even though it can only be wondered at how the survivors felt as they boarded their C47s with the smell of burning flesh still in the air.

On the morning of 9 September, with only the 2/25th and part of the now seriously under-strength 2/33rd Battalion at Nadzab, General Vasey ordered Eather's brigade to spearhead the 7th Division's advance down the Markham Valley towards Lae. While the enemy was not encountered initially, there were ample signs that they were in the area and that they would be contacted in the near future. The remaining troops of the brigade, delayed by bad flying weather, arrived at Nadzab in the next few days and joined in the advance as they became available. Until then, the 2/2nd Pioneer Battalion was attached to Eather's command to give him sufficient troops for his task. On Eather's orders the pace of the advance was pressed quickly, perhaps with the intention of denying the Japanese any opportunity to develop extensive defences as they had at Gona.

On 13 September the 25th Brigade approached enemy positions around Whittaker's and Heath's Plantations, 6.5 kilometres northwest of Lae, where, with the support of several artillery pieces, the Japanese intended to resist strongly from prepared positions. Indeed, both the Australian and Japanese commanders realised that the decisive fighting for Lae would occur here. Brigadier Eather's plan of attack was for the 2/25th Battalion to apply some pressure on those Japanese troops holding in front of Whittaker's. The 2/33rd would move around the flanks, avoiding the strong defences and setting up a blocking position behind the Japanese. They would then attack Whittaker's from the back of its defences, cutting the enemy's lines of communication and isolating the Japanese in the forward positions. The 2/31st Battalion was held in reserve, ready to press through and continue the advance. Even though they had not been expecting an attack to develop from behind them, the Japanese resisted strongly and the fighting was at close quarters, which largely negated the effectiveness of supporting Australian artillery and air attacks. In the end the Japanese commander had little choice but to withdraw his force if he did not want it to be totally destroyed. Heath's was also occupied that night after the Japanese had been severely mauled. The enemy abandoned the area in some haste and many weapons and much valuable equipment was discarded. Many enemy troops were killed but few Australians lost their lives in this fight. Eather's innovative tactics had paid off once more.

Both General Vasey and Eather closely scrutinised the action around Heath's Plantation, basing themselves at one of the battalion commander's headquarters. The presence of these senior officers, while it may have been intended to encourage their subordinates, could have put them under additional pressure while they were controlling a hard-fought battle. Japanese documents recovered from an abandoned headquarters' position suggested that the enemy were evacuating Lae. Armed with this important information, Eather further accelerated the rate of the 25th Brigade's advance. Although it had been planned that the 9th Division would actually take Lae, Eather and Vasey now saw an opportunity for the 7th Division to capture the town before the Japanese could escape.

Later, there would be some suggestion that part of the 2/33rd Battalion had failed to seal the Japanese rearguard in their positions around Heath's and Whittaker's and that some hundreds were able to escape. Apparently Eather was extremely angry about this, although the 2/33rd Battalion's historian has stated that his anger was misplaced. In any event, Japanese records obtained after the war indicate that not more than 80 to 100 Japanese escaped. Of these, some 64 were killed in a 2/31st Battalion ambush soon after.

For this campaign, the 25th Brigade had been issued with a number of jeeps. Eather made sure that some of these robust American vehicles were allocated to Brigade Headquarters and to the battalion commanders so that the senior officers could move about the area rapidly to assess the tactical situation. On one occasion Eather drove past one of his battalions and saw its commander walking with his troops. He called the officer aside and asked why he was not using his own jeep. The battalion commander replied that it was good for his men to see him sharing their discomfort, an explanation which would seem to tally with Eather's own philosophy. Despite this, Eather rebuked the officer, instructing him to use his vehicle for the purpose for which it was intended.

Unsatisfied with the progress of his brigade and sure that the Japanese were withdrawing, Eather continued to urge his troops to quicken their advance. Clearly, his intention was to capitalise on the initiative the brigade had taken from the Japanese. Several times he left his headquarters in exasperation and drove forward to the leading companies to personally tell the soldiers to 'get a move on'. He was an obvious target in his jeep, wearing his red-banded senior officer's cap, but he ignored the risk. On a number of occasions, parties of Japanese troops worked their way in behind the leading sections of troops he was with, but were killed by observant Australian soldiers. It was at this time, for his constant urging to move faster, that his troops gave him the nickname 'Phar Lap'. This was the name of an iconic 1930s Australian racehorse, but its use by the men was not always affectionate.

Eather's confidence and personal aggression in this campaign was reflected in the wording of some of his orders. One included the statement, 'press upon the enemy and annihilate him'. Another stated, in part, 'take no prisoners unless you are told we want one for questioning'.[5] Eather rationalised this order on the basis that prisoners were an encumbrance on the supply lines. It was a ruthless order, issued in a ruthless theatre of war where little quarter was asked or given by either side.

Eather made his own feelings about the enemy very plain in a letter to his parents on 9 October:

> As we advanced up the valley driving the Jap out they [the local indigenous people] came back to their deserted villages in droves. Hardly a day passes that doesn't bring one or two villagers back from the hills. They come with their dogs, pigs, children & household possessions. Of course many of their huts have been badly knocked about in driving the Japs out but even then they seem to be very pleased. I think the Jap gave them a bad time & I'm afraid the VD he has left behind will spread like a grass fire and take its toll. Naturally our medical people & those of the former administration are doing what they can for the poor devils.
>
> Things seem to be going very well overseas. The German is gradually being pushed out of Italy & the Russians are maintaining great pressure. In recent developments over there I see the beginning of the end but it will require some time yet to effect a thorough clean up. And then Master Jap will get his! I hope they are made wish they had never been born! My feelings regarding the Japs are most intense. They are hardly human. Never have I seen such filth & disgusting surroundings as obtain in the camps we drive them from. The few prisoners we take are wretched specimens. Now & then we lay hands on a diary which reveals on being translated their complete and utter beastliness. Some writings have related the circumstances surrounding the 'execution' of allied airmen who have been shot down & captured in enemy territory. These facts are known to our troops & they remember them when they meet him. The Americans are very bitter & I am sure determined to extract the full toll.

I can only hope that no misguided fools back home agitate for any let up in the total destruction of this vile beast. I'm afraid I've rather let my feelings run away with me but really one who has seen them & knows them as we have could not feel otherwise.

Yet despite his personal loathing, Eather's own actions sometimes belied his harsh words. In the advance on Lae he and his driver—acting as the forward scouts for the entire brigade—found two live Japanese in an abandoned car,[6] one of whom tried to attack them with a fork. Both were taken prisoner when they could have been legitimately shot. Later, a Japanese sergeant was found lying at the side of the road. There was some concern that he may have been concealing weapons or grenades under his body. Rather than having the Japanese soldier shot to reduce the risk of being killed by booby traps or ambush, Eather ordered a rope placed around one of his feet so that he could be dragged onto the road and searched more safely in the open. This soldier was also taken prisoner and, with his compatriots, provided useful information on the situation at Lae.

Early on the morning of 15 September, the 2/31st and 2/33rd Battalions over-ran Japanese positions at Edward's Plantation, leaving over 100 enemy dead. Again, Eather's orders to outflank the Japanese rather than commit to frontal attacks had proved successful and avoided heavy losses. The capture of Edward's paved the way for the 7th Division to enter Lae the following day—just hours ahead of the 9th Division, which had been held up trying to cross the Bumbu River. The 'Silent Seventh', with Brigadier Eather's 25th Brigade in the fore, had beaten their more famous 9th Division cousins into town and taken possession of its important harbour and airfield facilities. Lae had fallen sooner than planned and with less fighting than had been envisaged.

Recalling these momentous events, Captain W.G. Butler of the 2/25th Battalion recorded in David Dexter's *The New Guinea Offensives*:

Men are a bit nervous again and went [advanced] pretty steadily. Sick Japs along the track kept holding things up and we expected to run into something at any moment. Then along the track and into the middle of us came a jeep crowded with Brigade HQ. Passed me and [they moved] up to the leading platoon. The old Brig jumped out and started urging the troops to hurry along. The troops weren't very impressed as they thought the Jap was in front. Finally, the Brigadier, armed with a pistol, acted as leading scout, and the troops followed in column of route behind ... A brigadier is not an ideal section leader. The whole reason for his action was that he wanted the brigade to be first onto the beach. He managed it O.K. I had to send a patrol down to the beach and back so we have that honour—doubtful one—as there were no Japs. Unfortunately we advanced too quickly—due to no opposition—and the Yanks came over and strafed us.

Later, on reading a draft volume of the official history for the author David Dexter, Eather wrote of these events:

As time passed the reports I was receiving regarding the progress of the forward troops indicated to me that my orders for a speedy advance were not being carried out. Taking three Brigade HQ officers with me I moved forward to find the reason for the delay, there were reports indicating that no contact had been made with the enemy by the forward troops.

Arriving in the forward area I found that the advance was being made with undue caution & in fact there was no sign that an enemy was in the area. I spoke very sharply to the forward company commander [Butler] & got the advance going having regard for the absence of any indication of the presence of enemy.

This may well explain why Captain Butler was not happy with Eather's actions. Eather was also alive to the possibility of coming under friendly air attack and had requested the suspension of all air operations in front of his brigade well before the air attack mentioned by Captain Butler occurred. At one stage Eather was forced to withdraw his forward troops from Lae for two hours in the face of the 9th Division's artillery fire and friendly air attacks which caused some casualties. His signal had not been acted upon promptly enough to stop the air attacks and he later signalled General Vasey, 'am held up on outskirts of Lae by 5 USAF [sic; USAAF]; two casualties received from strafing. Can some action be taken to stop [the attacks]'.

LAE AND THE MARKHAM AND RAMU VALLEYS

Private Gerald Connelly's recollections are similar to Captain Butler's. He makes it clear that Eather was well forward with the lead troops:

> ...we were on the move again, and who came along in a jeep up with the forward soldiers but Brigadier Eather. We were getting close to Lae airstrip when about ten fighters—ours or American—began firing at the Jap planes on the ground. Shortly after our patrol arrived in Lae and we met no opposition there. The Japs had gone and Lae was in our hands.
>
> Brigadier Eather was credited with sending a message to the 9th Division who were working a pincer movement with us: 'Occupied Lae at 1000 hrs. Thanks for shelling it at 1100. Please don't knock our shithouse down!'[7]

The 2/33rd Battalion's unit history noted that Eather took great satisfaction in personally meeting 9th Division troops, who were unaware that Lae had already fallen and were cautiously advancing up Mt Lunaman while looking out for the Japanese. Instead of the enemy, they met Brigadier Eather smiling broadly and waiting for them in his jeep. As if to defy any Japanese in the vicinity, he had made a point of wearing his red-banded senior officer's cap—something which marked him as a conspicuous sniper target. Eather had already hauled down the Rising Sun flag which had flown on Mt Lunaman and replaced it with an Australian ensign.

Eather's decision to take so many personal risks in the lead-up to the fall of Lae was driven by neither bravado nor thoughtlessness. He was well aware that his soldiers were not convinced that the Japanese were on the run. While he was fairly sure that they did not intend to make a stronger fight for the town, he had to demonstrate to his troops that he was confident in that knowledge. The only way to do this was to be seen prominently forward with the lead troops whom he was asking to take the risk of increasing the rate of their pursuit. Previously, at Bardia and Imita Ridge, Eather had prominently placed himself forward on the battlefield so that his troops could see him sharing the danger they faced, assured of the outcome of the battle.

The fall of Lae made news around the world. Unfortunately, when commenting on the event on BBC Radio, British Prime

Minister Winston Churchill mistakenly gave the credit for this event to the 9th Division (no doubt Churchill had been briefed in advance about the plan for the campaign and the intention that the 9th would take Lae), much to the annoyance of the 'Silent Seventh'. Perhaps in answer to Churchill's error, an unknown 7th Division soldier later penned the following lines, which summed up their thoughts on the matter and their rivalry with the 9th Division:

> The Rats are in Finschafen,
> But they missed the bus at Lae,
> For the rabbits of the Owens,
> Had snatched the prize away.
>
> The 'Silent' jungle bunnies,
> Had sneaked up from the rear,
> And had surprised old Tojo,
> For more than he could bear.
>
> When the rats got into town,
> Much to their surprise,
> There was a welcome notice,
> Outstanding on the rise.
>
> 'twas put there by the rabbits,
> Whom the fighting Ninth forgot,
> And there wasn't any souvenirs—
> The rabbits had copped the lot.
>
> The notice read, 'Too late old sports,
> We know you'll get the cheers,
> But you can have the city march,
> And we'll drink all the beers'.

The reference to rats alludes to the nickname the 9th Division received at Tobruk. That division seemed to gain all the credit for the defence of Tobruk even though a brigade of the 7th Division also fought in the famous siege. The reference to rabbits relates to General Blamey's ill-advised speech to the 21st Brigade after it had been relieved on the Kokoda Track, which was interpreted by many to mean that the troops were cowards who had run like rabbits from the Japanese.

The Imperial Japanese Headquarters in Tokyo was stunned by the fall of Lae. Its loss, spearheaded by the 25th Brigade, had come at the end of a string of defeats. The Japanese leaders must have started to have serious misgivings about the general war situation and wonder when they would be able to take the initiative in New Guinea again. Not long before, such disasters would have been incomprehensible to a Japanese Army that had achieved some of the most spectacular victories of modern warfare. In December 1942, at a conference held in the presence of Emperor Hirohito, one of the decisions taken had been to reinforce Lae as it was considered a base too vital to give up. Consequently Lieutenant General Nakano Hidemitsu had laid down in his orders that Lae was to be defended to the death. This order was later countermanded and in August 1943 an evacuation began.

Even though the Japanese evacuation had been under way for some time, many of the enemy troops were exceedingly lucky to escape the 25th Brigade's rapid advance. Indeed, although the pursuit had not actually caught and destroyed most of the enemy force, the end result was very similar. Worried about the pace of the 25th Brigade's advance, the 8000 Japanese remaining in the area were hastily issued half rations, sufficient to last ten days of an expected sixteen-day trek to the North Coast. Soldiers too sick to attempt the crossing killed themselves or were abandoned. As events turned out, the journey lasted 26 days and some 2000 Japanese perished. The survivors endured such terrible privations that many never recovered.[8]

Following a rest at Nadzab, from 27 September on, Eather's troops started being flown by C47 into a landing ground near the village of Kaiapit and advanced into the Ramu Valley with the 21st Brigade. Initially the 21st and 25th Brigades pushed forward side by side. The 21st Brigade made the main thrust towards Shaggy Ridge while the 25th Brigade protected its left flank and acted in a supporting role.

After the capture of Lae an incident witnessed by several soldiers from the 2/31st Battalion caused some ill-feeling towards their brigadier. One of them recalled:

We had just captured Lae and were on our way to the Ramu Valley ... the object[ive being] Dumpu. We had passed through the village of Kaiapit. There was no road but the country was pretty flat in the valley and a jeep had no trouble travelling along it.

We were marching in the usual manner for protection from aircraft—one section on each side of the track with the length of a section between them. The track was very muddy. Along came Brig Eather in his jeep travelling in the same direction as our column was. The trailer on the jeep struck a pool of muddy water splashing it over a member of the nearest section. 'You bloody bastard' yelled the soldier. By this time Eather's jeep had travelled some distance to the head of the column where he commanded the officer-in-charge to halt. This accomplished, Eather came back to the unfortunate soldier in his jeep and trailer and put him on a charge for swearing at him ... While this was going on the other members of the section had a look see at what was under the cover in the trailer [no doubt with the intention of quietly helping themselves to anything of value—author]. It was later disclosed as an organ as used in a church and it was surmised that it came from the church in Kaiapit ... His action did not endear him to a lot of us foot soldiers.[9]

The supposition that the organ came from Kaiapit is probably correct but any inference that it was being taken for personal use or looted is highly unlikely. Such an action would have been out of character for someone of Eather's principles. The most likely explanation was that it had been recovered after being taken by the Japanese and was to be returned to town.

Describing the terrain encountered after Lae, David Dexter, the official historian noted:

> The Markham and Ramu Valleys, in which the 7th Division was now to operate, were like a giant corridor some 115 miles [185 kilometres] long running from south-east to north-west and separating the Huon Peninsula from the rest of New Guinea. From end to end of the river corridor towering mountains rose on the north and south. The valley itself was flat and kunai-clad and most suitable for airfields. Apart from the main rivers—the Markham and Ramu— there were many tributaries which in rainy weather would impede

LAE AND THE MARKHAM AND RAMU VALLEYS

progress, but movement up the Markham was relatively easy, except for the heat.

The advance continued despite some opposition. The Japanese were keen to delay the Australians while they withdrew the bulk of their troops through the Finisterre Range but the 21st and 25th Brigades vigorously pursued them into the mountains. On 10 October, the 2/33rd Battalion captured a 1250-metre high peak some 7.5 kilometres north of Kumbarum. This was a significant achievement and testimony to the troops' skill and tenacity, as they had to endure a five-hour climb before they could capture the area in a difficult night attack.

Dumpu, an important site for airfield development, had been captured by the 21st Brigade on 4 October. For a few weeks after this the Australians continued to pursue the Japanese into the mountains and then halted, having gained all the ground they needed to secure airfield sites at Dumpu, Gusap, Kaiapit and Nadzab.

After being withdrawn to Dumpu for a rest, on 9 November Brigadier Eather's troops relieved the 21st Brigade in the Faria-Uria Valley in what had now become a fairly static area of operations. With the 7th Division concentrated between Dumpu and Masawasa, the Markham and Ramu Valleys, with their important newly developed airfields and radar stations, were now secure from the Japanese, and a vigorous program of patrolling was undertaken forward of the occupied areas to gain information and keep the enemy out of the territory captured. Numerous small-scale—but at times bloody—engagements resulted from these patrols. Japanese intelligence sources knew they were operating against the 7th Division and Tokyo Radio broadcasts referred to the 7th Division as 'Vasey's Murderers'—a name the troops rather fancied.

Even when not actively patrolling, just holding onto some of the posts in the mountains could be a daunting proposition. At one stage, troops from the 2/33rd Battalion garrisoned part of the infamous Shaggy Ridge. At 1520 metres above sea level, this razorbacked ridge with almost precipitous sides, was only just over a metre wide at the top. Soldiers had to be very careful not to fall to their deaths out of their weapon pits or off the dangerous slopes surrounding the 'track' that led to their positions. To make matters worse, the forward

Japanese position was only 35 metres from the leading Australian two-man weapon pit. The 'Pimple', a cloud and mist shrouded pinnacle rising up sharply near the centre of Shaggy Ridge, was held by the Japanese and could only be approached along a one-man wide track. Without exaggeration, it has been said that the fighting on Shaggy Ridge was conducted on a one-man front.

So rough was the terrain that on some occasions Eather chose to make aerial reconnaissances in a small Piper Cub to see where his troops were operating. These flights were not without hazard, many an aircraft being lost over the New Guinea jungle due to bad weather, mechanical failure or enemy action. Aerial observation enabled Eather to assess the forward situation in a quick and relatively efficient manner, however.

Despite a strong emphasis on disease prevention and the stringent enforcement of anti-malarial precautions, in the lower lying areas malarial infection continued to cause casualties amongst the 25th Brigade. The Ramu Valley, in fact, was known to the local people as the 'Valley of Death', a reference to its highly malarious state. As usual in jungle fighting, mosquito-borne malaria and other tropical diseases claimed many more casualties than did the enemy.

Eather described the daily disease-prevention ritual in a letter to his mother:

> We are all as careful as possible regarding our anti-malarial precautions. Take Atebrin daily, sleep under nets, wear long pants & gaiters & have our sleeves rolled down as well as plastering ourselves with anti mosquito lotion, a lotion which is issued to us in bottles & is the goods in keeping the little beasts off. It's very much better than the old smelly lotions. I can assure you it is quite a ritual after the daily shower. Powder to prevent chaffing. Powder on the feet to prevent tinea. Repellent round the ankles & waist to keep off the [w]retched moccas [insects] which give one the dreaded scrub typhus & finally the mosquito repellent on exposed skin to prevent mosquito bites. Oh yes, quite a business is it not but necessary.
>
> I slept in pyjamas for the first time in over three months & got rather a kick out of it. I managed to get a pair from the Comforts Fund. They are pretty brilliant & not a very good fit for the size is marked EOS! The pants are shorts & no sleeves in the coat. Even so

it's a great change after being used to sleeping in ones clothes for so long. One objection is that it takes far longer to get into bed. Once all that was necessary was to kick off ones boots & loosen the belt & there you were ready.

Night fighting was a rare occurrence in this campaign, but on the evening of 12–13 December troops of the 2/25th Battalion came under strong attack. The soldiers were operating from a patrol base on high ground near Kesawai when, just after midnight, large numbers of Japanese were seen in the moonlight advancing towards them. Sentries gave the alarm and quietly the Australians prepared to meet the enemy. When the Japanese came within 35 metres, the Australians opened fire, causing heavy casualties. Both sides used machine-guns extensively but the Australians had an advantage in that they could simply roll hand-grenades down onto the Japanese as they climbed up towards them.

After suffering some casualties, the Australians began to run low on ammunition and withdrew before dawn. Although no strategically important ground had been lost and the Australians had acquitted themselves well, Brigadier Eather was unhappy that ground had been yielded, and the battalion commander later had to provide a detailed explanation of the matter.

Having satisfied himself as to the conduct of the 2/25th, Eather wrote of the action to his mother on 16 December:

> These past few weeks I've been much less bored with life. You may have read that fighting had flared up in the Ramu Valley. Gave one plenty to think about for a while & relieved the sense of boredom that was stealing over one. The little yellow . . . attacked us some days ago but we gave him such a thump that he has withdrawn to lick his wounds. No doubt he will come again but the chaps are very ready for him & I think will welcome the chance.

In a separate letter to his father, Eather described the battle in considerably more detail:

> I was delighted to be notified the other day that a number of awards for bravery in the face of the enemy which I had recommended for

the Lae show had been approved. My word, the Australian after being well trained & disciplined makes a wonderful soldier. I doubt he can be beaten unless things are overwhelmingly against him. Recently I had about 150 men out in front on an offensive patrol. They penetrated into enemy held country, ambushed four parties of Japs killing forty. Lord knows how many were wounded. The usual figure is about double the [number] killed.

These chaps of mine used to select a nice steep ridge and sit on top of it for a night as it is very difficult to do much in this country in the dark. On the second night an enemy patrol blundered into them and got shot up but an hour later the Jap attacked them and cut their phone line to me. In all they made three attacks on the chaps & each were beaten back. The firing was very heavy indeed. The sound rolled down the valley & woke me about 2.15 am. I was very anxious for a while for I knew that the Jap had cut the [telephone] line and must have had them surrounded. However, I knew they were in a strong position & as the firing continued on I knew they were giving as good, if not better, than they were getting.

After an hour of fighting I sent forty chaps out with extra ammunition with instructions to fight into them with the stuff which they would soon require. They got in too but just after that the Jap put in fresh troops against them, they estimated 400. They beat off that attack & the company commander decided it was time to get out before he had lots more about his ears. With great skill they managed to find and slip out through a small gap & get clear. Just as well for in half an hour the Japs put in an extra heavy attack against their empty position. He must have felt silly when he got there to find that the bird had flown.

These chaps came down the track and found the phone line behind the cut and [after repairing the break] told me all about it. I promptly shelled their old position with every gun I could bring to bear. Must have knocked the Jap about for when a scouting party returned there next afternoon they found twenty unburied Japs and lots of hastily dug graves. I calculate that little effort cost the Japs 200 & we had only two killed and we got back our five wounded as well as all our equipment. It's grand work like this that shows the worth of the Aust soldier. I'm hoping the company commander will get an MC out of it.

In the same letter Eather also touched on the international situation and domestic affairs in Australia:

> News from the other fronts continues to be very good. It's all leading up to the climax. Any day now I'm expecting to hear of bigger & better things. Still it is going to be a long business, another two years at least.
>
> Am wondering if anything will develop out of the reported peace feelers by the Bulgars? Hope so. Will be another nail in the Axis coffin.
>
> Things in Aust seem to be much the same as ever. Strikes & hold ups. Maybe we made a mistake in driving the Japs back over the Owen Stanleys. A couple of Jap Divisions on our mainland may have brought lots of people to their senses. A drastic measure I know but it would seem that they want a hell of a bump to awaken them to the fact that this isn't a time for making money. These lads of mine that did the fighting are getting five bob a day!

Despite the admiration for his troops which Eather expressed to his family, there were still occasions when individuals earned the wrath of their brigadier. On one occasion he noticed two soldiers in the distance shooting ducks, even though he had specifically banned the practice. Feeling that actions would speak louder than words, Eather borrowed a Bren gun from a nearby soldier, took careful aim, and let fly with a burst of fire near the miscreants. The effect was surprising: the two soldiers dropped to the ground, ducks flew from everywhere and several other soldiers who, unseen, had been stalking the ducks, opened fire on their rapidly disappearing dinners. When apprehended, two of the offenders were found to be members of the regimental police. No doubt numerous sentences of 28 days were handed down.

In the first days of January 1944, the 25th and 21st Brigades were relieved in New Guinea and returned to Australia on board HMAS *Kanimbla* for rest and retraining. By then, however, the campaign was a long way towards being complete.

Elsewhere, the Japanese were feeling the pinch of the rapidly developing American counter-offensive that they would prove unable to resist. In December 1943 American forces had landed on

New Britain, while in January 1944 the Marshall Islands in the Central Pacific were captured. Strong American naval, air and ground forces were moving forward, capturing islands and sections of coastline suitable for the construction of airfields and harbour facilities as they 'island-hopped' closer to Japan, leaving huge Japanese garrisons impotent and stranded behind them.

After its arduous service in the 'Valley of Death', the 7th Division was concentrated near Strathpine outside Brisbane. Its troops were hospitalised in large numbers, suffering from malaria and other tropical illnesses. Several months later, the division moved to the Atherton Tablelands where it trained for its next operation—an event destined to be a long time coming. As late as May 1944, Eather wrote to his mother saying that the brigade was 'not working very hard. Lots of chaps haven't finished their leave and are not yet back'. A month later he recorded that many of the troops were being given additional leave at a seaside rest camp which 'should do them the world of good'. This period was unremarkable except for the sheer length of time the 7th Division was kept idle by General MacArthur after it had been fully rehabilitated.

When General Vasey became seriously ill and was hospitalised in mid-June, Brigadier Eather acted as divisional commander for nearly three weeks until Major General E.J. Milford arrived as Vasey's replacement.[10] This was Eather's first, albeit short, divisional command. It came, however, with an unexpected benefit—he got to occupy Vasey's log cabin during what was a relatively cool winter. The cabin even had its own shower, wash basin and electric light. 'I'll be getting very soft if it goes on much longer' he told his family before Milford's arrival.

During this period, Eather was visited by Gavin Long, the official Army historian. They discussed many things, including the problem of training troops who had little prospect of seeing action in the immediate future. Long recorded Eather as saying: 'I don't believe in the idea that you reach a peak and then slide downhill. You reach a point where it is necessary to have a change of training and leave, after that, you can go back and improve.'[11]

This comment, however, was made at a fairly early phase of the 7th Division's inactivity. It would seem that, later, Eather would hold misgivings about the protracted delay in committing the 7th Division to further campaigns and the effect this had on both efficient training and morale.

On a personal level, at this time Eather got to see Adeline occasionally. At least once, Adeline came up to Queensland and stayed for several weeks in a flat. The couple met when they could and enjoyed a limited social life. At a nearby cinema they occasionally saw a movie, Eather noting that *Random Harvest* was a most enjoyable picture.

To a friend he wrote on 15 September 1944:

> The longer I stay in this Army of ours the more I'm finding to do and the busier I become. Have just come back into camp after a five-day exercise & tomorrow go out again for a further ten days. And are they long days too. Begin in the early hours and continue into the night...
>
> We are lucky enough to have a wireless & we are able to keep abreast of the news. And what grand news it is too! Am looking forward to the day when we can hear of the Jap getting his share of the good things at present being delivered to the German. It does look very much as if it is only a matter of time before it is all over...
>
> I ran into an old chap who had a cattle run in the 'back of beyond'. He was a very decent old stick & his main worry was that the Jap may throw in the sponge before he had received a thrashing. His view was understandable when one learned he had one son a POW in Malaya whom he hasn't heard from in eighteen months, another son killed in NG & twenty-seven other relatives serving!

During an exercise at this time, the 25th Brigade was receiving air support from some Boomerang aircraft. After directing a mortar shoot, one of the RAAF pilots circled Brigade Headquarters and dropped what was assumed to be a message. When opened by Eather, however, it was found to be the pilot's unpaid pre-war income tax assessment.[12] Presumably the pilot considered that Eather had more use for the Taxation Department's correspondence than he did!

The 7th Division had by now been out of action since January, so long a period that boredom, the isolation of the camps and the repetitive training for battles that might never be fought began to affect morale. In a letter to his mother in October 1944, Eather touched on this problem and some of the remedies:

> This camp we are in isn't so bad, it's in bush country miles away from anywhere. One of our worries is to provide some kind of amenities for the troops—something to keep them occupied at night for we cannot be training the whole time. We have the usual picture shows each week & now and then a concert. The Aust Army Educational Service are doing a splendid job for us. We have an Educational Officer on Brigade Headquarters & he does lots to keep those who desire employed. They teach all kinds of things from maths to handicrafts. At the moment there is a wave of enthusiasm for leatherwork which is sweeping through the camp. Even I have succumbed. Working the odd half hour now and then I have over the month produced a reasonable writing folder.

Eather's predictions on the war's end, though, must have made sobering reading for his mother:

> The news from overseas continues to be heartening doesn't it? Even so it begins to look as if the European war will last into the spring of next year. Then of course there is our own particular private war with the Japs to be concluded. I don't want to be pessimistic but I still see no reason to believe that the Jap will be defeated before 1947. Sounds pretty grim, doesn't it? I sincerely hope I'm wrong & that it is over much sooner. I shall be very glad to get back home for good.

In December, Eather predicted to his father an early return to action. Although he had been known as a kind-hearted young man in the 1920s, he had been deeply changed by the war. His blazing hatred of the Japanese was now deeply ingrained:

> The time is rapidly approaching when the AIF will leave Australia for, I hope, what is the last time. I do not think we are likely to return until the whole thing is over and, as you know, I am not labouring under any misguided optimistic ideas that Japan is going to be beaten easily or quickly. Most soldiers who have fought them in the field believe they will not be brought to think along the right

lines, the Jap soldier has a terrific ability to absorb punishment & I believe that is true of the whole race ...

Recently I have spoken to one of those fortunate chaps who was rescued from that torpedoed Jap POW ship [author's note: probably the *Montevideo Maru* or the *Rokyo Maru*]. The tales he tells, and they are backed up by other evidence, is hardly credible. Those yellow brutes treat those chaps of ours like they treat the subjugated Chinese & Koreans & that according to our ideas isn't a treatment to be given dogs ...

Throughout this long training period I have done my very best to inculcate into my troops my own hatred for the Jap race & I know I have achieved a great measure of success. There will be very few Japs left alive of those who confront these troops. God knows I suppose we shall pay a very dear price for it but to prevent our own people, who sometimes may not seem worth it [author's note: a reference to union strikes affecting the war effort and the generally relaxed and uncaring lifestyle of some civilians], from being enslaved as they surely would be if defeated by the Jap it will be worth the cost. There will be grief in lots of Aust homes yet before this is all over.

I may be wrong in my idea of how long it's going to take, I hope to heavens I am, but I don't see the sense of taking the view that it's going to be a 'push-over'. It isn't.

On Christmas Day 1944, Eather and his officers carried out one of the Australian Army's enduring traditions, rising early to inspect the kitchens and catering arrangements for feeding their troops. Satisfied that all was in order, he and his officers and NCOs later served the troops their Christmas lunch and then joined them in celebrating an important day away from their families and loved ones.

The beginning of 1945 saw the 7th Division still stranded in Australia. The war situation was progressing very well for the Allies. Germany was tottering on the brink of collapse, while Japan was fast approaching defeat. American forces had by now captured part of the Philippines and were pressing ever closer to Japan in large-scale amphibious operations. General MacArthur's subsidiary strategy, to keep the Australian forces relegated to a secondary role while American forces claimed the sole final victory, was also entirely successful. For almost a year Australia's elite striking force—the 7th and 9th Divisions—had been out of action. The American forces, having learnt from their failures in New Guinea, were operating successfully without Australian assistance and none but Americans would be in a position to claim the major part in the victory when Japan finally surrendered.

On 6 January, an unusual but pleasant interlude occurred when Eather stood in place for Sister E.L. Woodward's father during her wedding to Captain J.H. Mules at St Mary's Church of England at Atherton. This happy event is interesting as it shows the way in which some junior officers thought of their brigadier, inviting him to participate in such important private events.[13]

February saw the 7th Division visited by the Governor-General. This unusual event was recorded in a letter from Eather to one of his sisters:

> Last week we had HRH [the Duke of Gloucester] visit us. No doubt you have read of his visit in the press. He arrived on Monday afternoon and stayed with [Lieutenant General] Sir Leslie Morshead. The Corps Commander was kind enough to invite his Brigadiers to dinner that night to meet his guest. I found the Duke a very charming person. No sign of stiffness & he seemed very interested in the AIF. He isn't a very good domino player & throws a nifty dart.
>
> One Tuesday he came down into the camp area & had a good look 'round among the troops. I think most of them saw him. My word there was a great old upheaval in the area when it was known he would visit us. The whole place was gone over & cleaned up. Flower gardens came into being overnight. There are lots of funny stories going about over the visit & we had a good laugh over them.

In the same letter though, he also expressed his mounting concern over the fact that the AIF was being left out of the war: 'This waiting business is very trying on the troops. They feel that the job [the war effort] is not being got on with as quickly as it could be if they were used. Maybe they are right too . . .'

Eather's next letter to his mother on 12 March 1945 was sombre. The dragging out of the war without the 7th Division's participation, the length of time away from home and the loss of friends was clearly dispiriting:

> ... one does miss home. I hope it will not be long now before it is all over. Six years is a very long time to be away from home living rather like pigs. I think things look so well in Europe that it is pretty certain that the show over there will finish this year & then it remains to be seen just how long Master Jap will hang on by himself.
>
> We have been very upset about the loss of our late GOC Gen[eral] Vasey [killed in a plane crash with some of his staff]. I don't know of any general who captured the affection of the men under him as he did. Yesterday we held a memorial service and about ten thousand members of the Division attended. On Thursday last I went down to the funeral at Cairns. Gen's Vasey, Dours [sic; Major General Downs] and Lieutenant Colonel Bertram were buried in the Military Section of the Cairns Cemetery. There was a very big crowd there and Gen Blamey spoke in very glowing terms of them. Geo Bertram used to be my Brigade Major in the Middle East & when we first returned to Aust. Poor fellow leaves a wife and a three months old baby. It's a very sad business indeed.

Eather's affectionate remembrance of Major General Vasey was in sharp contrast to the restrained and concerned diary entries made on the Kokoda Track when Vasey replaced his good friend and commander Major General Allen in controversial circumstances. Clearly a strong bond of respect and friendship had developed between the two officers in the intervening period.

Over the years Eather also maintained contact with his good friend 'Tubby' Allen. In April 1945 the two had a reunion in Sydney. They marched together during the Anzac Day commemoration and afterwards ended up at Tubby's flat in Edgecliff. General Allen's teenage son, John, was at home when they arrived and he noted that the two had obviously had a good day. Of that meeting, in recent times John has recorded that he observed 'the closeness, trust and respect they had for each other. To use that well-known expression in its truest form, they were mates'.[14]

Also, in April, Eather was struck down by a relapse of malaria and hospitalised. This was of great concern as he expected that the

7th Division was finally to see action again. Fortunately, he recovered before the long-awaited embarkation orders were received.

Right up to the end, however, Eather continued to train the brigade hard. Recalled Frank McCosker of the 2/25th Battalion: 'On the last Brigade exercise on Atherton Tablelands prior to embarkation, the 2/25th Battalion and other units left base at Kairi at 3 am and arrived at our destination—Walsh River near Dimbula at 6 pm—a march of forty-two map miles [67 kilometres].'[15]

The 25th Brigade was well and truly prepared for action.

9
Balikpapan:
A final fight

I don't know how the Jap's treated them [the indigenous population] before they knew we were coming but after we landed his treatment of them has been brutal in the extreme. I have seen dozens of bodies of natives whom he has shot, beheaded or beaten to death. He adopts shocking methods of preventing them aiding us such as slicing off the soles of their feet to render them incapable of working for us. And there are people who wish to ease up on the brutes!

Brigadier Eather in a letter to his parents following
the Balikpapan campaign, 29 July 1945

The 7th and 9th Divisions were finally given another operational role in mid-1945. Their objectives, however, were in the Dutch East Indies—an area bypassed by American forces. The 9th Division was to seize the island of Tarakan on the north-east of Borneo and later Brunei Bay on the northern side. The 7th Division's mission was to invade Balikpapan on Borneo's east coast. After many broken promises and evasions by General MacArthur to give the Australian Army active employment in the Philippines and other forward locations, this task was a major disappointment.

The Australian Army everywhere was now being misemployed, fighting bypassed Japanese troops who were a threat to no one. The enemy were effectively isolated in their own camps where they grew their own food to survive and did little else. Nonetheless, the Australian Government had insisted that its troops keep fighting, and the decision to seize parts of Borneo reduced political pressure on General MacArthur to employ the highly trained AIF troops under his command. That there was no meaningful military requirement to seize the Dutch East Indies does not seem to have overly bothered either the Australian Government or MacArthur. The forthcoming operations would not bring the war to a conclusion a single day earlier than if they had not been mounted.

Despite the lack of military necessity—or perhaps because of it—the last major Allied amphibious operation of World War II would be carried out on a lavish scale. Codenamed 'Oboe II', the stated purpose of the Balikpapan operation was to seize naval anchorages, airfields and the oil-refining facilities which, prior to the war, provided an output of 15 million barrels a year. In the event, it would take over twelve months to get the refineries operating again once the damage caused by Japanese demolitions and Allied naval and air bombardments had been repaired. The war was long over before this could be done. Another reason given for the mounting of Oboe II was to liberate the indigenous populations from Japanese domination. Although the validity of this and other reasons for mounting the invasion are debatable, particularly in hindsight, Eather considered the operation worthwhile and an important step in the defeat of the Japanese.

While the 25th Brigade was at sea, Eather wrote to his mother from the assault ship HMAS *Westralia* on 28 June:

> Here we go again on our way to do another job which I hope will help bring things to a finish. I'm having the time of my life and thoroughly enjoying my sea trip. I've been on board now for several days & am eating like a horse. I have my meals with the captain in his cabin & these fellows live very well indeed. The troops too are very pleased with their food & if the chaps get plenty of good food they are as happy as school kids.
>
> They swarm all over the decks, stripped down to a pair of shorts & sometimes even less than that! They are getting a great old suntan up. Well they will have to wear all their clothes soon to stop the disease carrying mosquito getting at them so while at sea we let them be as comfy as they like.
>
> It's quite good weather, plenty of clouds, which is a good thing. The sea is very calm & the breeze quite cool most of the time but it's devilish hot below when the ship is closed down and darkened for the night. I'm always glad when daylight comes & I can open the porthole.

BALIKPAPAN: A FINAL FIGHT

> Since I've been aboard I have fallen into quite a routine. I spend the morning up on the bridge watching whatever there is to see, an island now and then. We struck one yesterday which had a hefty smoking volcano on it. About noon we generally have a pre lunch beer. After lunch I feel so satisfied that I have a nap for a couple of hours. Lazy habits I'm developing! ...
>
> It will be some time before I'll be able to write again. I expect to be pretty busy as soon as I land.

At around 7 am on 1 July 1945, the invasion force of over 100 vessels arrived off Balikpapan. A massive naval and air bombardment had preceded this event for several weeks and reached a crescendo on the morning of the landing. The smothering effect of the bombardment was so effective that the Japanese garrison near the beachhead (which was estimated to consist of 5000 troops) and their coastal batteries could offer very little resistance to the Australian landing parties. Consequently, casualties sustained by the assaulting 18th and 21st Brigades were minimal.

The 25th Brigade was designated the 7th Division's reserve and on the day of the landing remained afloat while its soldiers watched the bombardment and initial landing. One observer recorded:

> Never before had the Australians seen such destructive forces let loose by their side. The air and the sea shook and reverberated with the crashing discharge of hundreds of naval guns... whole buildings and trees were tossed grotesquely in the air...

Eather's headquarters was called ashore later on 1 July, with all the battalions landing the following day. The 25th Brigade was first given the task of taking over the centre of the Australian beachhead, but this changed on 3 July and the troops began advancing astride the Milford Highway (known locally as the Samarinda Road) on a wide front. The troops soon met with stern opposition from the Japanese who could fight more effectively away from the beachhead when the Australians could not call down massive naval gunfire support.

While Eather's three battalions (and an attached independent company) were opposed by only one Japanese battalion, the enemy fought tenaciously from hilltops and ridges and began to inflict, at times, severe casualties. Nonetheless the skilfully planned advance continued over succeeding days. Mindful of the unprecedented level of fire support available to him and hoping to keep casualties to a minimum, Eather warned his battalion commanders to move forward carefully and to make the maximum use of the available supporting fire. He ordered that patrols were to locate enemy strongpoints which were then to be destroyed by artillery fire, tanks or air attack. The days when he had earned the nickname Phar Lap for pushing his troops rapidly after the enemy were well and truly gone. At Balikpapan, there was no urgency.

Brigadier Eather points out a Japanese strongpoint to Major General Milford, commanding the 7th Division, on the 2/31st Battalion's front at Balikpapen, 4 July 1945.

Photo courtesy of the Australian War Memorial (AWM 111219)

BALIKPAPAN: A FINAL FIGHT

While the 25th Brigade continued to make good progress and rapidly achieved its assigned objectives, Eather's desire to avoid casualties was only partially successful. The Japanese gave little thought to surrender and under these circumstances it was inevitable that losses would continue to mount as the enemy was forced from or blasted out of its positions. When the 2/33rd Battalion's commander was wounded by shellfire, Eather was obliged to place his brigade major in charge until he could appoint a successor.

Recalling the fighting in the last days of the campaign, Private 'Doc' Waters from the 2/25th Battalion wrote:

> In one place we were held up for a bit. Much artillery and mortars were used by our side but nothing much gave. Then [came] an order to send a patrol to the area to see what was going on. It transpired that the Japs had well protected areas they used to retreat to when any shelling started. The officer with [the] patrol spoke to the men on the guns and asked them to raise their sights another 50 yards [46 metres]. This devastated the Jap position and we walked in the next day.[1]

Organised Japanese resistance declined in mid-July. By 21 July, the 25th Brigade had advanced towards Pope's Track and all the objectives allocated to the 7th Division in Oboe II had been attained. General Milford then advised Eather to advance no further and to simply patrol forward of the Australian perimeter rather than risk needless casualties pursuing the enemy. From then until the cessation of hostilities, patrolling was the main activity undertaken by the 25th Brigade. (Some weeks later, following the Japanese signing of surrender terms in Tokyo Bay on 2 September, outlying Japanese garrisons surrendered to local Allied commanders. General Milford accepted the surrender of Japanese forces on Borneo.)

Australian casualties at Balikpapan were 229 killed and 634 wounded. Ironically, of the 7th Division's three brigades, it was the 25th—the division's reserve brigade—which saw the hardest fighting and suffered the heaviest losses, some 360 killed and wounded. Nearly 1800 Japanese were known to have died in this meaningless campaign and some hundreds of others were probably also killed. Only 63 were taken prisoner. Undoubtedly thousands of civilians became casualties.

In a frank and disturbing letter to his parents on 29 July, Eather gave an account of the fighting and its aftermath:

> The show has gone remarkably well & my lads have had a great deal more fighting than was anticipated &, as always, have proved their mastery over the Jap.
>
> Until the other day I had not had the time to get about & had not seen anything of the town area. When we landed we began to fight our way north out into the country. Yesterday afternoon for the first time I drove round & had a look at the oil refinery & the town area. The damage done by both the Jap and our bombing is beyond description. It must be seen to be believed. This place has taken an awful punishment. It's most depressing to drive through & see what ravages the war has made. The natives too, have suffered. I don't know how the Jap's treated them before they knew we were coming but after we landed his treatment of them has been brutal to an extreme. I have seen dozens of bodies of natives whom he has shot, beheaded or beaten to death. He adopts shocking methods of preventing them aiding us such as slicing off the soles of their feet to render them incapable of working for us. And there are people who wish to ease up on the brutes!
>
> Now that we have all the ground we require & have pushed him back into the dense jungle the campaign is about over. We are still in contact with his rearguards however but we seemed to have knocked all the fight out of him & he won't start anything by himself. Of course he will scrap like the very devil if we push him but there is not any need to. We have got what we need and are prepared to let him exist in the jungle & allow sickness to take its toll. It was a short, sharp little show beautifully planned & carried out with dash and speed.

There was a lighter side to his correspondence, however:

> I am very comfortably installed in a nice house of my own design which some of my chaps built for me. It's of weatherboard & flywire gauze. There is any amount of building timber from wrecked houses about. Pop, you would have the time of your life among it, plenty of stuff to build fowl runs!

BALIKPAPAN: A FINAL FIGHT

Until yesterday I had a pet monkey, very young & a great source of fun. She used to climb all over one but was a holy terror if she got loose. She did one day & pinched my glasses. There was a great to do until they were found undamaged in the long grass nearby.

Well Pop, it looks as if the AIF as at presently organised has finished its job or nearly. With the release of the five year service chaps, & some have already gone, we will lose many battle trained & experienced leaders of all grades which of course must make a tremendous difference in the fighting efficiency of a battalion. I'm most grateful that we did not lose our fellows before we went into this operation. Our casualties would certainly have been far heavier than they were. There is nothing to bring the casualty rate up so much as untried & inexperienced leaders. In fact, it is my opinion that had they been taken out prior to the landing this force would not have been capable of doing the job at such slight cost.

I have received lots of cuttings from the papers on this subject. People seem to be making a political question of it. It cannot be denied that those with long service should be given the option of getting out. They have done a splendid job & deserve it & if it is the Government's policy to release them it's all to the good but it doesn't do to take the props from under a structure until the foundations are firm. It cannot be a sudden release for them without completely wiping the remainder off as a fighting force for a considerable period.

In the Balikpapan campaign Eather had displayed a markedly different style of operational command. Fully aware that there was no urgency to advance rapidly or to accept casualties to attain his objectives, the 25th Brigade's operations were typified by unhurried and steady movement using supporting fire from artillery, tanks and aircraft wherever possible. Patrols were used to probe forward carefully and locate areas of enemy resistance, after which the full force of supporting fire was applied to any enemy encountered. Under the circumstances, this was undoubtedly the best possible course of action to follow.

Eather was not at Balikpapan to witness the surrender of Japanese forces. On 26 July 1945 he was promoted to major general and appointed to command the 11th Australian Division on New Britain.

In the same letter in which he described the aftermath at Balikpapan, Eather told his parents:

> By the time this reaches you, you will have heard of my promotion. Of course it is very nice in a way but I do regret leaving this unit where I have made so many friends. In my new post I know a number of fellows who I have worked with before so I will not be altogether a stranger.

Although he was a very experienced and competent commander, Eather would not have been promoted to higher rank had it not been (indirectly) due to the untimely death of his old commander, George Vasey. The accident which claimed Vasey's life had occurred as he was travelling to New Guinea to take command of the 6th Division. In his place, Major General J.E.S. Stevens had been appointed and led that division during the drive to Wewak. However, following a request by his pre-war employer for an urgent release from the Army, the War Cabinet agreed to Stevens's retirement and the issue of the command of the 6th Division had been re-opened.

By this stage, there had been some criticism from both the media and politicians about the number of under-employed generals in the Australian Army. In these circumstances, Blamey appeared reluctant to fill the vacancy by nominating any brigadier for promotion. In the first instance he put forward Major General Bert Lloyd as Stevens's successor. Lloyd, a 61-year-old World War I veteran, was a friend of Blamey's who was keen to obtain some active service in this war before it concluded.[2] In attempting to appoint so elderly an officer to an active command, Blamey was clearly placing personal friendship ahead of the effective conduct of operations. At this stage of the war, Blamey no longer held the confidence of the Government and, in particular, the Minister for the Army. Indeed Blamey and the Minister had a strong dislike for each other.

In War Cabinet Minute 4294 dated 11 July 1945, Blamey was bluntly told that the Government would not approve the appointment of Lloyd. The minute stated in part: 'War Cabinet considers that a younger officer should be nominated for this post, in view of the desirability of his experience in an active field command being conserved to the AMF during the post war period.'[3] Blamey responded to the implicit criticism of his judgment in a letter to Frank Forde, the Minister for the Army, on 17 July. He justified his initial nomination of Lloyd on the basis that he believed that it was government policy not to promote any further officers to general rank.[4] He then went on to recommend that Brigadier Eather be promoted and appointed to fill the vacancy, giving a brief but glowing recommendation of his new nominee in the process. Blamey was on much safer ground here, as Eather was then the most senior brigadier in the Army and there was little chance that Blamey could be criticised for promoting him on the basis of friendship.

The War Cabinet approved this nomination. Eather would be the last Australian promoted to the rank of general in World War II. In a complex series of moves, he replaced Major General H.C.H. Robertson commanding the 11th Division. Robertson then took over the 6th Division, finally relieving Stevens who retired from the Army and returned to the Postmaster-General's Department.[5]

One factor that had the potential to prevent Eather's promotion and further embarrass General Blamey was the Government's plan to allow the early discharge of soldiers who had served for more than four years. Eather, while supporting the plan in general, was not prepared to take advantage of it himself.

To determine Eather's intentions regarding early release, Blamey needed to sound him out before officially putting his name forward for promotion. He did this on Morotai Island, just before the Balikpapan invasion force sailed. The reasons for his questions had to be guarded, however, in case his latest nomination, like Lloyd's beforehand, was not acceptable to the Government.

Of these discussions Eather told his parents:

Not so long ago while on Morotai I was asked personally by the C in C [General Blamey] what I would do myself. Of course there could only be one answer. I enlisted for the duration of the war (and it is nearly over now) & I could see no reason why I should weaken in my resolve to see the thing out. Gen Blamey seem[ed] pleased with the answer & this change is no doubt the result.

While the troops of the 25th Brigade knew that their brigadier of three and a half years had been promoted, this information did not become general knowledge in the rest of the Army for some time. When it did, his promotion was of small interest to the troops. More immediate and dramatic happenings were now having a direct bearing on their lives. Thus, a special 'sunset' edition of the Army's *Table Tops* newspaper on Wednesday 15 August had, as its almost exclusive topic, news of Japan's surrender. A small paragraph on the last page under the title 'Promoted to General on the Eve of Peace' announced Brigadier Eather's promotion. It was the only other news reported in the paper. In an understandable mistake the short announcement noted that 'news from Japan will probably prevent him taking command of an Australian Division'. In this the journalist was wrong, for Eather was already commanding the 11th Division on New Britain.

10
Overlord of a Japanese bastion

I have a big crowd of Japs in custody who are accused of war crimes & I'm waiting for [an] order to go ahead & try them. The order is on its way, I believe. I wonder if I will have to hang any of them? Many of them deserve it . . .

Major General Eather, in a letter to his parents from Rabaul, November 1945

On 26 July 1945, at the age of 44, Major General Eather took command of the 11th Division.[1] This Militia infantry division, with its headquarters at Jacquinot Bay on New Britain, comprised the 4th and 13th Infantry Brigades and supporting units.

Jacquinot Bay had originally been occupied by Australian troops in November 1944. From there, they had managed to cut the neck of the Gazelle Peninsula and, although heavily outnumbered, contain some 90 000 well-equipped Japanese troops. This strategy, which required no significant change after Eather's arrival, up to the war's end cost just 53 Australians killed in action.

After just a few days on New Britain, Eather received a signal from the commander of the 1st Australian Army, Lieutenant General Sturdee, warning of an impending cessation of hostilities; Sturdee advised that operations should be limited to those necessary for the maintenance of security and that Australian casualties were to be avoided if at all possible. Even before this signal had arrived, Eather and his troops had known that events of great import were afoot. After the Japanese Government refused to accept unconditional surrender, on 6 August an atomic bomb was dropped on Hiroshima, vaporising that city. Another atomic bomb had to be dropped on Nagasaki three days later before the Japanese were forced to concede the inevitable.

The situation was clarified a few days later while Eather was still settling into his new command. News of Japan's unconditional surrender on 15 August was greeted with jubilation when it was received the next day. Gavin Long recorded in the official history:

> In the Jacquinot Bay area the darkness was broken by coloured flares fired from ships in port; machine-guns rattled; tracers streaked up into the heavens. There was singing and shouting and long blasts from motor horns ... In the hospital wards, sisters and orderlies sang with the patients. By now several fires were visible as merry-makers ignited some disused buildings in the old camp sites. This joyous scene continued until almost morning.

On 6 September, during an impressive 40-minute ceremony on board the British aircraft carrier HMS *Glory,* General Sturdee accepted the official surrender of all Japanese forces on New Britain and New Ireland. The garrisoning and administration of the former Japanese stronghold then became the responsibility of General Eather and the 11th Division. As the designated military governor of the region and the vast Japanese fortress at Rabaul, Eather stood behind Sturdee as the formalities were completed and the surrender documents signed. During the ceremony, General Imamura Hitoshi asked to be allowed to keep his sword, as he was still expected to command his troops. This request was refused. When Imamura then attempted to hand his sword to Sturdee, he was pointedly told to lay it on the table. Perhaps Sturdee intended to reinforce to the Japanese commander that he was no longer in charge. This disdainful attitude would also be displayed by the 11th Division's commander.

It now remained for Eather to take a major role in planning the return of Australian forces to Rabaul. In a signal from Eather, General Imamura was warned that the Australians would be coming ashore on the morning of 10 September, south-west of the township. No Japanese except for some labourers and interpreters—all of whom were to be unarmed—were permitted within 900 metres of the landing point. The arriving soldiers were to be prepared for any treacherous attack although the likelihood of this type of action was considered to be small.[2]

Notifying Imamura of the forthcoming landing, Eather extended no military courtesy, merely addressing his signal to the 'C-in-C Jap Army' and ending it with the curt order, 'Acknowledge'.[3] Although he had been present at the surrender ceremony with Imamura, the new military governor did not bother to use his own name in this signal, simply sending it from the 'General Officer Commanding the 11th Division'. Imamura, who outranked the younger Australian general, must have understood from the tone of this signal who was now in charge. Eather had very good reason for making this point strongly. The Australian garrison would be substantially outnumbered by the Japanese who, at Rabaul, had not experienced defeat in battle before the end of the war.

In Administrative Order 99, Eather warned his troops not to loot from the Japanese; any who did, regardless of rank, would be severely punished.[4] Unfortunately, not everyone took heed of their new divisional commander's warning—perhaps they were unaware of his reputation as a strict disciplinarian. Several Australians would later pay a high price for this ignorance.

A convoy with air and naval cover was organised and, on 10 September, assault craft ferried elements of the 4th Brigade ashore past dozens of sunken or wrecked ships in Simpson Harbour. During this operation the possibility that renegade Japanese might oppose the landing could not be fully discounted so the troops were fully armed, as were the Corsair fighter-bombers of the Royal New Zealand Air Force that flew overhead. Naval gun crews were also at action stations, ready to open fire if necessary. Fortunately, the Japanese fully complied with the surrender orders, although some of them trained their large coastal defence guns on the landing craft as they approached the shore. This certainly raised the adrenalin levels of all concerned and was a particularly foolish act that could have led to tragedy had the troops or naval gunners panicked. Eather and his headquarters arrived on 13 September and, in a brief ceremony, the Japanese flag was lowered and the Australian ensign run up as New Britain and New Ireland again came under Australian administration. It must have been an intensely satisfying moment for Eather and his soldiers after so many years of bitter fighting.

Japanese guards were relieved of their duties and the Australian troops set up their own camps in and around the badly damaged and overgrown township that had once been described as 'not so much a town as a tropical garden'. Over 100 000 Japanese soldiers, sailors and civilian workers, including nineteen generals and eleven admirals, came under the command of a former Sydney dental mechanic who had left school at the age of fourteen. The principal Japanese fighting units now under Eather's control were the 17th and 38th Divisions, the 39th and 65th Brigades and the 14th, 34th and 35th Regiments. Naval combat units and support troops of both services were also present in large numbers. Eather also administered command of the 10 000 troops of his own division, together with 8300 Indian, Chinese, Malay and Indonesian liberated prisoners-of-war and the indigenous population, estimated at between 20 000 and 40 000 people. He was also responsible for the surviving members of the interned civilian population—several hundred Chinese and around 150 Europeans. His command was thus a very large and diverse one.

In the following weeks, the job of disarming the huge Japanese garrison and the occupation of New Britain and New Ireland got into full swing. The relatively well-fed but surly Japanese, in their newfound role as prisoners, contrasted starkly with their emaciated former captives, newly released from prison. The Japanese had developed their fortress to such an extent that there were approximately 240 kilometres of underground tunnels in the Rabaul area. Allied POWs had been used to work in these cramped tunnels. When they were released, it was found that they had been underground for so long that they had great difficulty in standing upright and adapting to sunlight.[5] All of them were in an extremely debilitated condition. The appalling condition of these prisoners further reinforced Eather's hatred of the Japanese.

Dumps of enemy munitions and equipment were located and either destroyed (often by dumping at sea) or utilised by the occupying forces themselves. One piece of enemy equipment which was not destroyed was a Japanese sub chaser—a small corvette-sized warship used, as the name implied, in a submarine hunting role.[6] On being made aware of this vessel's existence, Eather made it his personal barge and used it to travel to New Ireland and small outlying islands and difficult-to-access areas on New Britain itself. Japanese weapons and supply dumps provided a rich source of souvenirs for Australian troops prepared to ignore their commander's ban on such activities. Relations with Japanese prisoners were 'coldly

OVERLORD OF A JAPANESE BASTION

formal' and they were used to fill in trenches, bomb craters and other fortifications as well as on projects such as the digging of wells, unloading ships on the wharves, timber cutting and cleaning up the township.

The Japanese military units and command structures were maintained intact and Eather used these to administer control. This system seemed to work quite well, although it appears that military discipline among some of the Japanese began to break down as time went by.

Eather had to make some difficult decisions regarding the Japanese, particularly in view of his personal revulsion of them. In some outlying areas he agreed that a small number of Japanese could retain their rifles for self-defence until Australian troops could escort them to their prison camps. The Japanese had been such unpopular overlords since 1942 that it was considered possible that local people would murder them in retribution if they were fully disarmed and without Australian soldiers to protect them.

Another problem resulted from a group of Japanese marines who refused to capitulate with their comrades. For several weeks these fully armed soldiers would not come down from the jungle-clad hills and there was some concern that they might engage in some form of suicidal attack on outlying Australian posts or interfere with the indigenous population.[7] Japanese officers, with an escort of Australian military police, eventually tracked down this band of diehards and talked them into surrendering without bloodshed. Incidents such as this sorely tried the patience of the Military Governor. It says a great deal for Eather's character, however, that he could put his personal feelings aside and deal with the Japanese in an appropriate, if severe, manner.

Only too aware of the supply problems that confronted him, Eather carried out Lieutenant General Sturdee's directive that the Japanese were to make themselves as fully self-sufficient as possible. Consequently, they were made to grow their own vegetables and even had to make their own prison camps—thirteen in number, each able to house 10 000 prisoners (although some eventually held over 11 000 and others less than 10 000). One camp held Koreans and Formosans separately from the other prisoners; another camp operated as a headquarters to administer the activities of the rest of the Japanese.[8] The senior Japanese officers were housed in a small separate camp.

Eather also allowed the construction of a racecourse by the prisoners so that the Australians could organise race meetings using liberated Japanese Army horses!

Eather's purpose in authorising this particular project would have been twofold. First, it kept numbers of prisoners busy on a task that would have reinforced their subservience to the Australians. Secondly, he was already alive to the fact that his troops' morale could easily decline now that the war was over; the racecourse would thus provide a badly needed recreational outlet. The Japanese bitterly resented being used on projects like this—which perhaps was even more reason for being made to complete them. Certainly such activities reinforced the fact that they had lost the war and were no longer the overlords of New Britain.

The necessity of concentrating the Japanese within prison camps exacerbated the logistical problems of the Australian administration. The Japanese had previously been engaged in widespread crop production and had to start afresh in the vicinity of their camps. In some cases the soil in these new areas was not well suited to cultivation. It is recorded that crop production plunged by 60 per cent when the prisoners were relocated in their new camps and never fully recovered to previous levels. Nonetheless, the Japanese had to do the best they could as the Australians did not have the resources to supply their needs. The alternative of leaving the Japanese to spread over the island was, understandably, not considered by the administration. The Japanese camp leadership made numerous complaints about the problems they were having in growing their own rations, complaints which were almost laughable considering how they had deliberately starved and mistreated Allied prisoners at Rabaul right up to the last days of the war. They were not viewed sympathetically by Eather.

Perhaps, then, it was provident that through some sort of administrative error, large quantities of rations consisting of herrings in tomato sauce were continually delivered to Rabaul, despite requests that deliveries cease. The herrings were almost universally detested by the Australian troops and rarely eaten. Eventually a huge stack of them lay under tarpaulins on the parade ground. One day an exasperated staff officer complained to Eather, 'What on earth are we to do with these?' The comment came just after the Military Governor had received yet another complaint from General Imamura about the quantity of food available. A solution to the embarrassing joint problems was obvious. With the comment 'The bloody Japs are always complaining about wanting extra to eat—they can have them', a Japanese working party was summoned to take the rations to their various camps. The Japanese found these rations no more palatable than the Australians did and quickly tired of them, but this did not stop the herrings being issued, until they were all consumed.

Within days of his arrival, Major General Eather ordered the 13 000 Japanese troops on New Ireland transferred to Rabaul and Australian New Guinea Administrative Unit (ANGAU) officers then took over the local administration. As part of this process Major General Ito Takeo (Commander of Japanese forces on New Ireland) surrendered his sword to Eather in a brief ceremony on the sloop HMAS *Swan*. During the formalities, Ito and his staff must have been uncomfortably aware of the presence of a sailor with a Thompson submachine-gun at the ready in case there was any trouble. Any such act was unlikely in the extreme and no doubt Eather was being deliberately rude to his enemy. New Ireland's Kaivieng had been an important Japanese port, seaplane base and airfield, and had been virtually destroyed by Allied bombing.[9] Its rehabilitation would prove to be a major task.

Only one letter written while Eather was at Rabaul is known to have survived the intervening years. It was penned to his parents on 1 November 1945. Apart from discussing his duties, this letter again demonstrates his intense dislike of the Japanese now under his command. At the same time it also shows that he would not allow his troops to mistreat the enemy, despite his own obvious repugnance towards them:

Dear Mother & Dad . . .
I am kept very busy here. I get little time to myself, not that I'd have much use to put it to beyond a swim & a spot of fishing. There is quite good fishing up here, pike & mackerel. Some of our chaps have caught some but I haven't had time yet to go out.

Everyday brings its problems. Some things I am forced to spend time on make me hopping mad. Some darn fool writes home & draws a longbow about being ordered about by Jap officers & being fined for striking a Jap. Such stuff is nonsense. Then some bigger fool still takes it up and writes to his member [of parliament] about it who writes to the Minister who writes to the Army HQ who writes to me! Most of the writers are anonymous & the whole darn thing works because some kid writes a letter home trying to impress.

I regret to say I have had to court-martial several chaps on charges of robbery under arms. They stuck up Japs with a tommy gun & stole watches, pens and what not. The real 'Ned Kelly' act but even if it is the Jap, it's thieving & I won't have it. Why darn it, it makes Austs just as bad as the Jap himself when they do things like that. I wish to heaven I could use one of those atomic bombs & rid myself of all the Japs! [author's note: newsreels of the horrors of Hiroshima and Nagasaki had not yet reached the island; had Eather realised the terrible suffering of the civilian populations in Hiroshima and Nagasaki, he may not have made such a comment.]

I have a big crowd of Japs in custody who are accused of war crimes & I'm waiting for [an] order to go ahead & try them. The order is on its way, I believe. I wonder if I will have to hang any of them? Many of them deserve it . . .

Our Japs up here are still hard at work. It is marvellous to see the improvements in the place since we arrived here. Building[s] are going up everywhere. Camps are getting more & more comfortable & will become more comfortable as time goes on & material becomes available. The troops have plenty [of time] to do what [they want] with half of every day off for sport & swimming & educational studies. They spend the AM working in & about camp. Some of course have to work [longer] but as it's mainly guarding Jap working parties it's not very hard but it's long for the Japs [as their working] hours are from six to six.

One company of troops—with a large allocation of automatic weapons in case of breakout attempts—guarded each prison compound but the Japanese caused little trouble. However, the guards were wary of them, at times noting that the hatred and animosity towards them was almost palpable—feelings certainly reciprocated by many of the Australians.

In an article in the newspaper *New Guinea Gold*, titled 'Strict Discipline for Rabaul Japs', the following description of the administration of the Japanese was offered on 3 September:

A firm policy is being adopted toward the Japanese in Rabaul. They will be treated not as POW, but as disarmed enemy troops who have been beaten in combat. There will be no question of paying them for work performed.

Major General K.W. Eather, GOC 11 Aust Div, has announced that while working on construction and maintenance of camps, the Japs will be subject to strict discipline.

The Jap working parties would be called to attention by their Australian guards if any Australian officer passed, General Eather instructed. Japs would at all times salute Australian officers, who would not return the salute.

Australian troops were at all times to remember the treatment that Australian prisoners had received at the hands of the Japs.

There would be no fraternising, no bartering and no trading for souvenirs, while the Japs would not be offered cigarettes.

Hours of work for Jap labour have been fixed at 0630 to 1830 daily, except Sunday, with one hour for lunch and ten minutes rest morning and afternoon. If they are camped within one hour's march of their work they are not to be carried by motor transport.

By Australian standards Eather was a harsh administrator. By Japanese standards he was generous. While twelve-hour working days may not have been easy in the tropics, complaints of cruelty and ill-treatment of Japanese prisoners made after the war seem to have been the preserve of soldiers found guilty of war crimes. Of over 100 000 Japanese held at Rabaul in August 1945, 402 would die of illness, accident or natural causes before the last of them were repatriated in November 1947. When it is considered that they were held on an island subject to tropical diseases such as malaria, the total hardly seems excessive.

As Eather had forecast to his parents, war crimes trials commenced and the 1st Australian War Criminals Compound was set up at Rabaul to house suspects and the convicted. Rabaul became an important focus point for war crimes trials and punishment. War criminals found guilty and sentenced to jail in other areas under Australian administration were all incarcerated at Rabaul pending their removal to Japan for long-term imprisonment.

In no less than 188 separate trials, 390 Japanese and Korean defendants had their fates decided at Rabaul.[10] Typical charges included murder, rape, beating resulting in death, cannibalism, beating, ill-treatment and torture. Two hundred and sixty-six of those tried were found guilty. A significant minority of those convicted (93) received death sentences. Eighty were hanged; the remainder went before firing squads.[11] Four convicted war criminals died by accident or natural causes before their sentences could be carried out and another three committed suicide.

The details revealed in some of these trials were horrific. In one case during 1942, a Japanese doctor had a captured Australian officer brought to his field hospital and strapped to the operating table. The doctor proceeded to cut the heart out of the still-conscious prisoner, just to see what would happen. Some of the death sentences were passed, not surprisingly, against Kempetai troops—the infamous Japanese secret police. These soldiers had brutalised and murdered military prisoners, civilian internees and indigenous people alike. Even German missionaries—citizens of an Axis power—had been murdered on New Ireland.[12]

Others found guilty of lesser crimes received sentences of from five to 30 years' imprisonment. Some high-ranking Japanese officers were among those convicted. General Imamura, who had commanded the Japanese at Rabaul and was therefore ultimately responsible for all the crimes committed there during the period of his command, received a ten-year sentence.[13] In his role as military governor, Major General Eather was not personally involved in these trials, but it was his troops who executed the condemned.

Before his own trial commenced, in a meeting with Eather, General Imamura expressed the view that 'considerable fairness' was being shown by the Australians. However, he wanted the military courts to 'take the war circumstances into account' when making judgments.[14] In this, it seems, Imamura was asking that the Japanese forces' (and his own) repeated failures to adhere to the Geneva Conventions and the other accepted rules of war be put aside. Eather would never have agreed to this even if he'd had the authority to do so.

Not surprisingly, the administration of the indigenous population was a more pleasing task and Eather took a strong interest in their welfare. Documents relating to the reoccupation of Rabaul and the re-establishment of the Australian administration show a genuine—

if paternalistic—concern for the welfare of the local people. Plans were made to provide rations for up to 20 000 people per day during the early stages of the occupation, while medical assistance and relief supplies, including cooking equipment and utensils, clothing, blankets and gardening tools, were freely distributed in large quantities.[15] Eather never forgot that the people of New Guinea had suffered greatly in the war and that they had played an important role in assisting the Australians to win the vital 1942 campaigns.

For the Australians, with the possible exception of those involved in the war crimes trials, garrisoning Rabaul was not an onerous task. Apart from enjoying the races when they were not on guard duty or training, the troops watched movies, played sport and held concerts. Some volunteered for service in Japan as part of the British Commonwealth Occupation Force. Others commenced a variety of educational courses provided by the Army. Keeping the troops occupied and motivated was easier said than done, however. The war was over and they had had their fill of the Army and the tropics. Almost all wanted to go home, and as quickly as possible. Eather was well aware of this problem and urged his junior commanders to pay special attention to maintaining morale.

A number of social and ceremonial events were held with the former POWs and civilian internees. Eather attended a concert and inspected a parade of the Chinese soldiers with their commander, Lieutenant Colonel Woo Yen, which marked the 34th anniversary of the establishment of the Chinese Republic. The Indians also held a number of ceremonial events, and on at least one occasion invited Eather to a concert where they sang and performed sword dances in his honour.[16]

With the provision of adequate medical attention, some of these former prisoners recovered surprisingly quickly from their ordeals. Dressed in rags when recovered, they were initially re-clothed in Australian uniforms, and were grateful to their Australian allies. One senior Chinese officer—probably Lieutenant Colonel Yen—presented Eather with a ricepaper scroll, the only private possession he had been able to conceal from his captors. It had been rolled tightly, then flattened and kept sewn into a seam of his clothing for several years.

On 28 October, General Blamey visited Rabaul and a parade was called for the garrison. To fit Blamey's timetable and to avoid the heat of the day, the parade was held in the early morning. This meant, unfortunately, that some of the outlying garrisons were woken as early as 12.30 am to be ready and in place. Never a popular commander, Blamey was cursed by the soldiers as they marched to and from the parade ground, not realising that their own divisional commander was actually responsible for the early start time of the parade and that it had been planned this way for their own welfare as much as to fit in with the Commander-in-Chief's schedule.[17] Other ceremonial events held at Rabaul included smaller parades where Major General Eather presented gallantry medals for wartime service to some of his men, including members of the Papuan Battalion.

On 1 November Eather wrote to his parents of Blamey's visit:

> Gen Blamey was up here last Sat & Sun & we held a parade for him. To escape the intense heat of the day I held it at 7.30 am. It went off very well indeed & the C-in-C in his address to the men complimented them on it. He spoke of a number of things including 'going home' but he confessed he could not see how every one of them could go while over 100,000 Japs remained here.
>
> He seemed to be very fit & well & the attacks made on him [in the press and in parliament] do not seem to worry him in the slightest but I think he must feel it underneath. To me it is disgraceful to think that a great man who has done what he has for Aust in the last six years should be open to attacks as he has been.

On 28 December, Australian Prime Minister Ben Chifley also visited Rabaul—a visit Eather perhaps hosted with some concern as he was aware of the mood of his men. The Prime Minister chatted to the soldiers but specifically refused to answer any questions relating to their return to Australia. This made them angry and restless.[18]

By early 1946 however, the Japanese began to be repatriated in large numbers—the first draft set sail on the demilitarised aircraft carrier *Katsuragi* on 26 February. Even this first movement angered some of the Australian garrison, who felt the prisoners were receiving preferential treatment while they remained at Rabaul. Certainly, the Japanese headquarters was allowed to select the order in which their soldiers, with the exception of war crimes' suspects and witnesses, were to be repatriated.

Australian Prime Minister Ben Chifley is greeted by Major General Eather on his arrival at Rabaul, 28 December 1945. Visits by politicians and senior officers caused some difficulties for Eather, as they were unable or unwilling to give the men any idea as to when they would be returning to Australia.

Photo courtesy of the Australian War Memorial (AWM 120886)

The Australians, however, would be going home in the near future as shipping became available and the numbers of Japanese on the island dwindled. In this process, the 11th Division was kept relatively up to strength; replacement troops with less tropical service were brought in and substituted for those with long service, who were allocated a higher priority for return to Australia and discharge.

Unfortunately, most of the replacements sent to Rabaul did not wish to be there either. Of one group of 1300 who arrived at Simpson Harbour from Borneo, around 900 refused to disembark and demanded to be sent on to Australia. On being made aware of the problem, Eather tried to reason with them and promised that no charges would be laid if the men disembarked by the end of the day. He also told them that they could put their case for early return personally to the Minister for the Army, who would soon visit Rabaul.

As an additional 'inducement' to the decision-making process, the Military Governor ordered that no water or food was to be delivered to the ship until the matter was resolved. Fortunately, the soldiers straggled ashore in small numbers throughout the day before the incident assumed the nature of a serious mutiny. Unfortunately, the Minister could offer them no hope of an immediate return to Australia—something that Eather would have been well aware of when he made the offer.[19]

On 20 April 1946, the dwindling Australian garrison held the last meeting of the 'Rabaul Racing Club'. Although there were still some troops on New Britain, in June the garrison's work was essentially completed when the last Japanese prisoners sailed. A provisional civilian administration would now operate. New Britain was, in fact, the very last area of either Papua or New Guinea to be handed over to the civil authorities following the cessation of hostilities.

11
A celebration of victory

Although rather crowded, the ship is fairly comfortable & is feeding the Contingent like fighting cocks. Everybody aboard seems happy enough. All sorts of entertainment is arranged from quiz sessions to picture shows up on the quarter deck . . . It is very pleasant to sit up on deck & watch the flicks.

Major General Eather, en route to the United Kingdom on HMAS *Shropshire*

Major General Eather was not at Rabaul to see the end of the military occupation of the area, for the Australian Army had one last task for him to perform. The British Government had decided to hold a massive celebration in London to commemorate the first anniversary of victory in World War II, and all Allied countries were invited to send a combined Army, Navy and Air Force contingent. From his post in tropical Rabaul, more than half a world away from the London plans, Eather was selected to fill the appointment of General Officer Commanding the Australian Victory March Contingent. This appointment would be his last as an active officer in the Australian Army.[1] Records show he took up his new appointment on 28 March 1946, but there has been some suggestion that the 11th Division's commander was not aware that he had been given this duty. Indeed, it seems that when he left Rabaul the month after this official appointment was made, Eather was preparing for the termination of his military service and had begun to unwind a little, as the following anecdote suggests.

While attending a captain's party in Rabaul harbour on the supply ship *British Ambassador*, on which he was returning to Sydney, Eather was relaxing on deck with a group of officers of various ranks.

One junior officer who admired his general's reputation as a first-class fighting man quipped, 'I'd follow you anywhere, sir,' to which Eather replied, 'Very well then,' promptly stood up and, without warning, dived overboard. Once the others got over their shock, they reminded their junior colleague of his statement and told him he had better follow his general 'anywhere', which he reluctantly did—fully clothed, like Eather. For the rest of the voyage the junior officer was careful not to make any other rash statements which he might come to regret. The *British Ambassador* had for some time been chartered to make regular supply runs to Rabaul. The captain had got to know Eather and enjoyed his company, presenting him with an engraved silver cigarette case on this voyage as a token of their friendship.

It is interesting to ponder why Eather was selected for this high-profile ceremonial duty in London—a duty which many a senior officer would vie for in normal times. As a pre-war Militia officer, he could be assured that his military career would shortly be over. Simply put, there were now too many Staff Corps (regular officers) to find employment for in an army soon to shrink to miniscule proportions. As deserving as he was, it is possible that the appointment had been offered to other senior officers who had preferred to remain in Australia where they would be in a better position to influence their future prospects. In any event, Eather had made his own position clear in an interview shortly after his appointment was announced. 'Major General Eather has no ambition to be a permanent soldier', stated the *Age* on 18 April 1946.

In an interview which appeared in the *Sydney Morning Herald* in 1973, after stating he had no idea why he was selected, Eather recalled:

> At the time, I had just handed over my command—the 11th Australian Division in Rabaul—and I was on my way back to Australia in a fleet tanker.
>
> I must have omitted telling anyone I was going down [to Australia], because for a long time they couldn't find me to tell me that I had been chosen for the job.

The Victory March Contingent, comprising personnel—many of them highly decorated—from the Navy, Army and Air Force, gathered in Melbourne after about a month of individual service training. Among those selected were a number of Victoria Cross holders, including Private Richard Kelliher who had won his award with the 25th Brigade.[2] The breakdown of the Contingent was:

Royal Australian Navy	30 (including two women)
Australian Army	160 (including ten women)
Royal Australian Air Force	60 (including seven women)

The formation of the Victory Contingent had involved some controversy. When the issue was first raised in the media, members of the Women's Land Army and the Merchant Navy wanted to be included.[3] After some consideration the Government refused these requests, deserving as these groups were of representation, on the basis that the other participating countries were only sending military personnel. Elements of the Returned Services League agitated for the appointment of the now-retired General Sir Thomas Blamey as Contingent Commander, bluntly stating that it was disgraceful that he had not been appointed in the first place.[4] Blamey had stood virtually no chance of obtaining this ceremonial appointment, however. Even though the Government had given a commitment to re-enlist discharged veterans for this duty, Blamey had not had the Government's support while still serving and since retirement had been a vehement critic of Government policy.

A small advance party of two officers and two other ranks flew to the United Kingdom in the first days of April to look after administrative matters. The main body of the Contingent embarked in the RAN cruiser HMAS *Shropshire* and set sail on 19 April. Another small group selected from the Occupation Force in Japan also flew directly to London.[5] During the outward voyage, *Shropshire* stopped at Adelaide and Perth where the Contingent marched through the streets. While crossing the Great Australian Bight, *Shropshire* encountered a number of storms which did some damage to the ship and left many of its passengers seasick.

During the voyage Eather wrote to his mother:

> Although rather crowded, the ship is fairly comfortable & is feeding the Contingent like fighting cocks. Everybody aboard seems happy

enough. All sorts of entertainment is arranged from quiz sessions to picture shows up on the quarter deck. Fortunately the weather is warmer now than when we were in Melbourne & Perth & it is very pleasant to sit up on deck & watch the flicks.

I am living in the captain's day quarters [Eather outranked *Shropshire's* captain and as a courtesy he gave the general his quarters], he having moved to his sea cabin up under the bridge. The quarters consist of a sleeping cabin, bathroom, dining saloon & lounge & they are all right at the stern of the ship where one gets most of the ship's movement. Thank heavens I'm a pretty good sailor or the pitching & tossing would certainly have made me sea sick long ago. Each evening the Captain has a party of eight to dinner. Six of us eat all meals here, the Capt, Brig Moten who I know very well, young Bob Lyall my ADC, Matron-in-Chief Sage and Chief Officer Clements of the WRANS . . .

There are nineteen women aboard, members of the Army, Naval & Air Force Women's Services & they are fitting into the ship's routine very well. They all seem very nice girls. Just these last few days they are pestering everybody aboard to make one of those little felt animal toys which they hope to have a thousand of to present to some children's hospital on our arrival. Some of the animals are pretty weird and wonderful looking beasts too! So far I have not been tackled but I fear the worst!

Eather also reflected in this letter that while he was away his daughter Isobel would be married, and he would miss his father's birthday and Mother's Day yet again. For over six years he had spent very little time with his family. He wrote that he would be 'very glad when it's all over & I shall be home once again for good'.

While at sea, official war artist Geoffrey Mainwaring painted Eather's portrait. This fine work now hangs in the collection of the Australian War Memorial in Canberra. To help pass the time, Eather read extensively about Australia in case he was required to make any impromptu speeches while in London. He was also given £1000 by the Government with which he was to entertain the troops.[6]

Shropshire docked at Portsmouth on 30 May and the Contingent disembarked and was addressed by J.A. Beasley, the Australian High Commissioner to the United Kingdom. The Contingent was

A CELEBRATION OF VICTORY

quartered in a massive tent city in Hyde Park in company with the troops of the other countries. In the lead-up to the march the Australians socialised among themselves and enjoyed the generous hospitality of the British people and that of the other contingents.[7]

As a goodwill gesture to the British people, who were still suffering under wartime rationing conditions, *Shropshire* had been loaded with hard-to-obtain foods which were handed over to the authorities for distribution. The Australians' personal rations were often given away as well. Such 'luxuries' as fresh fruit were rarely seen in the United Kingdom at this time. One newspaper covering the Victory Contingent recorded the spectacle of Australian service personnel wandering about the parks looking for the most needy and giving away their food.[8] One young girl given an orange, after getting over her shock at seeing the fruit in the first place, burst into tears with gratitude. *Shropshire* came to be known as the 'grocery ship'.

The Australians were also visited by a number of dignitaries in the lead-up to the march. Wing Commander Rollo Kingsford-Smith, a distinguished RAAF bomber pilot and commander of the RAAF detachment, noted two of these:

> One day Winston Churchill came to visit us. He was no longer Prime Minister but he was the 'grand old statesman', the man who won the war. We fell in along a narrow road in the Park for the old man to inspect us ... He came to me and said how delighted he was to see such a fine body of men from the Free French Air Force. I was in my blue RAAF uniform with a clear 'Australia' patch on each shoulder and there had been thousands of us in London and in squadrons all over England for the four years until the previous June. The colour of the ... French uniform and its cut was nothing like ours. Astonished and somewhat upset I dared to tell him that we were Australians pointing to my shoulder patches. His minders were aghast at this and before they could whisk him away from the rude colonial he came back with 'Then why are you wearing a French uniform!' I did not reply—I was lost for words and he was led away before I could think of any.
>
> King George, Queen Elizabeth and the two teenage Royal Princesses next inspected us. The King even knew who we were and looking carefully at the campaign ribbons my men were wearing,

his comments indicated he was bewildered that the majority were wearing the ribbon of the Pacific Star. He seemed unaware that most Australian Forces had been involved in the life and death struggle in the Pacific against the Japanese.[9]

There were a number of official entertainments and receptions for the troops and officers. Wing Commander Kingsford-Smith recalled that the senior officers of all contingents were invited to a function at Hampton Court Palace where 'what I believe is the largest and oldest grape vine in the world was shown to me. We were the guests of the King and Queen. The Monarch was obviously relaxed and enjoying himself, showing that he was still one of the people'.[10] Eather attended this function and was presented to the King and Queen.

One of the other notable people Eather met in London was Admiral Lord Louis Mountbatten. With his senior officers, Eather was invited to afternoon tea at the admiral's town house. Arriving at the appointed hour, the Australians were met at the door by Lady Mountbatten. Telling Eather and his officers that the admiral was upstairs putting on his tie, she told her guests that she would tell Lord Louis they had arrived. Expecting Lady Mountbatten to disappear into the house, much to everyone's surprise she turned around and called up the staircase in a very loud voice, 'Oh Dicky, they are here now.' The Australians enjoyed a pleasant afternoon in the admiral's company.[11]

The Victory March was held on 8 June. Troops from 21 nations marched through the streets of London, which were lined by an extremely large and warmly cheering crowd. The King took the salute. Also present was Winston Churchill and the serving prime ministers of all the Dominions—with the sole exception of Australia. The Australian Contingent, led by Major General Eather, marched proudly through the streets with the soldiers wearing their conspicuous slouch hats and the Air Force personnel in their distinctive dark blue uniforms. As they approached the King, Eather gave the command 'eyes right' and smartly saluted Australia's head of state. It can only be assumed how pleased and vindicated Eather felt as he led his troops past the Monarch. His amazing journey from obscurity as a Sydney dental technician, through the North African Campaign, the bitter fighting in New Guinea and subsequent

Portrait of Major General Ken Eather, CB, CBE, DSO painted by Geoffrey Mainwaring on HMAS *Shropshire*, 1946.

Photo courtesy of the Australian War Memorial (AWM Art 26669)

campaigns which helped ensure Australia's security and the eventual defeat of Japan, was almost over.

Two days after the march, Eather wrote home to his father:

> As you know we landed here in Portsmouth on 30 May & have had a busy time ever since. The march is over now & I do not expect to have so much to do... I have been out to some official function nearly every night & will be glad when things do ease off. However,

I should not grumble for it has not been as bad as I anticipated it might have been.

From today the troops have nearly all gone on leave. Many of them have accepted invitations from people to stay in private homes while a number have just gone off about England sight seeing. They will come back to camp on the 29th.

Arriving back in Melbourne on the 22nd Aug. The trip back will be more interesting than the one we had coming over for we are spending two days at Gibraltar & Malta, one day in Port Said, two in Colombo, four in Perth and Adelaide. Later on in the month I am going over to Germany & Belgium for a few days to have a quick look see. It should be an interesting trip.

The food situation over here is not quite as bad as I expected. There seems to be plenty of food but it is very much of a sameness. Meat, fats & fruit are particularly scarce. In fact one never sees fruit at all.

I am staying in a Service flat in the city and have meals there. It is quite comfortable. The War Office has placed a car at my disposal, a new little Austin 14 & I can get about fairly easily. The crowds in London the last few days have been huge while on the day of the march the place was packed to such a degree that many were stranded and slept in the parks.

I have found it very cold here despite it being summertime and I will be very glad to get back to our own sunlight again. It is practically impossible to buy anything without coupons & we haven't any & prices are much higher than in Australia I think.

Have met hundreds of people since I arrived & expect to meet many more before I go. There were two or three receptions given for the leaders of the various contingents & among those I have attended there have been Poles, French, Indians, Egyptians, Greeks etc & of course those from our own dominions . . .

This morning I had an interview & made a recording at the BBC for broadcasting to Australia on my impressions of the march.

After the troops returned from leave, they re-embarked in the *Shropshire* and sailed for Australia. At Gibraltar, some of the troops clashed with local police. (As Eather had predicted to his father, the trip back to Australia would indeed be more interesting than the voyage over.) In what amounted to a mini riot, a substantial public relations problem for Australia, occurred at Gibraltar. The trouble apparently started when Victory Contingent members and some of *Shropshire*'s crew freed some sailors who had been arrested for disorderly behaviour from the local prison. Baton-wielding police attempted to intervene and the ensuing fracas eventually involved around 100 Australians, police and a few civilians. Several police and Australians were injured. Claims of excessive police force were made.[12]

After this incident, signals marked 'secret' flew between the British and Australian Governments. Eather was required to explain the charges against his troops to the Minister for the Army in detail. Eventually this saga would involve the attention of many notable persons, including the Australian Secretary for Defence, Sir Frederick Shedden, the Australian Resident Minister to the United Kingdom, the Prime Ministers of both Australia and the United Kingdom, the British Chief Justice and the Governor of Gibraltar. The British Government later decided to launch an inquiry into the affair but, after Australian Government intervention, the conduct of Australian personnel was specifically excluded from the terms of reference. Without this central issue being examined, the inquiry must surely have been farcical.[13]

The riot was widely publicised in the Australian media. While some newspapers took a favourable or neutral stand on the matter, the *Argus* noted on 9 July 1946: 'there can be no excuse for the disgraceful behaviour of members of the Victory March Contingent.'

Two days later in the *Age*, Frank Forde, the Minister for the Army, stated his own position (or perhaps, more accurately, Eather's) plainly, but with some evident reluctance. After commenting that the incident had been blown out of all proportion, he went on to note:

> Whilst I do not condone any misbehaviour on the part of Service personnel, I have the greatest admiration for the gallant men of the Australian Fighting Services and therefore, more readily, accept the temperate explanation by the trusted and reliable commanding officer, Major General Eather who is one of the most successful fighting generals in the Australian Army.

Eather's views on the matter were both clear and unequivocal. He did not believe that his troops had a case to answer. He refused to lay charges against any of them or to make any official apology to the British or local authorities. For an officer always known as a harsh disciplinarian this was an interesting stand to take. The Australians clearly had some responsibility for the riot. It seems most likely that Eather was unwilling to punish personnel with excellent war records who, for the most part, would be discharged on returning to Australia.

It is hardly likely that the British Government or civil authorities at Gibraltar shared either Forde's or Eather's views on the incident.

Major General Eather disembarked from the *Shropshire* at Adelaide on 16 August 1946, travelling on to Melbourne and finally to Sydney later in the month. On 18 September, no doubt after some 'tidying up' regarding the Gibraltar incident, he relinquished command of the Australian Victory March Contingent and was transferred to the retired list of officers. Eather had been a member of the AIF for 2532 days and within that period had been overseas for 1513 days.[14] His mission to London had been a most rewarding experience and a worthy, if slightly controversial, conclusion to a distinguished military career.

12

Farewell to all that

> *The Board commends the work of Major General K.W. Eather who retires at the end of July 1979 after his dedicated services to the Foundation since his appointment as our first Executive Director.*
>
> Dr Jack Beale, Chairman of the Water Research Foundation of Australia, 30 June 1979

Life out of uniform held significant challenges for General Eather. Although in many ways he was happy to leave military service behind, he had to readjust to civilian life and to a family that had seen little of him for several years. Indeed, his children had virtually grown up without a father in their most important years. Like many thousands of others, his family had been robbed by the war in various ways.

After having been involved in such momentous events, and having attained so much and travelled so widely, Eather now felt unable to return to his pre-war profession. Indeed, he felt he would not be happy with any form of indoor employment. Yet for a time a new occupation eluded him. His career options were also hampered by the less than comfortable financial situation brought about by his decision to sell his dental practice for much less than it was worth to accept an early appointment in the AIF. Although much better off than the rank and file soldier, an Australian general's pay was not substantial and Eather left the Army with limited savings.[1]

Nonetheless, those savings were sufficient for the eventual purchase of a poultry farm named Wilbetfarm near Penrith, to the west of Sydney. Eather may have made use of his repatriation benefits to help in this venture. The family moved from their former home at Bankstown and, in time, successfully built up the farm. It was an activity perhaps not entirely unexpected. For many years Eather's father had kept chickens and he had also developed an interest. The two occasionally corresponded on various aspects of this activity during the war.

Eather would now face a different and unpredictable enemy— the Australian environment. While being close to Sydney may have mitigated against some of the natural hazards of being a primary producer, he was not immune to the vagaries of the weather. In 1955 destructive floods affected much of New South Wales, while the following year what some described as the worst drought in 50 years commenced. Twenty months later drought conditions were still prevailing. It is not clear how badly these disasters affected Wilbetfarm but there must have been some impact.

The importance of maintaining a viable stock of birds would not have been lost on Eather. *The Australian Primary Producers' Advocate* noted in the early 1950s that 86 per cent of poultry farms held less than 500 hens and that on farms with less than 500 or 600 birds, poultry farming was supported by some other form of income generation. It seems likely that Eather would have wanted substantially more than 600 birds, even if not right away.

Along with the vagaries of the weather, the economic conditions of the times also adversely affected poultry farmers' ability to earn a living. In a background of declining production levels, in March 1955 poultry farmers asked the New South Wales State Government to introduce a system of licensing for all individuals owning more than twelve chickens, with the number of licences also very tightly controlled. This proposal was an attempt to increase the current low income of farmers brought about by a large proportion of their production being sold at low prices overseas. At the same time, the farmers contended, eggs sold locally (all eggs were sold to the Australian Egg Board) were being retailed at too high a price to encourage increased local consumption. The government saw things differently and turned down the request. The minister noted that Australia's rapidly increasing population under the migration program would eventually see more eggs consumed locally.

Significantly, Eather chose not to become involved with the Citizens' Military Forces (formerly the Militia) when that force was re-established in 1948. With his distinguished war record, Eather could easily have laid strong claim for appointment to the command of the CMF's 2nd (Infantry) Division as a major general. His decision not to continue part-time soldiering could have been due to a combination of reasons. His less than comfortable financial situation may have meant that he felt it necessary to devote all his time to establishing himself in civilian life. Equally, he may have been simply too tired of military life to put on a uniform again.

Despite the time it took away from his attempts to re-establish himself in civilian life, Eather agreed to numerous requests for assistance from Gavin Long, the general editor of the army volumes of the official history of Australia in World War II.² From 1946 to 1957 he read 'in confidence' drafts of various volumes and provided additional information, critical comment and various suggestions on the service details of the 2/1st Battalion, the 25th Brigade and the 7th Division. Fitting in with the various writers' deadlines and requirements proved to be a time-consuming task. Australian War Memorial records show that he assisted Long with *To Benghazi* and *The Final Campaigns*, and David Dexter with *The New Guinea Offensives*. From the surviving records it is apparent that Eather provided valuable information to the historians due to his habit of keeping a daily diary and other records, as well as providing personal recollections.

Surprisingly, there is no mention of Eather having helped Dudley McCarthy with *South West Pacific Area First Year—Kokoda to Wau*, the volume which told the story of the vital and controversial Kokoda Track fighting, for which he could have provided important insights. It may be that Eather did assist McCarthy but that the records have since been lost or destroyed. Alternatively, it is possible that McCarthy and Long (the general editor) may have made a decision not to involve the principal participants in these controversies. Although they would have sacrificed important insights on the campaigns, in this way they could work through and come to their own conclusions about the rights and wrongs of the commanders' decisions, free from potential bias or unpleasant pre-publication argument from aggrieved senior officers.

Wilbetfarm was close enough to Sydney to enable the Eathers to have regular contact with the rest of their relatives in Sydney and Chris Brookes, one of the general's nephews, recalls numerous visits as he was growing up:

Once, with my cousins, we helped collect the eggs but became so excited at the sight of so many eggs that we started to run to get them—and frightened the chooks. We were firmly pulled into line. I remember a pen for the sick chickens. It was called 'Belsen'. If they recovered they returned to their labours but, if there was little hope, they were put out of their misery.[3]

Shortly after he returned to Australia, Eather decided to join the Returned Services' League. Walking into his local branch, he asked a clerk if he could become a member. The clerk took out an application form and began to fill it out. When he got to the section containing military details he asked for Eather's service number and was told 'NX3'. The clerk wrote this down and paused, waiting for his visitor to supply the remainder of the number (most veterans' numbers were up to six digits long). When Eather said nothing more the clerk asked for the rest of the number but was told there was no more. Surprised, he moved on to the next section of the form and asked for his rank. On being told 'Major General', his mouth fell open and he summoned the club president to personally receive their distinguished new member![4]

Concern for the welfare of his men and for the many widows and children of those who were killed and wounded under his command led Eather to become an active member of the Legacy movement.[5] He also took a hand in the formation of the Association of the First Infantry Battalions, chairing the foundation meeting. It seems that he did not seek election as the association's president (although any claim he may have made to that office would have been compelling), perhaps for the same reason that he did not become active in the Citizens' Military Forces. Instead, he agreed to be one of the association's patrons—a largely honorary appointment.

An incident that occurred at Wilbetfarm showed a very different side to Eather's personality which might have surprised many of his soldiers. When the family's pet dog grew so old that it was in constant ill-health and pain, he came to the reluctant conclusion that it had to be put down. It was a decision that he had put off for some time but eventually he took the dog outside and shot it. After burying the dog, Eather quietly went inside, shut himself in a bedroom and wept for the pet that he had loved.[6]

Tragedy struck in 1948 when Ken Eather, Junior, was killed in a motorcycle accident. This was a devastating blow to the family, and particularly to the retired general. Eather later admitted that this accident was the worst thing that ever happened in his life. The farm now held painful memories and eventually he came to realise that he needed to find a new occupation to take him away from Penrith.

Eather became active in The Primary Producers' Association of New South Wales and in 1953, at the age of 52, was elected state president.[7] He held this appointment for five years, despite the amount of time it involved which could have been used in developing his own farm. Accepting this position as a public service would prove an important stepping stone in the next phase of his remarkable life, although this could not have been foreseen at the time.

In the mid-1950s, in his capacity as president of the Primary Producers' Association, Eather attended a seminar by a group promoting the wise and efficient use of Australia's limited water resources.[8] In 1955 the Water Research Foundation of Australia (WRFA) was formed as a result of the interest generated by this seminar. The fledgling organisation developed rapidly, and within a few years its board of trustees (all honorary) realised that to operate efficiently the WRFA would need a full-time senior manager. Subsequently Eather was appointed executive director of the organisation.

The executive director was responsible for the implementation of the board's policies and for the general administration of the Foundation. Thus an entirely different career commenced, one that would prove of great benefit not only to the organisation he had joined but to the Australian nation. In this new role, Eather's sense of service and leadership abilities would, once again, be fully utilised.

The WRFA was the first organisation in Australia solely devoted to research into water-related issues. Its formation had been prompted by, among other things, the implementation of the Snowy Mountains Scheme and the need to coordinate the various research projects being undertaken by the CSIRO, universities and other bodies. The WRFA also initiated new research projects under a system of research fellowships and published the findings of this research.[9]

The organisation itself later noted the importance of its role:

...to Australia, the driest continent, with its capricious rainfall, water has special significance. The effective management of this vital resource poses tremendous physical, economic, environmental and social challenges—at all levels of government and to all sections of the community.

Professor C.F. Munro, the research director of the WRFA, was rather more blunt when he was quoted in an edition of *The Australian Primary Producers' Advocate* in January 1956: 'Australians are living in a fool's paradise if they think all is well with the nation's basic water reserves.'

The WRFA's board, members and associates included leading researchers and scientists. While as a group and individually they provided a substantial contrast to Eather's previous working environment, he seems to have quickly established effective and harmonious working relationships with his new colleagues. Eather and Adeline later left the farm and moved to Kingsford in Sydney, closer to his work. In early 1965 the couple were living in a flat on Houston Road, Kingsford, although this may not have been their first residence in the area.[10]

In the course of time the WRFA became a truly national body, with committees in all states and regional committees in North Queensland, the Illawarra and Ballarat. The organisation also grew internally. Apart from the original Board of Trustees and Research Committee, a Publicity Committee and a Finance and Administration Committee were later formed.

Eather regularly had dealings with researchers, scientists, business representatives, public servants, politicians and dignitaries. During the 1960s he was even able to renew his acquaintance with Prime Minister R.G. Menzies, whom he had entertained over lunch at Tobruk in 1941.[11] The growing stature and importance of the WRFA was reflected in its burgeoning list of sponsors, which eventually included BHP, James Hardie Industries, Carlton & United Breweries, Commonwealth Bank, Esso, Comalco, Kraft Foods, Dalgety Australia, Western Mining and Australian Paper Manufacturers. There were many others in an impressive list which was a tribute to Eather's advocacy and passion for the organisation's work.

Although at times Eather had to work closely with politicians, he did not particularly care for them as a group, even those on the conservative side to which he had a personal leaning. Nonetheless, he took a pragmatic view of his necessary relationship, ensuring the aims and needs of the WRFA were always well represented. At social functions he was a charming and courteous host, but he did not suffer fools gladly.

While helping to develop an organisation he believed in, over time Eather managed to come to terms with the loss of his son. Adeline, who was perhaps even more devastated by the tragedy, took up the management of a small store in Lakemba as a way of filling in her own time and also of adding to the family income, which was still not generous. Eather helped out on weekends by delivering grocery orders to local residents.[12] These customers would have been surprised to realise that their delivery-man was the director of an important scientific organisation, not to mention a retired general!

Such action was typical of Eather. During the Great Depression, his Militia battalion had once marched through suburban streets to participate in some field training. Lack of funds meant there was no horse to pull the battalion's water cart and the soldiers had to take turns pushing the heavy vehicle to their destination. Although he was the commanding officer, Eather did not use his position to avoid a less than pleasant duty and one which many in a similar position would have considered beneath their dignity.[13] He took his turn with the privates and non-commissioned officers, pushing the cart through the rutted streets. Even visitors to the WRFA offices would not have known that they were associating with a highly decorated two-star general. His cluttered office held virtually no reminders of his service. Two cut-down artillery shell casings used as rather unconventional ashtrays were the only items that hinted at a military past.

Although he did prize the two chess sets (one a full-size set and the other a miniature travelling set) that had been presented to him by some of his soldiers during the war, he was generous with his other wartime souvenirs. Relatives and friends were given a number of Japanese swords that he had collected, possibly even the sword he took from General Ito when accepting the surrender of Japanese forces on New Ireland. An Italian Beretta pistol he had taken during the fighting at Bardia or Tobruk met an ignominious fate.

Concerned that the weapon was not registered with the police, one night he disassembled it and threw the pieces into the sea.[14]

While Eather enjoyed his role with the WRFA enormously, he still maintained a strong network of friends from his days in the Army. There was no closer friend than General Allen, his former Kokoda Track commander. Sadly, Allen's health had been seriously affected by his service in the two World Wars, and his death in 1959 was deeply felt. The passing of Eather's father two years later was also distressing.

Contact with his family was important to Eather. His nephew, Chris Brookes, recalls:

> My mother [Nancy] and father were very proud of Ken and, from a young age, this same pride was instilled in my brother and me. We used to see him quite a lot and he would spend Christmas Day with us at Dee Why. He was unaffected, unassuming and it was great for us (in our early twenties) to sit with him and my father on the front verandah and have a few beers and talk.
>
> Conversation sometimes turned to military matters but he did not comment very much on military commanders past or present but he did think it funny that 'Stonewall' Jackson had been an instructor at West Point [prior to the American Civil War] to many of the Union Commanders. Ken once said 'Stonewall knew if he went "boo" here or there exactly how they [the Union commanders] would react.'
>
> My mother and father were very fond of Ken and he of them. Even in her old age, my mother continued to hero worship her brother. On my father's sudden death in 1971, Ken was one of the first to arrive at Dee Why and stood by me when making the funeral arrangements.
>
> Every Anzac Day we would watch the televised march in Sydney—just to catch a glimpse of him. On one occasion, one of the commentators described him as 'one of Australia's best known fighting soldiers'.
>
> I once heard a younger soldier say that Ken 'did not cash in on his reputation'. Knowing him, he probably would have thought 'I only did my duty'.[15]

Eather loved to visit people and also to entertain at home. Typically, like many former infantrymen, he did not like to walk anywhere and invariably looked to his car when the need to travel more than a short distance arose. He had a preference for Australian-made Chrysler Valiants and owned several in succession. Although he enjoyed motoring, family members have noted that he was 'not generous' to other road users who cut him off or who were driving in what he considered a less than satisfactory manner.[16]

In the post-war world, Eather seems to have held fairly conservative views on most public issues. In the controversy that raged over the Vietnam War he took the view that it was up to the government to decide on policy and for the troops to carry it out. He was, however, active in supporting Vietnam veterans and their emerging problems at a time when the government and large segments of the community were either uninterested or actively hostile to their needs. When the full extent of the alienation of Vietnam veterans became apparent, Eather ensured that he never left an Anzac Day march early, waiting until the Vietnam veterans at the end of the parade had all passed by. In later years this became a tiring, self-imposed commitment, but he stayed on nonetheless, to help reinforce to Vietnam veterans that they were just as important as those from earlier wars.

In 1966 Eather suffered another terrible personal loss when Adeline, his wife of 43 years, died. A solitary and lonely life loomed ahead for the retired general but sometime later, while shopping in the city, he met Kathleen Carroll. A strong attachment developed and the couple married in 1968. Their happy life together would span 25 years. Eather accepted Kathleen's son Owen—a serving Army officer—as his own.

It was typical of Eather's modesty that he had not told Kathleen much about his background while they were courting. Only when Kathleen was watching television one night with her mother and was stunned to see her husband-to-be talking about the WRFA did she discover that not only was he the director of an important scientific body but also a retired general.

This was not Eather's only television appearance for the WRFA. He also appeared on the popular television program 'Where Are

They Now?', but in general he shied away from personal publicity and turned down a number of interview requests regarding his wartime service.[17]

When he noticed that some older veterans in Returned Soldiers League clubs were mocking Vietnam veterans by telling them they had not been to a 'real war', and were therefore not worthy to be members of the RSL, Eather took direct, if subtle, action to support the young veterans. He asked Kathleen's son Owen, a captain and Vietnam veteran himself, to act as his aide-de-camp and to stand at his side in the annual Sydney Anzac Day march. It was something that the two soldiers shared right through to 1992.

When Eather found that one of Owen's friends, Captain Don Dennis, had also been mocked in an RSL club, he promptly invited Don to become another of his ADCs on Anzac Day. Thus to tens of thousands watching the march each year Eather's support of Vietnam veterans was made very public. The highly regarded World War II commander had selected Vietnam veterans to stand at his side during Australia's largest commemorative service. Eather took his message further. If he attended any major RSL ceremonial function he always invited Owen and the two of them openly wore their medals on their mess kits.[18]

In the debate regarding Australia becoming a republic Eather's views were somewhat more radical than might have been expected of a highly decorated Army officer who had held a commission personally signed by the King. He believed a republic was inevitable and was not to be feared. However, he held strong views on attempts by republicans to change the Australian flag. He contended that the two issues were not related and that the Australian flag should never be changed.

During Eather's term with the WRFA, the organisation played a pivotal role in many initiatives including the establishment of Australia's first comprehensive Water Reference Library and the formation of three ministerial bodies: the Australian Water Resources Council, the Australian Forestry Council and the Australian Environment Council. Other major achievements included the completion of a major shallow aquifer investigation in New South Wales, an expanded national conifer planting program, national floodplain mapping and a national sewage treatment program.[19]

Additionally, some 55 major research reports of regional, state or national importance were completed. Topics were of a highly diverse nature and included such important environmental issues as desertification, beach erosion, the re-use of treated waste water, water pollution, water catchments and recreational use, floods and droughts, farm uses of water and the menace of aquatic weeds. Water-related workshops were held and information bulletins on related topics prepared and made available for researchers, primary producers, industry sources and other interested parties. Monthly newsletters—personally prepared by Eather and often typeset in his own time on weekends—were distributed to members. He was also known to take water samples home on the weekends where he prepared reports and other documentation on them. One member of his family recalled: 'I well remember Ken in the basement of the University of New South Wales Civil Engineering Building, setting type and plates with a competence that belied his status.'

Dr Jack Beale, Chairman of the Board of Trustees, noted that Eather was a quiet but firm administrator who got things done efficiently and promptly: 'He had an air about him that commanded respect and a wide-held respect for his war record materially assisted in the performance of his duties.' That respect was shared by the office staff who invariably addressed him courteously as 'General' although they did not have to do so. Wherever Dr Beale and Eather travelled interstate, it seemed there was always some serving or former army colleague nearby to assist them if needed. Dr Beale also recalled that Eather worked far longer hours than was expected of him and that it was several years before he could be induced to take his first substantial period of annual leave.[20]

As much as he loved the WRFA, as the years went by Eather began to feel the need to retire. He first raised the issue with the Board of Trustees in early 1977. The Board, however, pressed him to stay on, clearly demonstrating their satisfaction with their executive director, and he allowed himself to be talked into staying. However, this could not continue indefinitely.

In January 1978, Eather's resignation was finally tendered. The conclusion of this letter stated: 'Because of my great interest in the Foundation and its important work I am reluctant to leave suddenly and would, if so desired, continue to act as executive director for a limited period to advise and assist any new appointee.'[21] The WRFA readily accepted this offer, although the eighteen months he stayed on may have been longer than he had planned or really wanted. Eather supervised the recruiting process for his replacement and finally, in June 1979, the executive director's position was re-advertised for the first time since 1958. Another retired Army officer, Brigadier E.S. Swinbourne, was selected and officially became Executive Director the following month.

After 21 years' service to the WRFA, at the age of 78 (long after most Australians had left the workforce) Eather retired. Up to the time of its closure in 2002 the WRFA had become an internationally respected organisation and its work was recognised and of value around the world. Much of its success was owed to Eather's capable and efficient administration. In honour of his achievements and selfless service Eather was made an Honorary Life Councillor of the WRFA. Only three other individuals—all of them scientists—have been granted this honour.[22]

In retirement Eather spent time, as many people do, in the company of family. With his grandson Eamon he could often be found on all fours down on the floor acting as a horse, to the delight of his young protégé. When Eamon turned seven, the retired general began to teach him how to play chess on an old chess set made in an army workshop during World War II. He also passed on to Eamon his mechanical skills and a love of reading. Owen relates that, as a result of this tutelage, Eamon now 'reads voraciously, has better mechanical skills than anyone in the family and plays such a withering chess game that, for the life of me, I still can't beat him'. Just as Colonel Lees, many years before, had played a strong role in developing an interest in military service for the future major general, so too was a similar interest passed on to Eamon. Thus, Eamon later joined the Army Reserve and subsequently volunteered for active service in East Timor where he was based at Balibo.

Of the retired general's character Owen also notes that:

> He could take infinite pains when there was time but make a point, or act, firmly and with unhesitating speed, often in the least expected manner, when that was the only way to go.
>
> Those who met Ken invariably fell to his unassuming charm,

from government ministers, to grizzly friends of mine, to hard bitten journalists, to teenage friends of his grandson. He was a 'good man' in all senses of that term. He only ever spoke harshly, and deservedly, once to me. He could, though, speak sternly when necessary and with a sternness that was biblical and final. But mostly it was a quiet admonishment of 'nick up' [a term Owen does not recall being used by anyone else] to soften family discussions that were tending to overheat.

The retired general's character and sense of duty had a major impact on the lives of many who had contact with him including stepson Owen (left), seen here at Bein Hoa, South Vietnam in 1968, and grandson Eamon, on patrol in Balibo East Timor in 2000.

Eather also spent time in his workshop constructing a working steam engine, two elaborate miniature railways and a steam-powered model boat. His early training in detailed dental work greatly assisted him in these complex and time-consuming projects. He also used his workshop to make wooden toys for underprivileged children which he passed on to the St Vincent De Paul Society for distribution. He enjoyed boating, astronomy, playing cards—especially cribbage—and attending Army reunions.[23]

He was not afraid of new technology and was an early purchaser of an Omega digital watch and of a new (German-made) colour television set.

Eather also had a love of animals, particularly birds and dogs, and maintained an aviary. (On Balikpapan his pet monkey had the disconcerting habit of drinking the ink from his fountain pen. It was also found guilty of stealing the possessions of the other officers in Brigade Headquarters!) He read widely, both non-fiction and fiction. He frequently consulted his own set of volumes of the official history of Australia in World War II, and he maintained an interest in military matters. He also enjoyed fishing—although he was noted for bringing an empty basket home. With Kathleen he would sometimes hire a cabin cruiser and spend time relaxing on Broken Bay. Eather also enjoyed playing board games, particularly if they involved strategy and calculations. He rarely lost a game of chess to anyone. The couple also occasionally went to theatre restaurants in the Sydney area.

As Kathleen was a keen racegoer, Eather became a member of both the Sydney Turf Club and the Australian Jockey Club.[24] He often went to the races on Saturdays with his wife and family, although this was more for the company than for any strong interest in racing. It may well have been while he was at the races that Eather met, or possibly renewed his acquaintance with, Sir Robert Askin, the then Premier of New South Wales and a former sergeant who had served with the 25th Brigade under Eather's command. Notwithstanding their shared service, it is probable that Eather, who already had a healthy dislike for politicians, would have had little time for Askin, who had immersed himself, and his government, in numerous scandals. As related in Appendix III, it seems that Askin would later play a significant role in ensuring that Eather's exceptional service to the WRFA was not acknowledged by an appropriate award.

It is interesting to note that while Eather experienced no conflict in finally trading in his Australian-made Valiant and purchasing one of the first German Volkswagen Golfs sold in Sydney, when Owen sold his Australian-made car and replaced it with an imported Japanese model, Eather was visibly shocked. Although he was a pragmatic man, at times he found it hard to accept Japan's growing post-war relationship with Australia.

A keen astronomer, in 1986 Eather watched the appearance of Halley's Comet with considerable interest, as did millions of people around the world. Unlike most of those watchers, Eather was one of a much smaller group viewing this spectacle for the second time. He told Owen that the comet appeared much brighter on the first occasion he viewed it in 1910, sitting in a dinghy in Manly Cove with his father.

For many years, Eather led the Sydney Anzac Day March—the largest Anzac commemoration in Australia. On 25 April he would be seen, although advancing in years, standing proudly in an Army Land Rover as he led the veterans of all wars through the streets. His ongoing involvement in Anzac Day reflected his close association with his former soldiers and a concern for their welfare. He intended that those who had died in their country's service would not be forgotten.

Like many of his soldiers, Eather's health had been affected by the war. Pneumonia induced by dust inhalation, rough living and exhaustion, combined with the effects of numerous malarial attacks, resulted in a susceptibility to illness, particularly during the cold of winter. As time went by, the recovery period for these illnesses increased. During the 1980s he became desperately ill and nearly died from the effects of influenza. As his health deteriorated, he was granted a part disability pension by the Department of Veterans' Affairs which was eventually increased.[25]

At one time during the Hawke Government's administration, a public servant with the Department of Veterans' Affairs sought to have Eather's pension reduced on the grounds that he was not sick enough to be entitled to it. Even the final correspondence from the Department, which conceded that he could keep his pension, was calculated to hurt and offend. The tone of this document implied that Eather should consider himself grateful for this favourable treatment and the cover letter was rudely addressed to 'Mr Eather', even though the assessment documentation attached made it clear that the Department knew it was corresponding with a high-ranking and distinguished Army officer.[26] The affair hurt Eather and his family deeply, a hurt made worse by the fact that for several years he had refused to apply for the veterans' pension—which entitled him to substantially more than the aged pension—as he did not wish to be a burden to the taxpayer.

In early 1992 Eather's health deteriorated alarmingly. He did manage to attend and lead the Sydney Anzac Day March once more, the event that meant so much to him, but the effort exhausted him and greatly alarmed his family. The parade commander remained to watch the entire march after his own official duties were completed. Towards the end, when the Allied forces had marched past, he said to Owen, 'It would be wonderful if, one day, all our old enemies could come and march with us.' Time is a great healer. General Eather had forgiven his wartime Japanese enemies.

The year 1992 also saw the death of Eather's remaining sister, Nancy (Dulcie having died earlier). Eather's nephew Chris came to tell Ken and Kathleen the bad news. He was nonplussed to find his uncle alone at the time:

> I gave him the news about his sister. He gave me a beer and he had a whisky and took the news like the fine soldier he always was. I was concerned about leaving him alone and when I said this he replied 'You go, Chris, you have a lot to do and I'll be OK'. The following day he came to Mum's funeral with Kath.[27]

By the end of the year, the Department of Veterans' Affairs suggested that Eather should be admitted to Mosman Nursing Home to receive constant care. Five months later the end was very near, and he knew it. Nonetheless, he remained in good heart and 'stirred up' his nurses, who were often seen laughing with him. On 8 May, he bade Kathleen a fond farewell and told her gently and calmly that he would not be there the following day. As he had predicted, on 9 May 1993, Major General K.W. Eather, CB, CBE, DSO, DSC died peacefully in his sleep with his family about him. He was 92 years old. His two sisters, first wife and son had all predeceased him.

The day before he died, Owen and his family were, as usual, with him at the nursing home. Owen recalled that:

> We talked for a bit and, for the first and last time, I put my hand on his. He dozed for a while, waking every so often saying 'Who's that,

who's there? Are they back?' and pointing to the end of his bed. I tried to calm him but he remained restless. The third time, in a flash of inspiration, I answered 'The rearguard, that's all of them back' as I thought Ken might have remembered the fateful Imita withdrawal and all that rested on it. Amazingly, this calmed him and he slept soundly.

Was he thinking of his soldiers still? I think so and at the time of starkest danger some of his last thoughts were of the men he commanded, I am sure.

Five days later, on 14 May, his family, the Australian Army and the Australian public paid their last respects to this gallant and capable soldier and distinguished administrator when he was farewelled with full military honours in a moving funeral service at St Andrew's Anglican Cathedral, Sydney. The cathedral was filled to capacity and many mourners had to wait outside to pay their respects. Three companies of infantry from the 3rd Battalion, Royal Australian Regiment, a band and an artillery battery provided the military component for the funeral of Australia's last remaining World War II general. General Sir Francis Hassett, former Chairman of the Chiefs of Staff committee, read the eulogy and eight generals acted as pallbearers. When the service was completed, the funeral cortege with its escort of over 300 troops marched in slow time through large crowds of mourners and onlookers. Sydney's busy George Street—the same street along which Lieutenant Colonel Eather had proudly led the 2/1st Battalion prior to embarkation for North Africa in 1940—was closed from the Town Hall to Market Street. Over 1000 veterans lined George Street as an additional honour guard. At the Northern Suburbs Crematorium, North Ryde, the awaiting artillerymen fired an eleven-gun salute and the Last Post was played. Phar Lap's last race was run.

Postscript

There are a small number of modest reminders of Major General Eather's achievements. Eather Street at Ingleburn Army base, where he formed the 2/1st Infantry Battalion in 1939, is one. A memorial plaque also exists in the New South Wales Garden of Remembrance, adjacent to the Sydney War Cemetery at Rookwood. Eather Reserve, a park containing some trees, bench seating and a plaque in Bankstown, is the most substantial memorial in existence.

Appendix 1
Command assessments

As a commander of troops and an officer who played a pivotal role in the battles which decided the fate of New Guinea and, ultimately of Australia, how was Eather's command ability seen by his peers?

The official Army historian Gavin Long first met Eather in August 1944, when he visited 25th Brigade's Headquarters at Petrie to discuss the Syrian Campaign and the subsequent occupation. In one of his diaries, now held at the Australian War Memorial, he made the following annotation:

> A very happy and, I think, efficient staff [at the 25th Brigade]. This staff has a great admiration for Eather. He is quiet but very definite and commanding, reputed to read all the paperwork very carefully, seldom hammers officers down, but when he does, hammers them like a tack. Easy going Mess... They say he is very hard physically, and to me it is interesting to see officers in their 40s looking so spare and fit in contrast to the American officers of the same age, who are mostly soft and sagging...[1]

Long also made the penetrating observation that the staff in 7th Division Brigade Headquarters were of a higher standard than those of the other AIF divisions.

Major General George Vasey, commander of the 7th Division from late 1942 to mid-1944, was also in an excellent position to comment. In a discussion with journalist Reg Glennie and Gavin Long during 1944, 'he mentioned Eather was a fine commanding officer and brigadier who would *not* [author's emphasis] be able to cope with higher rank'.[2]

This was an interesting assessment, but how valid was it? In the savage and utterly vital Kokoda Track fighting, Eather had successfully, if somewhat controversially, commanded a force sometimes closer to two brigades than one in strength. He had proved to be a commander able to disregard pressure from senior officers and politicians, as evidenced by his difficult decision to initiate a withdrawal to the better defensive position at Imita Ridge. The campaigns he participated in were all ultimately successful. Indeed, American historian Eric Bergerud deemed the battle of Oivi–Gorari to have been one of the main turning points in the land war against the Japanese. Eather's 25th Brigade—with his old 2/1st Battalion attached—played the key flanking role in that shattering victory.

Perhaps Vasey's view was clouded by memories of pre-war days, when highly capable regular officers (of whom he was one) were made to play second fiddle to part-time Militia officers. Despite having substantial combat service and having won promotion in World War I, Vasey was—like other regular officers—reduced in rank after the war. Eather, on the other hand, despite being commissioned in only 1919, by 1933 was a lieutenant colonel commanding his own infantry battalion while Vasey—a well-trained, capable veteran decorated for gallantry—was not promoted to major until 1935.

The controversial manner in which Vasey assumed command of the 7th Division after the dismissal of Major General Allen also needs to be considered. Eather was a good friend of Allen and the two had known each other for many years. Allen had reluctantly supported his Brigadier's decision to withdraw to Imita and Eather had led his brigade successfully along the Kokoda Track. Notwithstanding the fact that he had not attended a high-level staff course, he was an experienced and successful commander who may well have been seen as a potential rival to Vasey for the command of the 7th Division. Vasey's comments were made towards the end of World War II when peace was in sight. Although a bond of friendship had developed between Vasey and Eather, it was clearly not in the regular officer's interests to see any attempt to resume the pre-war policy with regard to Militia officer preference. These fears may have played a part in his less than flattering performance appraisal.

APPENDIX 1: COMMAND ASSESSMENTS

Despite Vasey's ungenerous assessment, Eather was promoted to major general just before the close of hostilities; ironically, it was Vasey's own untimely death which indirectly led to this promotion. Although his command of the 11th Division occurred too late for Eather to lead that formation in any major action, the new command was a substantial one. Eather proved an able divisional commander and administrator not only of his own force, but of many thousands of freed Allied prisoners of war and civilian detainees of different races, the local population and over 100 000 Japanese prisoners of war. For military, political and social reasons, his was an extremely complex command.

Commenting on the dark days of 1942 and the time when Eather's career could have been destroyed along with those of Brigadier Potts, Major General Allen and Lieutenant General Rowell, Brigadier Chilton, a highly regarded AIF commander, noted:

> I think the general consensus is that it [the decision to withdraw to Imita Ridge] was a good decision but it apparently panicked some headquarters people back in Melbourne.
>
> The campaign in the Owen Stanleys was one of the most remarkable in history due to the incredible terrain and entire lack of communications, and, of course, a formidable enemy.[3]

Lieutenant Generals Sir Leslie Morshead and Sir Frank Berryman also seem to have had differing views to Vasey. In 1947 or 1948 the two distinguished soldiers were travelling to London via the Qantas flying-boat service. Stopping overnight at Cairo, the pair caught up with Major General Allen who was then retired and representing institutions promoting increased trade between Australia and the Middle East. Along with General Allen's son, they met at a houseboat hotel moored near the flying-boat base. Recalled John Allen:

> There is only one topic of conversation that I remember with absolute clarity and it concerned General Eather. General Berryman was fulsome in his praise of Eather and my father's role over the years in his development. He said to my father, 'If you had done nothing else in the war but produce Ken Eather you would have done a good job.' It was a two way compliment but I took it as a

stunning appraisal of General Eather's ability as a soldier and I have never forgotten it.[4]

Brigadier Phil Carey, the historian of the Royal New South Wales Regiment, has noted of Eather:

> We know he was tough minded and very determined, but I also believe he was a 'thinking' commander. That is to say, he could think in concepts and clearly understood how he wanted the battle to develop. Accordingly, his decisions would reflect both an anticipation of what the enemy might do and how he could forestall him. He thought ahead effectively. At the same time he was alert to the need to change his plans when the battle did not go as expected and any change he instituted was done speedily and with minimum disruption to his battalions. So he watched the battle carefully down to at least company level. Equally, he was always mindful of the logistics problem and how difficulties of maintenance and resupply could affect his tactical planning and operations. He understood the 'manoeuvre battle' very well.
>
> As an example, his conduct of the advance from Imita Ridge, as well as his decision to withdraw to that feature in the first place, was a model of control, determination and wise offensive action. It combined positive action with appropriate prudence. In my opinion it was sound tactics cleverly done.
>
> Another example is his decision to move two battalions around the Japanese strongpoint south of Gorari to attack the Japanese main position while holding the first position with the other two battalions. A sound calculation of risk and use of maximum force I think, and a classic case of using his manoeuvre units in concert.
>
> It is always interesting to look at the relationship between Eather and Vasey. The latter did not always look kindly on senior Militia people. He was a notable protagonist in the Staff Corps/Militia feud, initially in 6th Division. He could well have seen Eather's appointment to raise 2/1Bn adversely and I sense that their first meeting on the Kokoda Track might have been strained. There are obvious reasons for that, of course. Clearly though, they came to respect each other and it seems that Vasey believed Eather was more worthy of Divisional command before someone like Ramsay in late 1943 . . .

APPENDIX 1: COMMAND ASSESSMENTS

The criticisms of the slowness of the advance across the Owen Stanleys are quite unfair and say more about the critics than the operational commanders. The commanders and troops in Papua were learning as they went. It says a great deal for their capacity that they were able to win so thoroughly in six months or so, and after some very substantial setbacks. The conditions, weather, climate, terrain and disease were worse than in any other theatre. A fierce enemy was enough to deal with without these other factors. The strain on commanders and resources, the devastating effects on the soldiers are hard to imagine for anyone who has never seen the country. Therefore the demand for the ablest leadership was intense...

Ken Eather played a key role in winning the campaign. He began the fight back in a thoroughly professional way and he carried it through. But he did not do it alone. I believe he would be one of the first to give the credit to his men. What's more, good leaders feed off each other and 7th Division had a great command team right through the South West Pacific War. Allen, Vasey, Dougherty and Eather were a most effective combination, and Lloyd, though technically 6th Division, contributed to 1942 very well.[5]

Many front-line soldiers also seemed to have a high regard for Eather's abilities, courage and leadership. Noted Captain M.L. Roberts of the 2/33rd Battalion:

> The Brig was a superb commander and the men of every battalion had great faith in his ability. Both he and Major General Vasey won universal respect when they made a point of moving amongst units to congratulate them after a successful battle. Gorari is an example...
>
> He was an outstanding commander who, in my opinion, was never adequately rewarded for his success.[6]

An interesting view of Eather's dealings with his own officers and his human qualities was offered by Sir William Prentice (formerly Brigade Major of the 25th Brigade and in more recent times the Chief Justice of Papua New Guinea):

> He was a very human, basically kind man, but not one to shirk decisions after most earnest thought and discussion with his

commanders, his Brigade Major and Intelligence Officer. He did not interfere with the detailed work of commanders or staff, but demanded their best. Having made decisions he let them get on with the job and was liked and respected accordingly. On the other hand he was not afraid to challenge troops who publicly and improperly questioned his actions. In the Ramu Valley he leapt out of the only jeep, that was carrying his command group, to check a soldier complaining of having to trudge [while Eather was driving] explaining to him the desirability of his getting ahead to recce and disperse the Units in the most effective and safest manner. On another occasion he himself put a stop to duck and pigeon shooting 'behind lines' in the Ramu Valley (causing alarms) by a careful aimed-off use of a Bren towards the visible miscreants.

As a soldier he worked hard and played hard. I remember refusing his 'order' to attend a 'session' in the brigade Officers' Mess quite late at night (I was working late and getting out movement orders and tables). A further (illegal) order followed a little later, resulting in my being carried in my bed (protesting) into the mess. The 'play' continued.

Everyone gave him loyal support. He was admired by Command, his staff and the troops for the clear-sighted, able, firm and fair commander that he was. He was undoubtedly one of the outstanding unit and formation leaders of World War II. Many [soldiers] of the 2/33rd Battalion, other commanders of general rank and senior citizens believe he was not sufficiently recognised and honoured by his country.[7]

General Sir Thomas Blamey seemed to have little doubt as to Eather's ability, notwithstanding the extreme discomfiture the withdrawal to Imita Ridge caused him. Despite this damaging incident, Blamey did not have Eather removed from his command at any stage during the Kokoda and Gona fighting (as he had removed Rowell, Allen and Potts). In a letter dated 17 July 1945 to the Minister for the Army, requesting Eather's promotion and appointment to the command of the 11th Division, he wrote: 'Brigadier Eather is the senior brigade commander in the AMF and is suitable, from every point of view, to be promoted and given a divisional command.'[8]

Appendix ll
Promotions and command appointments

Promotions

31 June 1919	Second Lieutenant
31 May 1923	Lieutenant
23 February 1926	Captain
27 November 1928	Major
1 July 1933	Lieutenant Colonel
27 December 1941	Colonel and Temporary Brigadier
26 July 1945	Major General

Command appointments

1 July 1933–1 August 1937	Commanding Officer 56th (Infantry) Battalion, Australian Military Forces
1 August 1937–31 July 1938	Commanding Officer 3rd (Infantry) Battalion, Australian Military Forces
13 October 1939–27 December 1941	Commanding Officer 2/1st (Infantry) Battalion, Australian Imperial Force
18 June 1941—30 August 1941	Acting Commanding Officer 16th (Infantry) Brigade, Australian Imperial Force

27 December 1941–26 July 1945	Commanding Officer 25th (Infantry) Brigade, Australian Imperial Force
16 June 1944–4 July 1944	Acting General Officer Commanding 7th Australian Division
26 July 1945–28 March 1946	General Officer Commanding 11th Australian Division
28 March 1946–18 September 1946	General Officer Commanding Australian Contingent, Victory March, London

Appendix lll
Honours and awards

Distinguished Service Order (DSO)

For conspicuous gallantry and devotion to duty during the attack on Bardia during the period from 2 January 1941 to 5 January 1941.

He gallantly and successfully led his Battalion in a night attack on 2/3 January capturing all objectives and several thousands of prisoners. He re-organised his battalion and continued to gain further ground and prisoners.

On 4 January he continued to lead his battalion with great daring and exploited the success of the first day and again captured several thousands of prisoners.

On the morning of 5 January he again led his battalion and completed the capture of the sector allotted to his battalion in the northern sector of the Bardia perimeter.

During the whole period of the attack, Lieutenant Colonel Eather set a fine example of initiative which was an inspiration to his battalion and his general bearing throughout brought forth the admiration of his men. His careful planning of the initial attack was a masterpiece that can well be followed by others and contributed largely to the success of the whole battle.

During the initial attack, the officer in charge of Bangalore Torpedoes was wounded and it looked as if things might go wrong. Lieutenant Colonel Eather was on the spot and his coolness and advice restored confidence in the sergeant in charge of the party.

At mid-day 4 January when the advance in part of his sector appeared to have been held up, he moved forward to ascertain the reason. After a quick appreciation he picked up a rifle and with a light machine gun detachment moved forward to a suitable position which he held thus restoring the confidence of his men and brought the company forward.

Commander of the Order of the British Empire (CBE)

For gallant leadership, outstanding devotion to duty, sustained untiring effort and conspicuous skill and ability in the Owen Stanley Range, New Guinea Campaign, during the period from 12 September 1942 to 29 October 1942.

Brigadier Eather led his Brigade in the successful attack on Ioribaiwa Ridge and the subsequent advance on Alola. During this advance his Brigade was successful in several attacks on the enemy's strongly defended positions in the Templeton's Crossing area.

Throughout this arduous campaign, Brigadier Eather set an example of tenacity and endurance which was an inspiration to all who came within his influence and he efficiently demonstrated that he was at all times in complete control of the situation which confronted him, proving himself a commander who at all times was able to display sound judgment, coolness and mental clarity which were conducive to excellent planning and quick decisions.

Since taking over the 25th Brigade approximately twelve months ago, Brigadier Eather has raised the standard of its training very considerably. His personal ability, enthusiasm, and skill as a trainer of infantry is in a great measure responsible for the very efficient work done by his Brigade in the campaign, the success of which was very materially assisted by the qualities displayed by him.

Distinguished Service Cross (DSC) [United States award]

For extraordinary heroism in action in New Guinea, during the Papuan Campaign, July 23 1942 to January 8 1943. As commander of the 25th Infantry Brigade, Australian Army, Brigadier Eather displayed extraordinary courage, marked efficiency and precise execution of operations during the Papuan Campaign.

APPENDIX III: HONOURS AND AWARDS

Companion of the Most Honourable Order of the Bath (CB)

Brigadier K.W. Eather commanded the 25th Australian Infantry Brigade at the assault on Balikpapan. Landing on 2 July 1945, he became responsible for the sector including the Balikpapan–Samarinda Road, to become the main axis of enemy strength. The enemy quickly recovered from his confusion caused by the preliminary bombardment and assault and formed strong rearguards supported by artillery and determined to fight to the death to resist our further advance in this area.

Brigadier Eather with his Brigade, trained and fit to a very high degree, relentlessly forced the enemy back, inflicting heavy casualties and permitting little time for the enemy to readjust his forces. Brigadier Eather, by his capacity to command, by his drive and by the skill with which he manoeuvred his Brigade, contributed in no small measure to the final defeat of the enemy at Balikpapan.

Mention in Dispatches

Eather was twice mentioned in dispatches. The first occasion was on 9 May 1941 for his conduct during operations in the Middle East. The second occurred on 31 May 1944 for 'gallant and distinguished service' in the South West Pacific between 1 April and 30 September 1943. Australian War Memorial records indicate that he may have been awarded a third MID during 1942 but his service records make no mention of this.

On 23 June 1943, he was awarded the Australian Efficiency Decoration (ED).

Knighthood and Order of Australia nominations

Several attempts were made to have Eather knighted or bestowed with the Order of Australia but no such awards eventuated. The Water Research Foundation of Australia is known to have initiated a knighthood nomination, as did several retired generals and other senior officers.

There has since been controversy about the WRFA nomination as the Premier of New South Wales at the time (Sir Robert Askin) had immersed himself in numerous scandals and seemed to have close connections with organised crime in the state. Apparently, paying bribes for knighthoods, among other corrupt acts, occurred regularly in this period. During the Commonwealth Royal Commission into Drugs, allegations were made by one witness that several prominent knighthoods in New South Wales were arranged for a fee of $60 000. After Eather had been nominated for his knighthood by the WRFA he was approached by Askin and asked to pay a bribe for his own nomination to proceed. This was probably the first that Eather would have known of his nomination. Nonetheless, his response was immediate and the conversation was terminated as a disgusted Eather bluntly told the Premier that 'he earned his awards and did not pay for them'. Eather confirmed only years later that this had happened, when he told immediate family members and two of his former officers.[1]

Members of Eather's family, as well as some of his former officers and friends, have no doubt that the award was then stopped by Askin. The WRFA, however, was a federally recognised body and this nomination was certainly processed through Federal Government channels and not through the New South Wales State Government where interference could most easily have occurred. It seems likely, however, that the Premier made use of colleagues in the Federal Government or Public Service (the same political party was in office at both State and Federal levels) to ensure that this and all future nominations for any high awards would be unsuccessful. Certainly, nominations put forward by his former officers in 1989 and 1992 to have Eather knighted were unsuccessful, as was an Order of Australia nomination in 1993.

Ironically, it seems likely that apart from being insulted by the bribe attempt, Eather did not have any great interest in honours or awards for himself. In many ways he was still the same man who, as a Militia officer, helped his soldiers push a watercart through Sydney streets, who as a brigadier slept with his men in the mud on the side of the Kokoda Track and later, as a retired general, delivered groceries from his wife's store to local residents.

Notes

Chapter 1
1. J. St Pierre, *The Eather Family in Australia*, Eather Family History Committee, 1990.
2. ibid.
3. Eather Family Newsletter (No 146), September 1999.
4. Letter: Mrs M. Reynolds to author, 10 March 2000.
5. Letter: Chris Brookes to author, 28 June 2001.
6. Letter: Ms Avril Condren to author, 28 March 2001. Information taken from K. Cook, *The Railway Came to Ku-Ring-Gai*, 1991.
7. Letter: Chris Brookes to author, 28 June 2001.
8. ibid.
9. ibid.
10. J. Barrett, *Falling In: Australians and 'Boy Conscription' 1911–1915*, Hale & Iremonger, Sydney, 1979.
11. Letter: Mrs Isobel Elliot to author, 5 September 2001.
12. K.W. Eather papers.
13. Service record: NX3 K.W. Eather.
14. Letter: Mrs M. Reynolds to author, 10 March 2000.
15. Letter: Mrs Isobel Elliot to author, 5 September 2001.
16. G. Long: *To Benghazi*, Australian War Memorial, Canberra, 1952, p. 24.

Chapter 2
1. Interview: Lieutenant Colonel Wally Delves, 2 November 2000.
2. Letter: Captain William Travers to author, 4 November 2000.
3. E.C. Givney, *The First at War: The Story Of The 2/1st Australian Infantry Battalion 1939–1945*, The Association of First Infantry Battalions, Sydney, 1987.
4. For differing versions of this incident see *The First at War* (Givney, F.C.) and *To Benghazi* (Long, G.).
5. Interview: Lieutenant Colonel Wally Delves, 2 November 2000.
6. Telephone interview: Captain Owen Eather, 14 July 2002.
7. Letter: Lieutenant Colonel John Burrell to author, 9 October 2000.
8. ibid.
9. Telephone interview: Patrick Lawry, 14 September 2000.

10 Letter: Reg Pane to author, 10 August 2000.
11 Telephone interview: Captain Owen Eather, 14 July 2002.

Chapter 3
1. E.C. Givney, *The First at War: The Story Of The 2/1st Australian Infantry Battalion 1939–1945*, The Association of First Infantry Battalions, Sydney, 1987.
2. AWM 67 67/2/56, diary 56 of Gavin Long.
3. Interview: Lieutenant Colonel Wally Delves, 2 November 2000.
4. Letter: Major General Paul Cullen to author, 14 November 2000.
5. Interview: Lieutenant Colonel Wally Delves, 2 November 2000.
6. Ivan Chapman, *Iven G. Mackay: Citizen and Soldier,* Melway Publishing, Melbourne, 1975.
7. Letter: Mr Barry Hennessy to author, 29 October 2000.
8. *The Operations in Northern Africa: Sidi El Barani,* Volume 1, The Official History of Italy in World War II. Stato Maggiore Dell' Eserciton, Reporto Affari Generali, Ufficio Storico.
9. E.C. Givney, *The First at War.*
10. Interview: Lieutenant Colonel Wally Delves, 2 November 2000.
11. Letter: Barry Hennessy to author, 29 October 2000.
12. AWM 67 67/2/56.
13. Interview: Lieutenant Colonel Wally Delves, 2 November 2000.
14. ibid.
15. E.C. Givney, *The First at War.*
16. Service record: NX3 K.W. Eather.
17. Telephone interview: Captain Owen Eather, 5 September 2000.
18. E.C. Givney, *The First at War.*
19. Service record: NX3 K.W. Eather.

Chapter 4
1. E.C. Givney, *The First at War: The Story Of The 2/1st Australian Infantry Battalion 1939–1945*, The Association of First Infantry Battalions, Sydney, 1987.
2. Private diary of K.W. Eather.
3. ibid.
4. ibid.
5. ibid.
6. Letter: Captain M.L. Roberts to author, 27 October 2000.
7. Private diary of K.W. Eather.
8. ibid.
9. *Forever Forward*, newsletter of the 2/31st Battalion Association, December 2000, p. 7.

10 Private diary of K.W. Eather.
11 ibid.
12 ibid.
13 ibid.
14 ibid.
15 ibid
16 ibid.

Chapter 5
1 R. Paull, *Retreat from Kokoda*, Heinemann, Melbourne, 1958, p. 222.
2 Private diary of K.W. Eather.
3 ibid.
4 ibid.
5 Julian Waters, *Doc's War*, self-published memoir, 1988.
6 Private diary of K.W. Eather.
7 Colin Kennedy, *Port Moresby to Gona Beach*, self-published, 1992.
8 Jill Sykes, 'Phar Lap of World War II', *Sydney Morning Herald*, 16 January 1973.
9 Private diary of K.W. Eather.
10 R. Paull, *Retreat from Kokoda*, p. 224.
11 Julian Waters, *Doc's War*.
12 For a detailed account of these higher level events see David Horner's *Crisis in Command*, Australian National University Press, 1978.
13 Private diary of K.W. Eather.
14 Telephone interview: Captain Owen Eather, 10 July 2002.
15 R. Paull, *Retreat from Kokoda*.
16 Private diary of K.W. Eather.
17 ibid.
18 ibid.
19 ibid.
20 ibid.

Chapter 6
1 Private diary of K.W. Eather.
2 ibid.
3 ibid.
4 ibid.
5 ibid.
6 ibid.
7 ibid.
8 Letter: Captain M.L. Roberts to author, 27 October 2000.
9 Private diary of K.W. Eather.

10 ibid.
11 For a detailed account of the fighting in the Owen Stanleys and afterwards see Lex McAulay's books *Blood and Iron: The Battle for Kokoda 1942* (Random House Australia, 1992) and *To the Bitter End: The Japanese Defeat at Buna and Gona 1942–43* (Random House Australia, 1992). These works provide an excellent account of the campaigns from both the Australian and Japanese perspective. They also detail how the high level of 'Ultra' signals intelligence information was used by MacArthur's headquarters.
12 ibid.
13 ibid.
14 David Horner, *General Vasey's War*, Melbourne University Press, 1992.
15 Private diary of K.W. Eather.
16 ibid.
17 AWM 52 8/3/39, War Diary 3rd Battalion.
18 Private diary of K.W. Eather.
19 ibid.
20 Julian Waters, *Doc's War*, self-published memoir, 1988.
21 Private diary of K.W. Eather.
22 ibid.
23 ibid.
24 ibid.
25 ibid.
26 ibid.
27 *Forever Forward*, newsletter of the 2/31st Battalion Association, December 2000.
28 For a highly detailed account of the battle of Gorari and also of this particular incident see William Crooks, *The Foot Soldiers: The Story of the 2/33rd Australian Infantry Battalion*, 2/33rd Battalion Association, Sydney, 1971.
29 Masaru, Moriki, *Battle for Kokoda*, self-published memoir, 1998.
30 Letter: Major General Paul Cullen to author, 14 November 2000.

Chapter 7

1 Private diary of K.W. Eather.
2 ibid.
3 ibid.
4 ibid.
5 Telephone interview: Captain Owen Eather, 14 July 2002.
6 For a detailed account on 'Ultra' intelligence see Edward Drea, *MacArthur's Ultra: Code Breaking and the War Against Japan 1942–1945*, University Press of Kansas, 1992.

NOTES

7 Private diary of K.W. Eather.
8 ibid.
9 ibid.
10 ibid.
11 ibid.
12 ibid.
13 ibid.
14 ibid.
15 ibid.
16 ibid.
17 ibid.
18 ibid.
19 War Diary 2/16th Battalion.
20 Private diary of K.W. Eather.
21 ibid.
22 ibid.
23 Quoted from *Forever Forward*, December 2000, p. 28.
24 Private diary of K.W. Eather.
25 Service record: NX3 K.W. Eather.
26 See Peter Brune, *Those Ragged Bloody Heroes: From the Kokoda Track to Gona Beach*, Allen & Unwin, Sydney, 1991; Frank Sublet, *From Kokoda to the Sea*, Slouch Hat Publications, McCrae VIC, 2000.
27 Private diary of K.W. Eather.

Chapter 8

1 Edward Drea, *MacArthur's Ultra: Code Breaking and the War Against Japan 1942–1945*, University Press of Kansas, 1992.
2 Service record: NX3 K.W. Eather.
3 Letter: Captain M.L. Roberts to author, 27 October 2000.
4 John Barrett, *We Were There: Australian Soldiers in World War II*, Viking, Melbourne, 1987, p. 241.
5 Crooks, William, *The Foot Soldiers: The Story of the 2/33rd Australian Infantry Battalion*, 2/33rd Battalion Association, Sydney, 1971.
6 AWM 93.
7 Letter: Gerald Connelly to author, 18 September 2000.
8 Edward Drea, *MacArthur's Ultra*, p. 85.
9 Letter: 'Hook' Anderson to author, 10 September 2000.
10 Service record: NX3 K.W. Eather.
11 AWM 67/2/56 Gavin Long diary 56.
12 ibid.
13 Photographs held at the Australian War Memorial depict this event.
14 Letter: John Allen to author, 11 April 2001.
15 Letter: Frank McCosker to author, 18 September 2001.

Chapter 9
1. Julian Waters, *Doc's War*, self-published memoir, 1988.
2. Australian Archives GP 21-1283, Release From Service of Major General J.E.S. Stevens.
3. ibid.
4. ibid.
5. ibid.

Chapter 10
1. Service record: NX3 K.W. Eather.
2. AWM 54 80/3/7 ANGAU Reoccupation of Rabaul.
3. ibid.
4. ibid.
5. Ron Blair, *A Young Man's War: A History of the 37th/52nd Australian Infantry Battalion in World War II*, 37th/52nd Battalion Association, Melbourne, 1992.
6. Interview: Captain Owen Eather, 24 January 2001.
7. Ron Blair, *A Young Man's War*.
8. Professor Tanaka Hiromi, Self-sufficiency in Rabaul, paper presented at *'Remembering the War in New Guinea' Symposium*, October 2000.
9. Peter Ryan, *Encyclopaedia of Papua and New Guinea*, Melbourne University Press, 1972.
10. Peter Dennis et al., *The Oxford Companion to Australian Military History*, Oxford University Press, 1995.
11. Peter Stone, *Hostages to Freedom: The Fall of Rabaul*, Ocean Enterprises, Yarram VIC, 1994.
12. Australian Archives B4175, [Japanese War Crimes] Senior Officers' Trials.
13. ibid.
14. ibid.
15. AWM 54 80/3/7, ANGAU Reoccupation of Rabaul.
16. AWM photographic files record these events.
17. Ron Blair, *A Young Man's War*.
18. ibid.
19. John Barrett, *We Were There: Australian Soldiers in World War II*, Viking, Melbourne, 1987.

Chapter 11
1. Service record: NX3 K.W. Eather.
2. AWM 123/24 Victory March in London—Australian Participation.
3. ibid.
4. ibid.

NOTES

5 AWM 113 MHI/174 Victory March London.
6 ibid.
7 Letter: Wing Commander Rollo Kingsford-Smith to author, 10 October 2000.
8 AWM 123/24 Victory March in London—Australian Participation.
9 Rollo Kingsford-Smith, *I Wouldn't Have Missed it for Quids*, self-published memoir, 1999, pp. 111, 112.
10 ibid.
11 Interview: Captain Owen Eather, 24 January 2001.
12 AWM 123/24 Victory March in London—Australian participation.
13 ibid.
14 Service Record: K.W. Eather.

Chapter 12

1 Interview: Mrs Kathleen Eather, 26 January 2001.
2 AWM 93 Correspondence with Major General K.W. Eather regarding information for and comments on the official history.
3 Letter: Chris Brookes to author, 28 June 2001.
4 Interview: Captain Owen Eather, 24 January 2001.
5 ibid.
6 Telephone interview: Captain Owen Eather, 14 July 2002.
7 Private papers of K.W. Eather.
8 Telephone interview: Dr Jack Beale, 19 December 2000.
9 ibid.
10 Private papers of K.W. Eather.
11 Telephone interview: Dr Jack Beale, 19 December 2000.
12 Interview: Mrs Kathleen Eather, 26 January 2001.
13 Letter: Major General Paul Cullen to author, 18 September 2000.
14 Interview: Captain Owen Eather, 24 January 2001.
15 Letter: Chris Brookes to author, 28 June 2001.
16 Telephone interview: Captain Owen Eather, 14 July 2002.
17 Interview: Mrs Kathleen Eather, 26 January 2001.
18 Telephone interview: Captain Owen Eather, 14 July 2002.
19 Various Water Research Foundation of Australia annual reports.
20 Telephone interview: Dr Jack Beale, 19 December 2000.
21 Water Research Foundation of Australia papers passed on to author.
22 ibid.
23 Interview: Captain Owen Eather, 24 January 2001.
24 ibid.
25 ibid.
26 Private papers of K.W. Eather.
27 Letter: Chris Brookes to author, 28 June 2001.

Appendix I
1   AWM 67/1/6 diary 6 of Gavin Long.
2   David Horner, *General Vasey's War,* Melbourne University Press, 1992.
3   Letter: Brigadier Chilton to author, 25 October 2000.
4   Letter: John Allen to author, 11 April 2001.
5   Letter: Brigadier Phil Carey to author, 10 August 2002.
6   Letter: Captain M.L. Roberts to author, 27 October 2000.
7   Private papers of K.W. Eather.
8   Australian Archives GP 21-1283 Release From Service of Major General J.E.S. Stevens.

Appendix III
1   Telephone interview with 2/1st Battalion Officer A, 9 October 2000, telephone interview with 2/1st Battalion Officer B, 10 November 2000, and interviews with family members confirmed this incident. The endemic corruption then occurring in New South Wales is well documented. David Hickie's *The Prince and the Premier: The Story of Perce Galea, Bob Askin and Others Who Gave Organised Crime its Start in Australia* (Angus & Robertson, Sydney, 1985) provides a disturbing account of the state of affairs in the state when Eather was nominated for his knighthood and mentions the knighthoods for cash scandal.

Bibliography

Official histories

Dexter, David, *The New Guinea Offensives*, Australian War Memorial, 1961.

Hasluck, Paul, *The Government and the People 1939–1941*, Australian War Memorial, 1952.

——, *The Government and the People 1942–1945*, Australian War Memorial, 1970.

Hermon Gill, G., *Royal Australian Navy 1942–1945*, Australian War Memorial, 1968.

Long, Gavin, *To Benghazi*, Australian War Memorial, 1952.

——, *Greece, Crete and Syria*, Australian War Memorial, 1953.

——, *The Final Campaigns*, Australian War Memorial, 1963.

McCarthy, Dudley, *South West Pacific Area First Year: Kokoda To Wau*, Australian War Memorial, 1959.

Mordike, John, *An Army for a Nation*, Australian Army in conjunction with Allen & Unwin, Sydney, 1992.

Walker, Allen, *Clinical Problems of War*, Australian War Memorial, 1952.

The Operations in Northern Africa: Sidi El Barani, Volume I, (The Official History of Italy in World War II). Stato Maggiore Dell' Esercito, Reporto Affari Glenerali, Ufficio Storico.

Official records, reports and documents

Australian Archives

AIF Service record	NX3 Major General Kenneth William Eather
File B4175 —	[Japanese War Crimes] Senior Officers' Trials (Judge Advocate's diary)
File B4175—	[Japanese War Crimes] Senior Officers' Trials (Judge Advocate's notes on law and for summing up)
File GP 21-1283	Release from Service of Major General J.E.S. Stevens

Australian War Memorial

AWM 52 8/2/1	War Diary 2/1st Battalion
AWM 52 8/2/25	War Diary 2/25th Battalion
AWM 52 8/2/31	War Diary 2/31st Battalion
AWM 52 8/2/33	War Diary 2/33rd Battalion
AWM 52 8/3/39	War Diary 3rd Battalion
AWM 52 8/3/67	War Diary 16th Battalion
AWM 8/2/16	War Diary 16th Brigade
AWM 8/2/21	War Diary 21st Brigade
AWM 8/2/25	War Diary 25th Brigade
AWM 54 80/3/7	ANGAU Reoccupation of Rabaul
AWM 54 1010/9/22	Australian Military Forces War Crimes Trials—Nominal Role of Japanese War Criminals in Rabaul Under Sentence, 1947
AWM 54 225/2/5	Letters from Lieutenant General S.F. Rowell, G.O.C. New Guinea Force to Major General G.A. Vasey
AWM 54	1st Australian Army, Admin Instructions Including Movement Control—Rabaul
AWM 54	Register of Native Trials at Rabaul, Indictable Offences, ANGAU Jurisdiction in

BIBLIOGRAPHY

	Territories of Papua & New Guinea 1942–44
AWM 67 1/6	Gavin Long Diary 6
AWM 67 67/2/56	Gavin Long Diary 56
AWM 93	Correspondence with Major General K.W. Eather regarding information for and comments on the official history
AWM 113 MHI/174	Victory March London
AWM 123/24	Victory March in London—Australian Participation
MSS 743	Private Records, Hideo, Katayama
MSS 0768	Private Records, Benson, James, Father
MSS 1089	Private Records, Imamura, Hitoshi

Water Research Foundation of Australia

Third Annual Report and Balance Sheet for the year ended 30 June 1958.
The Treatment & Disposal of Water-Borne Colliery Wastes, Report 39, WRFA, 1972.
Twenty-Fourth Annual Report for the year ended 30 June 1979.
Forty-Fifth Annual Report 1999/2000.

Private papers

Personal diary kept by Brigadier K.W. Eather for period Jan–Dec 1942.
Private papers of Major General K.W. Eather held by Captain Owen Eather.
Private papers of Major General K.W. Eather held by Chris Brooks.

Books

Badman, Peter, *North Africa 1940–1942: The Desert War*, Time-Life Books (Australia), 1988.
Barrett, John, *Falling In: Australians and 'Boy Conscription' 1911–1915*, Hale & Iremonger, Sydney, 1979.

——, *We Were There: Australian Soldiers in World War II*, Viking, Melbourne, 1987.
Bergerud, Eric, *Touched With Fire: The Land War in the South Pacific*, Viking, Melbourne, 1996.
Blair, Ron, *A Young Man's War: A History of the 37th/52nd Australian Infantry Battalion in World War II*, 37th/52nd Battalion Association, Melbourne, 1992.
Brune, Peter, *Those Ragged Bloody Heroes: From the Kokoda Track to Gona Beach*, Allen & Unwin, Sydney, 1991.
——, *Gona's Gone: The Battle for the Beachhead*, Allen & Unwin, Sydney, 1994.
——, *The Spell Broken: Exploding the Myth of Japanese Invincibility*, Allen & Unwin, Sydney, 1997.
Budden, F.M., *The Chockos: The Story of the Militia Infantry Battalions in the South West Pacific 1941–1945*, self-published, 1987.
Chapman, Ivan, *Iven G. Mackay: Citizen and Soldier*, Melway Publishing, Melbourne, 1975.
Charlton, Peter, *The Thirty Niners*, Macmillan, Sydney, 1981.
——, *War Against Japan 1942–1945*, Time-Life Books (Australia), 1989.
Crooks, William, *The Foot Soldiers: The Story of the 2/33rd Australian Infantry Battalion*, 2/33rd Battalion Association, Sydney, 1971.
Dandy, Phillip, *The Kookaburra Cut Throats Vol 1*, self-published, 1995.
——, *The Kookaburra Cut Throats Vol 2*, self-published, 1998.
Dennis, P., Grey, J., Morris, E., Prior, R. and Connor, J., *The Oxford Companion to Australian Military History,* Oxford University Press, 1995.
Drayton, A.W., *Men of Courage: A History of the 2/25th Australian Infantry Battalion 1940–1945*, 2/25th Battalion Association, Chermside QLD, 2000.
Drea, Edward J., *MacArthur's Ultra: Code Breaking and the War Against Japan, 1942–1945*, University Press of Kansas, 1992.
Edgar, Bill, *Warrior Of Kokoda: A Biography of Brigadier Arnold Potts*, Allen & Unwin, Sydney, 1999.
Fernside, G.H. & Clift, K., *Dougherty: A Great Man Among Men*, Alpha Books, Sydney, 1979.

Givney, E.C., *The First at War: The Story of the 2/1st Australian Infantry Battalion 1939–1945*, The Association of First Infantry Battalions, Sydney, 1987.

Hickie, David, *The Prince and the Premier: The Story of Perce Galea, Bob Askin and Others Who Gave Organised Crime its Start in Australia*, Angus & Robertson, Sydney, 1985.

Horner, David Murray, *Crisis of Command: Australian Generalship and the Japanese Threat 1941–1943*, Australian National University Press, Canberra, 1978.

———, *General Vasey's War*, Melbourne University Press, Melbourne, 1992.

———, *Blamey: The Commander-in-Chief*, Allen & Unwin, Sydney, 1998.

Kennedy, Colin, *Port Moresby to Gona Beach: The 3rd Australian Infantry Battalion, 1942*, self-published, 1992.

Kingsford-Smith, Rollo, *I Wouldn't Have Missed It for Quids*, self-published, 1999.

Laffin, John, *Forever Forward: The Story of the 2/31st Australian Infantry Battalion*, 2/31st Battalion Association, Newport NSW, 1994.

McAulay, Lex, *Blood and Iron: The Battle for Kokoda 1942*, Random House Australia, Sydney, 1992.

———, *To the Bitter End: The Japanese Defeat at Buna and Gona 1942–43*, Random House Australia, Sydney, 1992.

Maitland, G.L, *The Second World War and Its Australian Army Battle Honours*, Kangaroo Press, Sydney, 1999.

Mayo, Lida, *Bloody Buna*, Doubleday, Sydney, 1974.

Moriki, Masaru, *Cowra Uprising: One Survivor's Memoir*, self-published, 1972.

———, *Battle of Kokoda*, self-published, 1998.

Paull, Raymond, *Retreat from Kokoda*, Heinemann, Melbourne, 1958

Rowell, Sydney, *Full Circle*, Melbourne University Press, Melbourne, 1974.

Ryan, Peter, *Encyclopaedia of Papua and New Guinea*, Melbourne University Press, 1972.

Saburo, Hayashi and Cox, Alvin, *Kogan: The Japanese Army in the Pacific War*, (English translation), The Marine Corps Association, Quantico VA, 1959.

St Pierre, John, *A History of the Eather Family in Australia, Volume 1 (Thomas Eather and Elizabeth Lee)*, Eather Family History Committee, 1990.

———, *A History of the Eather Family in Australia, Volume 5 (Thomas Eather Junior and his Descendants)*, Eather Family History Committee, 2002.

Stone, Peter, *Hostages to Freedom: The Fall of Rabaul*, Ocean Enterprises, Yarram VIC., 1994.

Sublet, Frank, *From Kokoda to the Sea*, Slouch Hat Publications, McCrae VIC, 2000.

Waters, Julian, *'Doc's War'*, self-published, 1988.

Wilcox, Craig, *For Hearths and Homes: Citizen Soldiering in Australia 1854–1945*, Allen & Unwin, Sydney, 1998.

Wilmot, Chester, *Tobruk 1941*, Halstead Press, 1944.

Conference and research papers

Brennan, Major M.J. 'Major General K. Weather, CB, CBE, DSO, ED, DSC (USA)—A study of his command and staff methods, Australian Army command and Staff College, 1993.'

These papers all presented at the 'Remembering The War In New Guinea' *Symposium*, Australian National University, Canberra, October 2000:

Frei, Professor Henry, Why the Japanese Were in New Guinea.

Gray, Dr Jeffrey, The Coming of the War to the Territories: Forced Labour and Broken Promises.

Horner, Professor David, Strategy and Command in Australia's New Guinea Campaigns.

Iwamoto, Hiromitsu, Japanese and New Guinean Memories of Wartime Experiences at Rabaul, 1942–1946.

Johnson, Dr Mark, 'Yet They're Human Just As We Are': Australian Attitudes Towards the Japanese in the South-West Pacific, 1942–1945.

Kaima, Sam, Ammak Tapduk: Kaiapit-Saidor Track During the Second World War.

Low, Dr Morris, Japanese Perceptions of the Enemy.
Tanaka, Prof. Hiromi, Self-sufficiency in Rabaul.

Newspapers/magazines/newsletters

Forever Forward, 2/31st Australian Infantry Battalion (AIF) Association (NSW) newsletter, Dec. 2000.

Forever Forward: Special News Bulletin Commemorating 50 Years Since The Owen Stanley Campaign, 2/31st Australian Infantry Battalion (AIF) Association (NSW) newsletter, Sept 1992.

MacFadyen Barry, 'Full Honors for Major General', Obituaries, *The Herald Sun*, 15 May 1993.

The Australian Primary Producers' Advocate, the Primary Producers' Union (NSW Division) 1 Feb 1952.

The Australian Primary Producers' Advocate, the Primary Producers' Union (New South Wales Division) newspaper, various editions, 1946–1958.

The 'Military Mourns Kokoda Conqueror', *The Australian*, 14 May 1993.

Reynolds, Mildred (ed), Eather Family Newsletter, No 146, September 1999.

'Strict Discipline for Rabaul Japs', *New Guinea Gold*, 3 September 1945.

Simonds, Derry, 'Having the Right Connections', Eather Family Newsletter, June 2000.

Sykes, Jill, '"Phar Lap" of World War II', *The Sydney Morning Herald*, 16 January 1973.

Table Tops, Australian Army Newspaper, No 73, 15 August 1945.

Teh-Kallim, 25 Brigade News, Volume 4, No 9, December 1980.

Water and the Environment, No 347, Feb 2000, Newsletter of the Water Research Foundation of Australia.

Water and the Environment, No 348, May 2000. Newsletter of the Water Research Foundation of Australia.

Index

2/1st Battalion
    at Bardia 25–31; at Oivi–Gorari 97–100, 104; at Tobruk 34–9; forms 11–14; in Greece 41–2
25th Brigade units
    advance on Lae 133–7; at Balikpapan 156–9; at Gona 107–20; at Ioribaiwa Ridge 62–6; at Oivi–Gorari 96–12; at Templeton's Crossing 84–5; capture of Lae 137–40; in Syria and Palestine 46–8; in the Markham and Ramu Valleys 142–7; occupies Kokoda 94–6; *passim* 123–7; recaptures Ioribaiwa Ridge 76–9; soldiers killed in Liberator crash 133; withdraws to Imita Ridge 66–71
11th Australian Division
    reoccupies Rabaul 167
Abbotsholme College 3
Alexandria 21–22, 40
Allen, A.S. 7, 12, 16, 30, 42, 55–6, 60, 65, 67, 68, 70–1, 74–78, 81–4, 86–8, 93, 97, 122, 126, 153, 208, 209, 211, 212
    death 196; photo 78; relieved of his command 87; signals between Allen and Blamey 88–92
Allen, John 153, 209
Alola 89, 91
Amiriya 22, 39
Anzac Day 18, 196–8, 203–4
Askin, Sir Robert 202, 218
Australian Victory March Contingent
    forms 180–1; Gibraltar riot 186–8
Awala 106

Balikpapan 155–9, 161–3, 202
Bardia 24–5, 28, 30–3, 42, 139
    map 29
Beale, Jack 199
Beasley, J.A. 182
Bergerud, Eric 65, 103
Berryman, Sir Frank 68–9, 122, 209
Bertram G.A., 47, 153
Blamey, Sir Thomas 12, 14, 39, 56, 58, 60, 62, 70, 72–3, 77, 81–3, 86–8, 122–3, 128, 131, 140, 162–3, 175–6, 181, 212
Boase, A.J. 42, 44
British Ambassador 179–180
Broardbent, Ray 122
Brookes, Chris 4, 191, 196, 204
Bumbu River 137
Buna 90, 97, 105, 110, 113–4, 121, 125, 128, 131
Butler, W.G. 137–8

Buttrose, A.W. 57, 75–6, 99, 106, 115

Cadets 4
Cairo 21, 23
Cameron, A.G. 75, 84–5, 93, 106, 115, 118
Cape Endaiadere 122
Cardigan, Lord 4
Carey, Phil 210
Caro, A.E. 75
Carroll, Kathleen *see* Kathleen Eather
'Chaforce' 111
Channell, Doug 25
Chifley, Ben 176
    photo 177
Chilton, F.O. 1, 41, 209
Churchill, Winston 48, 50–1, 140, 183–4
Clements, Chief Officer 182
Clowes, Cyril 68
Compulsory military training 4
Connelly, Gerald 139
Crooks, Bill 65, 93
Cullen, Paul 16, 26, 85, 100, 104
Curtin, John 50–1, 73

Delves, Wally 11, 17, 38, 39
Dennis, Don 198
Dexter, David 137–8, 142, 191
Dougherty, Sir Ivan 1, 87, 117, 119–20, 126, 211
Duke of Gloucester 152
Dumpu 142–3,
Dunbar, C.C. 75–6
Duntroon 5

Eather, Adeline Mabel 5, 14, 16, 51–2, 54, 74, 100, 124, 149, 194–5
    death 197; photo 6
Eather, Dulcie 2–3
Eather, Eamon 200
Eather, Elsie Isobel 5, 51, 54, 124, 182
    photo 6
Eather, Isabella Theresa 2–3
    photo 6
Eather, Kathleen 197, 202, 204
Eather, Ken
    accepts surrender of Japanese forces on New Ireland 171; acts on inaccurate and misleading intelligence 108–9, 111, 113–5, 125; advance from Imita to Ioribaiwa 76–7; appointed military governor of New Britain

INDEX

and New Ireland 166; appointed to AIF and command of 2/1st Battalion 11; appointed to command of Australian Victory March Contingent 179; at Balikpapen 157–61; at Bardia 26–8; at Middle East Tactical School 22–3; at Oivi–Gorari 97–101; at Tobruk 35–9; becomes executive director Water Research Foundation of Australia 193; becomes poultry farmer 189; birth 2; birth of children 5; commands 3rd Battalion 7; deals with potential mutiny of troops 177; death 204; dental mechanic career 5–6, 8; faulty planning in support of 21st Brigade 118; front line leadership 26, 28, 35–6, 63, 135, 137–9; Gibraltar riot 186–8; growing up 3–4; hospitalised 124; hospitalised in Alexandria 39–41; in Syria 44–6; in the advance on Lae 134–9; Ioribaiwa/Imita controversy 61–76; knighthood and Order of Australia nominations 217–8; marriage 5; militia service and commissioning into 53rd Battalion 5; nicknamed 'Pharlap' 135–6; occupies Kokoda 94–7; orders blowing of wire defences at Bardia 26, 32; photo arriving at Port Moresby 57; photo at Balikpapan 158; photo at Ioribaiwa 78; photo meets Prime Minister Chifley at Rabaul 177; photo with family 6; president Primary Producers' Association 193; promoted to brigadier 46; promoted to lieutenant colonel and commands 56th Battalion 7; promoted to major general 161–3; pursuit to Gona 106–8; records Japanese cannibalism 84; retires 199–200; retires from Army 188; retrains 25th Brigade 52; returns to Australia 48; temporary command of 16th Brigade 42–3; training of troops 14, 16–7, 42, 55–6, 131–2, 148–51, 154; transfers to unattached list 7

Eather, Ken Junior 5, 54
   death 193
Eather, Nancy 2–3, 204
Eather, Owen 75, 198, 200–4
Eather, William 2–3
   photo 6
Edwards Plantation 137
Efogi 82–3, 89
Eichelberger, Robert 113–4
England, V.T. 41
Eora Creek 91

Faria-Uria Valley 143
Forde, Frank 52–3, 163, 187–8

Gaza 18
Giruwa 115
Glennie, Reg 207
Glory 166
Gona 97, 105–17, 119–21, 123, 125, 128, 131, 212
   criticisms of Gona Campaign 124–7
Gusap 143

Harding, Edwin 55, 113
Hassett, Sir Francis 205

Heath's Plantation 134–5
Helwan 21
Hennessy, Barry 28, 36
Henry T. Allen 129
Herring, Sir Edmund 77, 95, 122–3
Holt, Harold 3
Hombrom Bluff 68
Honner, R 126
Honner, Ralph 119, 126
Horii, Tomitaro 72, 74, 102
Horner, David 68, 111, 128

Ilimo 97
Imamura, Hitoshi 166–7, 170, 174
Imita Ridge 61–2, 68–72, 74–6, 139, 205, 208, 210
   photo 67
Ingleburn 12, 17
   riot 13–14
Ioribaiwa Ridge 60–2, 64–79;
   passim, 81, 96, 110, 131; photo 67
Ismailia Canal 23
Isurava 94
Ito, Takeo 171, 195

Jackson, 'Stonewall' 196
Jacquinot Bay 165–6
Jaffa 18
Jericho 18
Jerusalem 18, 19
Julis 16, 17
Jumbora 106

Kagi 91
Kaiapit 141–3
Kanimbla 147
Kantara 16
Katoomba 56
Katsuragi 176
Kelliher, Richard 181
Kenny, George 69
Kesawai 145
Kingsford-Smith, Rollo 183–4
Kokoda 88–97, 102, 212
Kokoda Track 7, 58–9, 61, 79, 102, 130, 141, 153, 208, 210
Kumbarum 143
Kumusi River 97, 100, 102, 105

Lae 129, 131–5, 137–42, 146
Lavarack, Sir John 9
Lawry, Pat 18
Leaney's Corner 98
Lees, Isabella Theresa *see* Eather, Isabella Theresa
Lees, James 4, 200
Lewis, Adeline, Mabel *see* Eather, Adeline Mabel
Lloyd, Bert 162
Lloyd, J.E. 85, 88–9, 211
Long, Gavin 9, 31, 36–7, 148, 166, 191, 207
Lyall, Bob 182

MacArthur, Douglas 58, 60, 62, 71, 73, 79, 83, 86–8, 90–1, 93, 108–9, 111, 113–14, 119, 123, 127, 129, 148, 151, 155–6
MacArthur Onslow, D. 34

Mackay, Sir Iven 40
Madang 133
Mainwaring, Geoffrey 182
   his portrait of General Eather 185
Manella, Petassi 35
Markham River 131, 142
Markham Valley 129, 133, 142–3
Marson, R.H. 63, 97, 99–100, 107, 115
Masawasa 143
Mayo, Lida 67, 74
McCarthy, Dudley 191
McCosker, Frank 154
McMahon, Sir William 3
Menari 82, 84
Menzies, Sir Robert 10, 39, 194
Mersa Matruh 39–40
Middle East Combined Training Centre 42
Middle East Tactical School 22
Milford E.J. 122, 148, 159
   photo 158
Milford Highway 157
Miller, Jim 97, 100, 105, 108, 114–5
Moriki, Masaru 102
Mount Batten, Lord Louis 184
Mount Vernon 48–51, 132
Moreshead, Sir Leslie 152, 209
Morotai 163
Mt Lunaman 139
Mules, J.H. 152
Myola 85, 87–9, 91–2

Nadzab 131–2, 134, 141, 143
Nakano Hidemitsu 141
Nauro 79, 81–3
Neptune 1–2

Oboe II 156, 159
Oivi–Gorari 93, 96–103, 110, 126, 208, 210
   maps 98–99, 101
Operation Cartwheel 129
Orford 14–15, 49
Ower's Corner 60, 72

Pane, Reg 18
Pongani 90
Pope's Track 159
Popondetta 122
Porter, Selwyn 1, 47, 57, 60, 62, 65–8, 75–6, 119
Porter, Tom 122
Port Moresby 3, 54, 56–7, 59–63, 68–9, 72–4, 79, 85–6, 92, 97, 122, 129–30
Potts A.W. 57–61, 66, 69–70, 126, 209, 212
   relieved of his command 87
Prentice, Sir William 211
Primary Producers' Association of New South Wales 193

Rabaul 129, 167–8, 170–6, 179
Ramu River 142
Ramu Valley 133, 141–5, 212

Redding, Don 101
Returned Services League 192, 198
Roberts, M.L. 50, 83, 132, 211
Robertson, Bruce 112–3
Robertson, H.C.H. 163
Roosevelt, D 50
Rowell, Sir Sidney 68–70, 126, 209, 212
   relieved of his command 77

Sage, Matron-in-Chief 182
Salamaua 131, 133
Samarinda Road *see* Milford Highway
Sanananda 97, 105, 114, 119, 121, 128
Seregina 91
Shaggy Ridge 141, 143–4
Shedden, Sir Frederick 187
Shropshire 181–3, 186–8
Sidi Barrani 24
South Seas Force 72–3, 102
Spry, Chas 76, 115, 117
Staff Corps 11, 42–3, 180, 210
Stevens, J.E.S. 162–3
Street, G.A. 10
Sturdee, Sir Vernon 165, 169
Sublet, Frank 124–6
Suez Canal 31
Sutherland, Richard 68
Swan 171
Swinbourne, E.S. 200

Tarakan 155
Tel Aviv 18–20
Templeton's Crossing 84–5, 110
Tobruk 24–5, 32–7, 40, 42, 140
Travers, Bill 11

Vasey, George 87, 92–7, 106, 110–11, 115, 117, 119, 122, 126, 133–5, 138, 148, 162, 208–9, 211
   death, 153
Vernon, Dr, G.A. 75
Vickery, Ian 117

Wairopi 97, 106
War Criminal Trials 173–4
Water Research Foundation of Australia 193–9, 202, 217–8
Waters, Doc 62, 70, 96, 159
Wavell, Earl 24, 48
Westralia 156
Wewak 162
White, Tom 122
Whittaker's Plantation 134–5
Willoughby, Charles 76
Wilmot, Chester 33
Withy, C.B. 63, 75, 85
Woodward, E.L. 152
Wooten, George 16, 122

Yen, Woo 175
Yoshinobu Tomita 109